# For Reference

**Not to be taken from this room**

# CLASSICAL ARCHITECTURE

# Classical Architecture

## A COMPREHENSIVE HANDBOOK TO THE TRADITION OF CLASSICAL STYLE

### ROBERT ADAM

*Illustrations by Derek Brentnall*

HARRY N. ABRAMS, INC., PUBLISHERS
*New York*

Library of Congress Cataloging-in-Publication Data
Adam, Robert, 1948–
    Classical architecture: a comprehensive handbook to the tradition
of classical style / Robert Adam; illustrations by Derek Brentnall.
    p.    cm.
    ISBN 0–8109–3166–4
    1. Architecture, Classical— Handbooks, manuals, etc.   I. Title.
NA260.A26      1991
722′.6—dc20
                                                                90–38210
                                                                    CIP

Copyright © Robert Adam, 1990

First published in 1990 in the United Kingdom and Commonwealth by Viking

Published in 1991 by Harry N. Abrams, Incorporated, New York
A Times Mirror Company

*Printed and bound in Great Britain*

FOR
SARAH, JAMIE AND CHARLOTTE

# ACKNOWLEDGEMENTS

This book would not have come into being if Alan Powers had not first had the idea and asked me to join him in its preparation. Alan later decided not to pursue the project due to pressure of work and his original concept has changed a little as it progressed. I hope Alan approves of the final product and I must extend my thanks to him for our first discussions which set out the structure of the book and for his continued encouragement after his active involvement had ceased.

One of the principal problems in research has been the gathering of accurate information. Many people have helped me with details of individual buildings or by suggesting possible sources. In particular I must thank Vincent Bouvet of the CNMHS in Paris, Jorn Grabowski of the Staatliche Museen zu Berlin in the DDR, Paul Wingfield of Gaius College Cambridge, Professor Geoffrey Broadbent and Liza and Brian Stanley in New York. My fellow directors at Winchester Design, John McKenna, David Strugnell and Charles Walker, have given me essential moral support. My staff have shown great interest in the progress of the book and have also assisted me with information and suggestions for material. In particular I would like to thank Tony Harrison, Roderick MacLennan, Nigel Anderson and Andrew Howarth and his wife. I am particularly grateful to Amanda Claridge of the British School at Rome and Dan Cruickshank for their assistance in reading the final manuscript and their helpful comments.

*Winchester 1989*

# CONTENTS

# USING THE BOOK

Classical architecture is a familiar part of our everyday lives. For two thousand years the tradition of classical building has been an essential part of western civilization and this long association has given us all a deep-rooted understanding of its language.

Like literature, a classical design can take many forms and can be expressed in countless different ways. Like a great novel, a great classical building will have a simple message for everyone while offering the knowledgeable spectator layer upon layer of more profound meaning. This handbook will help to guide the reader into the creative depths of the works of art that we inhabit.

In common with the spoken language, classical design draws its strength and variety from its history. From this history have grown myths and symbols which colour even the simplest designs. Methods of construction and small details each have their own story to tell. *Classical Architecture* will look at this history and introduce all of these elements, tracing their evolution through the centuries and offering practical advice for their use.

The richness and diversity of the great heritage of classical buildings are first examined in relation to their historical context and use. The book goes on to describe the different formal systems of design, or orders, which lie behind all classical architecture. Parts of buildings and types of decoration are then examined one by one to create a comprehensive picture of the classical building in all its aspects.

Each page of text is a self-contained essay and is placed opposite a page of drawings, usually to scale, which have been prepared specially to illustrate the text. This format allows the reader to study the book chapter by chapter or to select pages or sections of specific interest.

As it is a specialized subject, classical architecture has a large number of technical words. The division of the book into a series of linked essays means that the reader may not know or have read previously the definition of some of the more obscure but unavoidable expressions. Where these are not defined on the same page a short definition can be found in the glossary. The index gives directions to pages where the subject is discussed in more depth.

The reader will soon realize just how vast and complex is the study of classical architecture. This handbook can only be an introduction. When many of these pages can be the subject of several books, the choice of material has to be highly selective. The selection is intended to be objective and there is no significance in the inevitable list of omissions. Examples have been chosen to show the variety, depth and dynamism of classical architecture and to trace the evolution of the tradition as it changes with the society it serves.

# 1. CLASSICAL HERITAGE

## ORIGINS

From the earliest days, when men learnt to till the soil and herd their animals, tribes settled the fertile regions around the eastern perimeter of the Mediterranean Sea. The life and legends of these prehistoric peoples became the foundations of western civilization. In rough villages they housed their gods in the same primitive dwellings they built for themselves, and in these houses and temples lie the roots of classical architecture.

As these tribes emerged from illiterate obscurity they jealously preserved their sacred ancestral traditions and recorded their already ancient spoken tales of gods and heroes to create the fountainhead of western literature. As their houses and temples grew to reflect the increasing sophistication of their lives, memories of the simple structures of their forebears were woven into the design and decoration of new buildings.

The stone temples and tombs of Egypt often imitate in their shape, carvings and painted decorations the reed houses of the first farmers of the Lower Nile. Even today, similar dwellings (b) can be found in riverside villages in southern Mesopotamia.

In the ninth century BC, pottery models of buildings were offered to the goddess Hera, near Corinth in Greece. The reconstruction illustrated (a) is probably a model of such a temple. In the seventh century BC, the Latin tribes that settled the hills that were to become Rome buried the ashes of their dead in miniature huts of clay and illustration (c) is a reconstruction of a hut based on the remains of these vessels.

Made from the natural materials of the countryside, buildings such as these still house migrant shepherds in the lands where classical architecture was born. To this day they can serve as permanent homes in the poorer regions of the world. In antiquity not only would everyday rural dwellings have served as a constant reminder of the ancestry of stone temples, but up until the first century AD, ancient thatched temples were reverently preserved in both Athens and Rome.

Throughout the long history of classical architecture the influence of these inherited origins has lain below the surface, sometimes half-forgotten, sometimes emerging to the surface to revitalize the strain, but never totally absent. Every classical building is a descendant of these primitive huts and the use of classical architecture is a living bond with the cultural origins of western civilization.

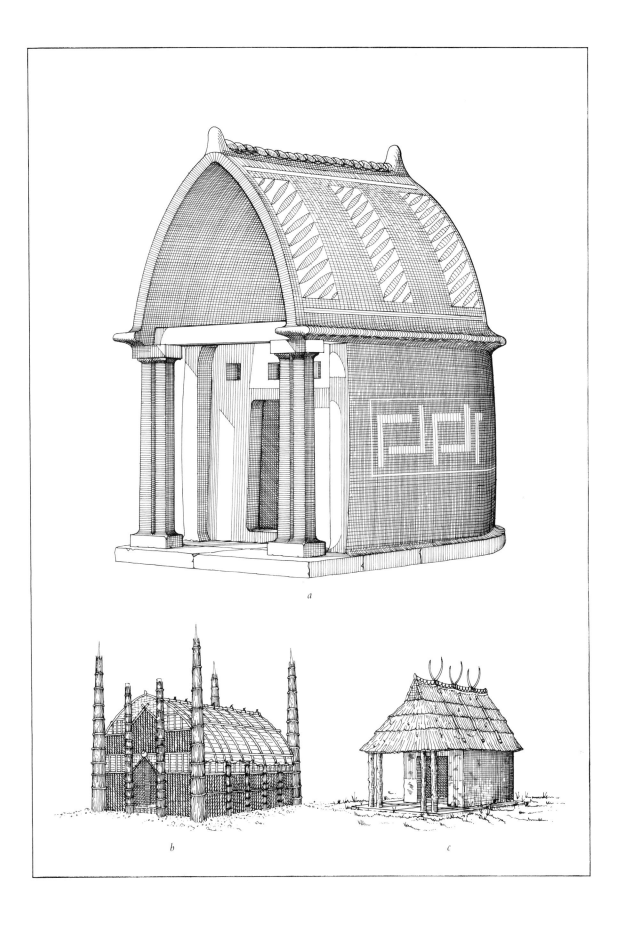

*a*

*b*

*c*

# EGYPT

---

The foundations of western monumental architecture were laid in Egypt. By the time the first signs of civilization began to emerge in Greece, Egyptian architects had been building massive structures for fifteen hundred years.

Soil of unusual richness was carried down the River Nile and the exploitation of this resource produced a wealthy civilization ruled by god-kings, or pharaohs. A complex religion consumed the surplus labour force in the erection of huge buildings dedicated to half-animal gods and the afterlife of the pharaohs.

A preoccupation with eternity and the creation of permanence dominated the architecture of ancient Egypt. Royal tombs were temples for the worship of the deceased pharaoh. By about 2800 BC huge, artificial, stone-faced mountains, or pyramids, were built over rooms containing the elaborately embalmed body of the pharaoh and his valued worldly possessions. The pyramids were the first major monuments in the western world to be constructed with cut stone.

The pyramids were famed throughout the ancient world, but due to their solely sepulchral function and huge size they had no practical influence on the emerging Greek civilization to the north. The great enclosed stone temples on the other hand, that sometimes accompanied and sometimes stood apart from the pyramid complexes, must have made a greater impression on Greek traders and mercenaries.

The Temple of Khons at Karnak (a) was built in 1198 BC and is quite a small example (the nearby Temple of Amon is six times the size), but typical. It stood inside a large walled enclosure (not shown) which would have contained service buildings and a sacred lake. The temple faces inwards to the sanctuary containing the sacred barge, which is approached on an axial processional route by way of a large door between two tall pylons, an open court and a colonnaded room, or hypostyle hall. The sanctuary is surrounded by a corridor giving access to chapels.

We shall see how individual features of Egyptian architecture had a major influence on the development of the classical style, and how details came to be incorporated in Roman architecture. Yet, although it remained virtually unchanged for fifteen hundred years, no Egyptian style became established outside Egypt in antiquity. It was, it seems, too specific and too conservative for adaptation to the needs of the poorer surrounding cultures. The Treasury of Atreus (b) of about 1300 BC, from the Greek Minoan and Mycenaean civilization, and the Temple at Prinias (c), erected in Crete by the emerging Greek peoples six hundred years later, illustrate the contrast between the advancement and wealth of Egypt and the comparative backwardness of its northern neighbours. We must look rather to the adoption of finely dressed stone for buildings of importance, the use of the column and beam system (trabeation) for temples and an appetite for large and impressive structures as the most significant contributions of Egyptian architecture to the mainstream of classicism.

4

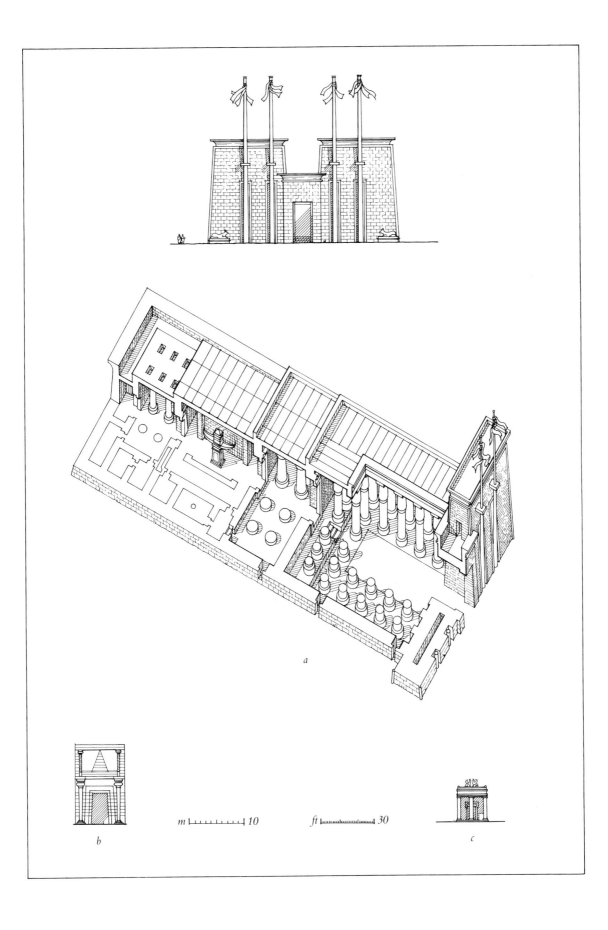

*a*

*b*

$m$ |—————| *10*          $ft$ |—————————| *30*

*c*

# THE GREEK TEMPLE

The Minoan and Mycenaean civilizations were destroyed in 1100 BC and Greece descended into four centuries of obscurity. By 800 BC the Greek peoples had dispersed and city-states were created in Greece, the Aegean islands and on the west coast of Turkey. In the next two centuries these cities in turn colonized Sicily, southern Italy, the south of France and the Black Sea.

The Greek states came to profit from their position on the rich trade routes of the Mediterranean and by about 700 BC were unified in culture but not in government. These diverse communities were to create a civilization where freedom of thought combined with internal rivalry to bring about an intellectual and artistic revolution.

The rise of Greek civilization launched the western world into a political, intellectual and artistic current which has carried it forward for two and a half thousand years. The dawn of rational thought did not, however, dispel the savage gods that followed the Greeks out of their dark past, and the houses that were built for them became the touchstone of western architecture.

From the mud-brick and thatched buildings illustrated on page 3 a new temple design evolved. The first temples had flat mud roofs or thatch, but in the eighth century BC, the invention of large clay roof-tiles made it more practical to build a simple rectangular plan with the shallow roof and gable-end, or pediment, which characterize classical buildings. On more important temples this roof came to be carried on an open colonnade which surrounded the temple.

All of these new features can be found in the Temple of Apollo at Thermon in Greece (a), built in about 630 BC. This temple was constructed with wooden columns and a timber roof. Its basic form remained the pattern for all major temples for centuries to come, but within forty years the builders of temples such as that of Artemis in Corfu (b) had translated all the exposed timber features into stone.

There followed one hundred and fifty years of refinement and enlargement. Small changes were tried out and, as confidence increased, more slender proportions were used, but major temples never strayed far from the basic type illustrated by the Temple of Hera at Paestum in Italy (c) of 460 BC. An enclosed sanctuary housed the image of the god; if necessary, rows of inner columns helped to support the roof; it was entered through a porch, which was often repeated on the back, and the whole structure was surrounded by columns. When a building was of such a huge size that the columns could not support the roof, such as the Olympieum at Agrigento in Sicily (d), an imitation colonnade was added as decoration to the supporting walls.

Ancient Greek architects spent more than two centuries trying to perfect just one building type and created an architecture of such enduring excellence that it has survived for more than two thousand years as a universal ideal.

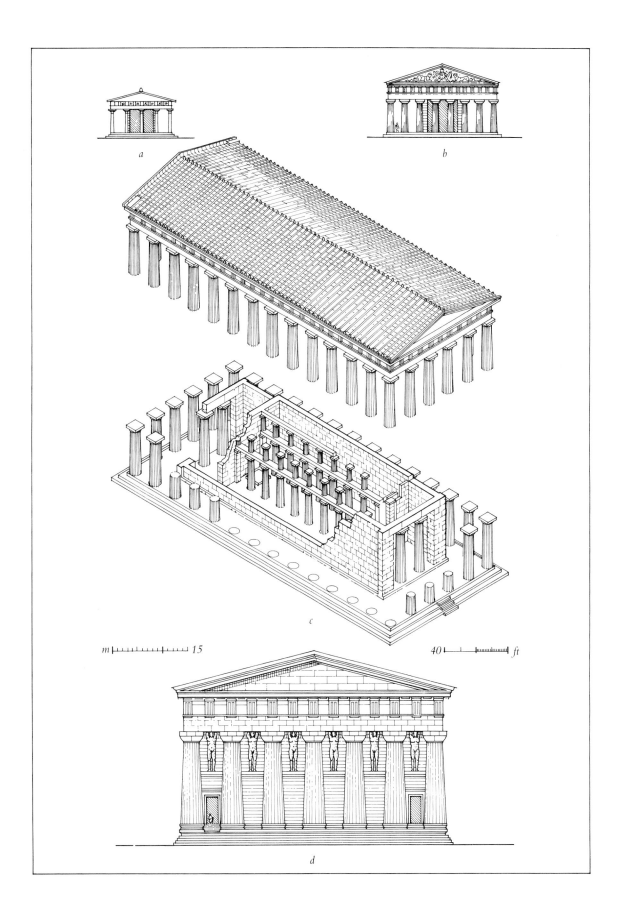

a

b

c

m |——|——|——|——|——| 15          40 |——|——|——|——| ft

d

# THE PERFECTION OF GREECE

When the Greek peoples turned back the Persian Empire in the middle of the fifth century BC, their unique civilization realized its accumulated wisdom in a century of wealth and power. Literature, art and philosophy flourished, and new buildings displayed such a level of refinement that their details became prototypes that would influence all future development in western architecture.

Skilful leadership and naval power gave the city of Athens dominance over the alliance that defeated the Persians, and the peace that followed. The appropriation of allied naval subscriptions by Pericles, the Athenian demagogue, to cultivate a popular power base in Athens generated a public building programme that produced architecture of unprecedented sophistication.

The greatest of these buildings was the new temple to the goddess Athena, the Parthenon (a), often considered to be the peak of the development of the traditional Greek temple and of the architectural system, the Doric order, that had evolved with it. The new temple, dedicated in 438 BC, was richly decorated with sculpture and was the work of two architects, Callicrates and Ictinus.

The design incorporates several optical devices, often not in themselves visible to the human eye, but probably intended to correct undesirable visual effects created by rectangular forms. These devices include a subtle tapering of the column, a minute rise to the centre in the surrounding steps, an equally gentle rise in the floor, an inward slant to the columns, variations in the column spacing, an increased thickness of the corner columns and an outward slant in the upper part of the building.

Seventeen years later, work began on a nearby temple called the Erechtheion. This building had an unusually complicated plan, perhaps suggested by the uneven ground on which it was constructed and its multiple dedications. It had three different porches, one of which is illustrated (b), and two of them have a quite different decorative system, or order. This order, the Ionic, is most notable for the spiral details, or volutes, on the capitals over the columns, for its more elegant proportions, compared with the Doric, and for its richer details.

In 334 BC an Athenian called Lysicrates won a prize for his choir and decided to build a monument to celebrate his victory. This exquisite little building (c) is the earliest surviving exterior use of another architectural order which had been invented for the interiors of Doric temples about eighty years before. Similar to the Ionic, this is the Corinthian order. It is characterized by columns that are made more slender by replacing the spiral volutes with a tall decoration of finely carved leaves.

While the Greek city-states enjoyed the brief peak of their fortunes, they created for posterity the architecture we call classical. The three principal orders were established and, although great changes would be made in the following millennia, classical architecture would always draw its spiritual energy from this pure spring.

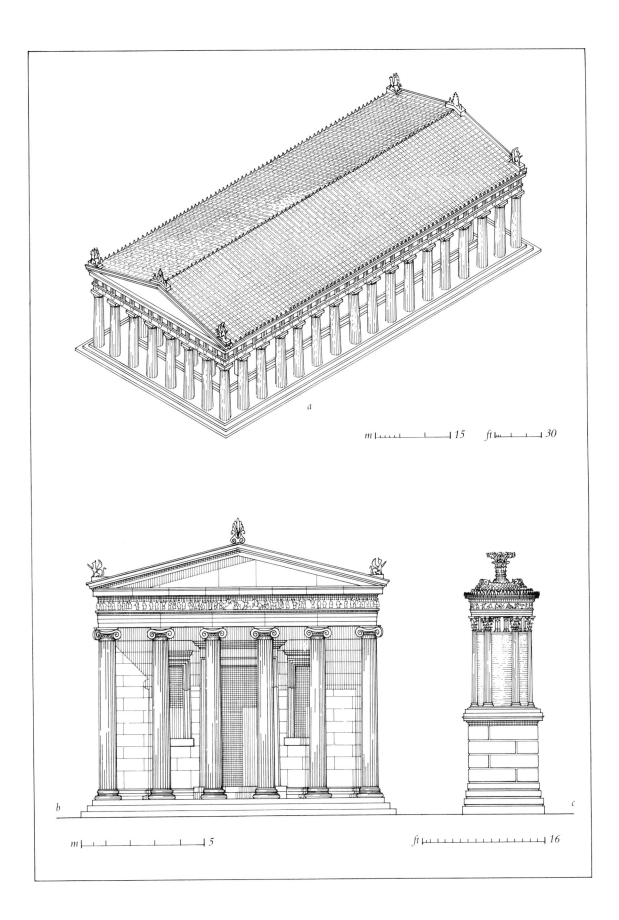

*a*

m |⊢⊢⊢⊢⊢|⊢⊢⊢⊢⊢| 15    ft |⊢⊢⊢|⊢⊢⊢| 30

*b*

*c*

m |⊢⊢⊢|⊢⊢⊢| 5    ft |⊢⊢⊢⊢⊢⊢⊢⊢⊢⊢⊢⊢⊢⊢⊢⊢| 16

# HELLENISM

The independence of the Greek states was their undoing. Rivalry led to bloody wars until in 338 BC the Greek mainland fell to the army of a half-barbarian king from the north, Philip of Macedon. Although monarchy was abhorrent to the republican mentality of the Greeks, their Macedonian conquerors were absorbed into the mystique of Greek culture, and when Philip was assassinated only two years after his conquest, both his dominance and veneration of Greece were inherited by his young son, Alexander. In a brief and brilliant thirteen-year reign, Alexander took his armies and his adopted Greek culture to the east as far as India. In the Mediterranean he created an empire that would ensure the continuation of the cultural revolution instigated by the small republics his father had defeated.

With Alexander's legendary reign begins the one-hundred-and-fifty-year epoch we call Hellenistic. On Alexander's death his empire was divided among his generals and this new Greek civilization developed to accommodate the more diverse world beyond the introspective states of Greece.

Greek architecture had been based on the development of one building, the temple. This building type could not be used for all the different functional requirements of the more complex society that was now emerging. Temple architecture had already been adopted for simple meeting houses, gates and tombs, but now a much more significant adaptation took place that would establish the temple architectural system as an appropriate decorative form for all building types. This adaptation lies at the root of all subsequent developments in classical architecture.

The Council House at Miletus (a), built in 170 BC, is two temple forms adapted to act as a gate and a large covered hall, linked by a colonnaded courtyard. The altar enclosure at Pergamon (b) was built at about the same time and is a dramatic departure from Greek tradition. Altars were originally long narrow platforms outside temples, but Hellenistic altars set new standards of grandeur and ostentation. At Pergamon the altar is dominated by its platform and surrounding colonnade.

By about 200 BC the citizen armies of Rome and its Italian allies had finally defeated the Carthaginians and were making advances into the weakening remnants of Alexander's empire. At first an outpost of the Hellenistic world, Rome's expansion brought it into the centre of civilization and luxury. Before long Rome had abandoned its provincial version of Greek Doric architecture and Roman architects started to adapt their temples to the more cosmopolitan style of their Hellenistic Greek neighbours. The Temple of Portunus in Rome (c), built in the late second century BC, retains the entrance steps and solid side-walls of the traditional Roman temple, but adopts the appearance of a Greek Ionic temple. When the progress of classical architecture passed to Rome, the inspiration was not the by then historic monuments of the Greek republics, but the living architecture of the Hellenistic kingdoms.

a

b

a

b

c

m └─┴┴┴┴┴┴┴┴─────────────┘ 20          ft └┴┴┴┴┴┴─┴────┴────────┘ 60

# IMPERIAL ROME

For two centuries the city of Rome struggled to reconcile its progressive domination of the Mediterranean world with its own city-state democracy. The temptations of great power and the enormous wealth of conquest led to civil war and the emergence of a new kind of monarchy, born out of an elaborate pretence of democratic conformity. The new monarchs, or emperors, consolidated their power to rule for five centuries over a vast and complex empire which stretched from the Atlantic to the Persian Gulf and from Scotland to the Upper Nile.

At about the time of the creation of the imperial monarchy, at the end of the first century BC, the use of a volcanic sand mixed with lime revolutionized building construction and transformed classical architecture. This natural cement was laid inside a brick skin and hardened to create a solid durable mass; it was not suited to the beam and post system of Greek architecture, but worked best when moulded into arches and domes. Roman architects extended the range of the architectural system that had come down to them from the Greeks to accommodate the new material.

The emperors inherited a democratic obligation to maintain the buildings and their own popularity in the city of Rome. The wealth of the empire allowed successive emperors to erect vast buildings for the entertainment of the people and the adornment of the city.

Perhaps the most famous of these is the Colosseum (b), begun in AD 70 by the Emperor Vespasian. This huge structure seated some 50,000 spectators for the brutal entertainments of the amphitheatre. The solution of the functional and structural problems inspires respect to this day and the tiers of columns and arches decorating the exterior added a new dimension to classical architecture (see page 128).

The Roman fondness for what we would call Turkish baths provided another outlet for imperial munificence in architectural splendour. A series of ever larger baths was built and came to include libraries, lecture halls, gymnasia and even enclosed parks. The Baths of the Emperor Caracalla (c), built in AD 216, are typical and could accommodate 1600 bathers. These vast public buildings required large, roofed halls and a structural and architectural system evolved for unsupported spans of up to 27 metres in vaulted concrete.

The Temple to the Pantheon of the Gods (a), built by the Emperor Hadrian in AD 120, gives us the most complete impression of the great buildings of the emperors. Its conventional temple porch sits in front of a huge brick-clad concrete drum covered with a 40-metre-wide dome creating a dramatic top-lit space decorated with rows of coloured marble columns and arches. This new concentration on interior spaces, and the adaptation of the Greek and Hellenistic tradition to the new opportunities of concrete construction, transformed the classical tradition and, supported by the prestige of the empire, would continue to influence its further development.

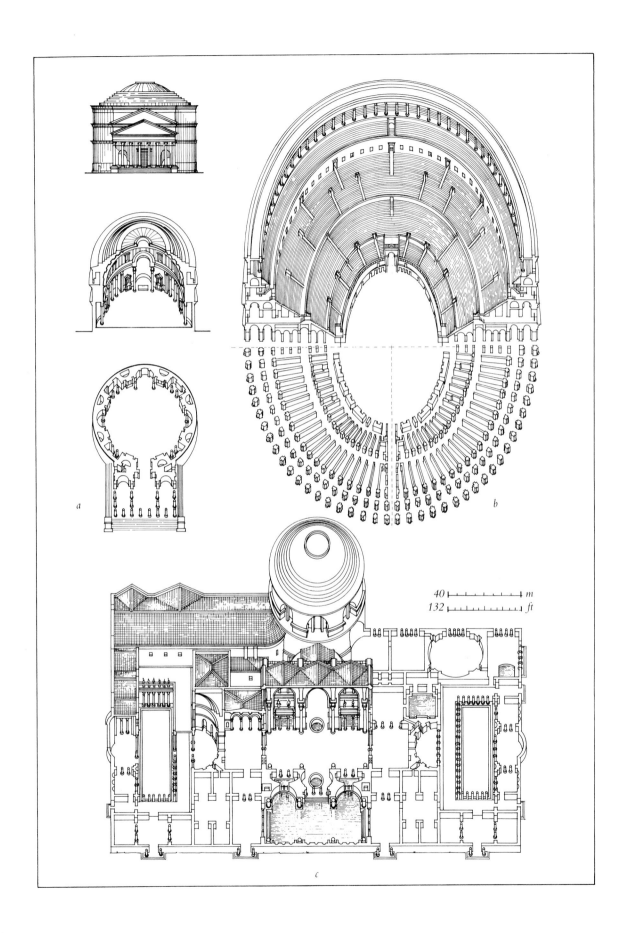

*a*

*b*

40 ⊢———————⊣ *m*

132 ⊢—————————⊣ *ft*

*c*

# LATE ROME

The Roman Empire became too large to be dominated by its founding race and, within a century, power had passed beyond the shores of Italy. In the third century AD, pressure from peoples beyond the northern and eastern borders brought warfare, plague and, finally, invasion to the heart of the empire. As the armies grew in numbers they came to be dominated by barbarian mercenaries who created emperors out of their ranks and fought civil wars as damaging as invasions. Inflation and taxation began to destroy the city-based culture that had characterized the civilizations of the ancient world. The old religions were reduced to ceremony as mystery cults from the Near East gripped the insecure population.

As the third century drew to a close, the Emperor Diocletian instituted reforms to divide, transform and save the empire. His successor Constantine formalized the division by founding Constantinople (Istanbul) and established one of the new cults, Christianity, as the official religion of the state.

Once the empire was restored, classical culture was no longer in the hands of the old Mediterranean races. The Greek tradition had become a distant memory, craftsmen had died out and power lay with dour soldiers educated in the austere discipline of the camps. Yet the strength of the imperial idea and its expression through great buildings survived.

The Emperor Diocletian's reforms foresaw his own retirement and in the year 300 he built himself a palace in his homeland in Yugoslavia. As large as a town, the palace took the form of a fortified military camp. The entrance court to his apartments (b) displays provincial classicism characteristic of the Syrian provinces, but leads to buildings that deliberately echo the monuments of an earlier, imperial age.

Constantine defeated the Emperor Maxentius outside Rome in 312 and assumed power. Maxentius' unfinished public hall, or basilica (a), in the Forum was modified and completed as part of Constantine's building programme for the city. This large and open hall with its plain exterior and bold geometric interior was quite unlike traditional galleried basilicas and owed its origins to the central halls of baths.

Constantine's daughter was buried in Rome and her Christian mausoleum (c) combines the same exterior simplicity with a rich and geometrically complex interior, decorated with fine, but traditionally pagan, mosaics.

Late Roman buildings draw their inspiration not from a distant Greek source but from earlier imperial buildings and the impure interpretations of the provinces which now gave Rome her rulers. Complete familiarity with the geometric possibilities of the concrete vault and arch and the adoption of regional innovations, such as the arch rising directly off the column, added to the classical tradition and produced the first specifically Christian buildings. It was this period that the following thousand years of western Christendom would view with particular devotion.

14

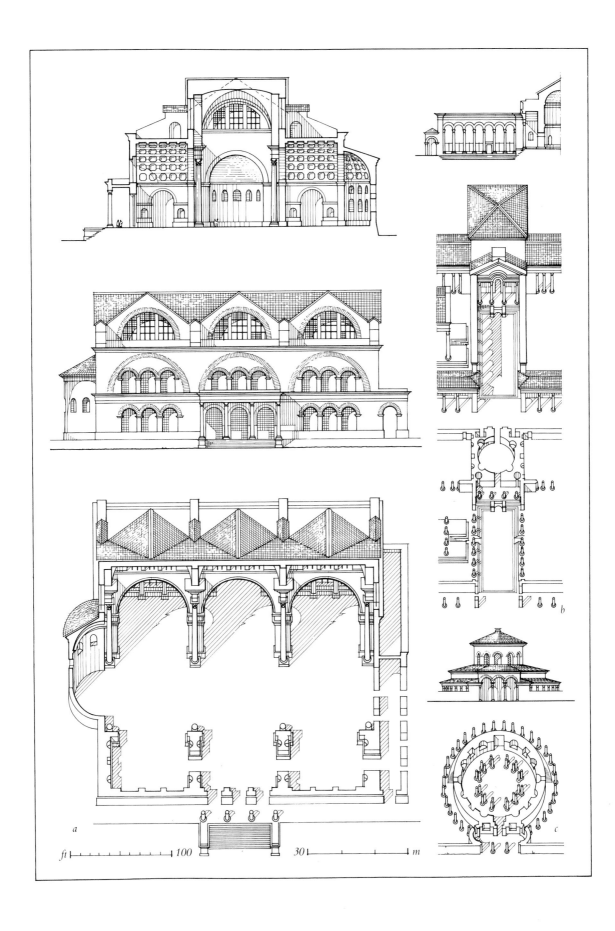

a

ft ⊢———————⊣ 100    30 ⊢————————⊣ m

b

c

# BYZANTIUM

When the Roman Empire in the west finally succumbed to invaders in 476, the imperial badges of office were sent back to the eastern emperor in Constantinople, or Byzantium. The Byzantines considered themselves to be the successors of the first emperors in Rome and Byzantine architecture is a direct, if geographically limited, continuation of the classical tradition.

Early Byzantine buildings, such as the church of St Demetrius in Thessalonica (e), built in about 475, differ little from other examples in the late Roman Empire. The large churches or basilicas built in Rome a century earlier were designed to an almost identical pattern. But in the details of the interior, distinctly eastern features have started to appear, with abstract patterns in multicoloured stone and golden mosaics, and leaf decoration over the columns cut like lacework.

The eastern emperors were prevented from reunifying the empire by war on their eastern borders, but in 532 the Emperor Justinian signed a treaty with the Persians which freed his army to reconquer – albeit briefly – the lost provinces of Africa and even Rome itself.

In this its most glorious period, the greatest building of the Eastern Empire was erected, Hagia Sofia in Constantinople (d). This huge domed structure takes the interior geometry of late Rome to its conclusion. It is no accident that the architects, Anthemius and Isidorus, were known as mathematicians. The 55-metre-high dome sits on a square plan supported by huge arches and flanked by two half-domes each containing three more half-domes. The audacious structure allows windows to be placed high up in the dome and its supporting arches so that the dome appeared to contemporaries to float in the air. The geometry overshadows the transformed classical details. Rows of columns and arches are faint memories of the ordered classical interiors of earlier Rome. Roman cement had by now fallen out of use and the great domes are made of solid brick.

A distinct Byzantine interpretation of classicism had now emerged and is illustrated by novel versions of the traditional column capitals. The carving in (a) takes the old upright leaf pattern and sweeps it round as if blown by the wind, and in (b) all the traditional details have gone, to be replaced by abstract pattern and Christian symbols.

Barbarian invasion in the west and the rise of Islam in the east soon turned victory into a long retreat. But for the following nine centuries the great age of Justinian lived on in small buildings whose architects continued the pursuit of increasingly complex geometry, such as in the domed brick structure of the church of the Holy Apostles in Thessalonica (c) of 1315.

When the last Roman emperor left Constantinople in 1453, Byzantine classicism ended, but its legacy endured in the buildings of eastern Europe and even in those of its Turkish conquerors.

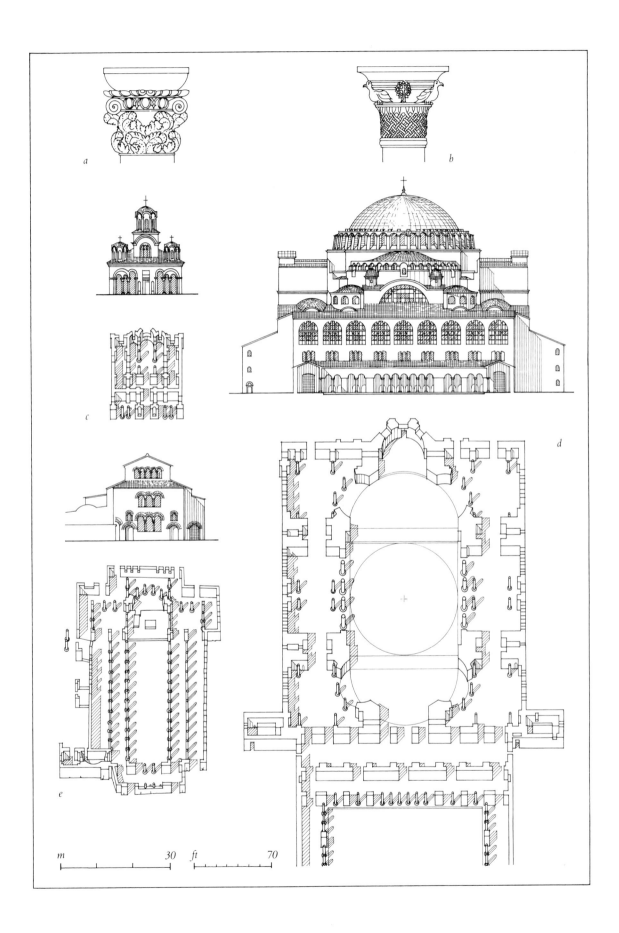

*a*

*b*

*c*

*d*

*e*

m                    30    ft            70

# OUT OF THE DARK AGES

When the Western Empire came to its weary end, Roman citizens had been living alongside increasing numbers of barbarian settlers for two centuries. In France, Italy and Spain these uneasy neighbours came together under local tribal rulers, and the fragmented nature of the Western Empire in its final years became a recognized fact.

The political ideal of the empire lived on and the buildings served as a constant reminder of the lost skills and settled life of organized civilization. Barbarian kings longed for the status and territorial control implied by the imperial title and in their crude buildings tried to imitate the great architecture they had come to inhabit.

Amid the turmoil of migration and war, the king of the Frankish tribes, Charlemagne, gained control of France, Germany and much of Italy. In Rome in 800 he was crowned by the Pope as the emperor of the west, the Holy Roman Emperor. Charlemagne set in motion a remarkable revival of Roman culture in literature and painting. His buildings were a sincere if rudimentary attempt to copy the greatness of Rome; the abbey gateway at Lorsch (c), for example, struggles to revive the splendour of the triumphal arch.

The Holy Roman Empire fell quickly into disorder with internal division and external pressure from Scandinavians, Slavs and Arabs. The Roman Church and the Pope, the Bishop of Rome, became the only stable organization in a divided Europe. Strengthened by a growing passion for monastic life, by the conversion to Christianity of each new barbarian influx and by papal control over the still potent title of Holy Roman Emperor, the western Church became Europe's greatest builder.

Out of the ruins of Rome, and Charlemagne's brief rule, inspired by late Roman buildings and incomplete knowledge of the great architecture of the Eastern Empire, a European barbarian classicism emerged. In recognition of its Roman inspiration, this new architecture is called Romanesque. In Britain it is called Norman.

An obsession with the magical powers of the mortal remains of saints brought the possessors of these doubtful relics great wealth from the hordes of pilgrims who sought them out. Great churches such as Santiago de Compostela in Spain (a) of 1080 were built to house these pilgrims and to raise the status of the powerful bishops who controlled them. Building skills improved and stonemasons attempted to recapture the great interiors of the decaying Roman buildings that surrounded them.

Massive stone structures were designed in such a way as to follow the forms of the lost skills of concrete construction and, in their decoration, tried to imitate with barbarian geometry the themes inherited from ancient Greece. As far north as Durham in England (b), and as far south as Sicily, architecture emerged from a dark age. The lost traditions were revived with a naïve power that achieved a kind of greatness and launched European architecture into the Middle Ages.

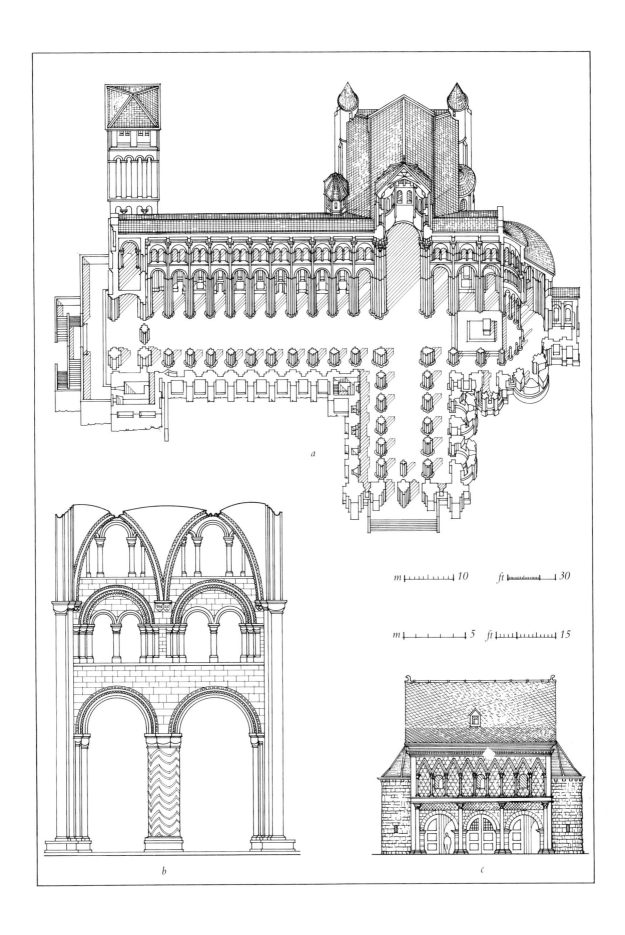

*a*

*m* 10    *ft* 30

*m* 5    *ft* 15

*b*

*c*

# THE BIRTH OF GOTHIC

After centuries of invasion, war and destruction, in the twelfth century the West settled down to a period of relative peace and stability and centres of learning developed in cathedral cities. The crusades halted Arab expansion and allowed safer travel in southern Europe and the Holy Land. Attention turned again to the intellectual achievements of Rome, preserved in monastic libraries. Latin, still a living language, was purified by a revival of the literature of antiquity, and the science and philosophy of the ancient authors became the cornerstone of education. Wealthy and sophisticated clerics, visiting the classical churches of Rome and Constantine's monuments in the Holy Land, saw their own churches, with their massive piers, crude decoration and squat interiors, as barbaric.

The intervening centuries had not destroyed the spell of Rome, but the unbroken continuity of civilization had been lost. The sense of the progress of history had gone and artists innocently depicted ancient figures in modern dress. Superstition and a mystic form of Christianity turned minds to a cryptic world of symbol and myth which gained a reality equal to the physical world. When the builders of cathedrals sought to recreate ancient buildings they had no interest in exact reproduction, but duplicated symbolic dimensions and numbers of architectural features.

In eastern France in 1089, Cluny (a), the headquarters of the powerful order of Cluniac monks, was rebuilt to rival St Peter's in Rome. The new building was rich in classical decoration but included an early example of the pointed arch, copied from Arab buildings seen in Sicily, Spain or the Holy Land.

The difference between these arches and round Roman arches was not regarded as significant and the fashion for pointed arches spread. At this time the rich Cluniac bishops of northern France were asking their architects to open up the walls of their churches for large areas of stained glass to cast a mystic light on elegant internal rows of classical columns. To achieve this architects reduced the weight of stone vaults by crossing arches diagonally between columns. These arches, or ribs, then pushed the weight they carried outwards to half-arches, or flying buttresses, leaning against the outside walls.

Remarkable structural improvements were developed which, together with the constructional advantages discovered in pointed arches enabled architects to create higher and higher buildings with ever larger windows. As the structure improved from Noyon Cathedral (b) to Laon (c) the unbroken row of columns, such as those found in late Roman churches, was finally achieved.

By the end of the century, the Latin revival was over. In the cathedrals the structural innovations had opened up new opportunities. At Chartres Cathedral (d) the classical ideal was overwhelmed by height and glass. Medieval architecture now had its own style for inspiration, but it was a style born of a clouded vision of Rome.

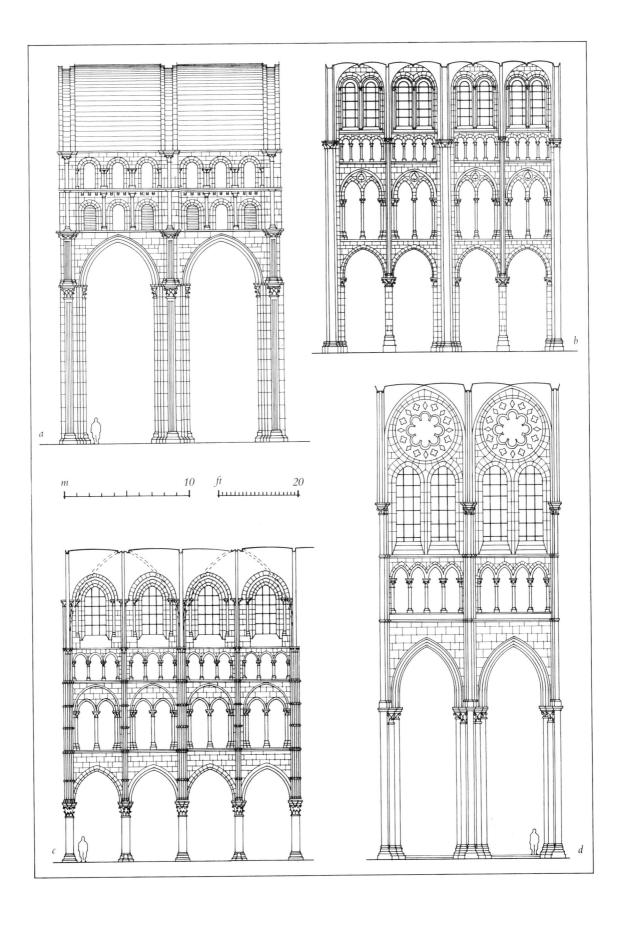

a

m ⊢——————— 10  ft ⊢——————— 20

c

b

d

# THE RENAISSANCE

Italian city life survived the devastation of the Dark Ages and, in the Middle Ages, some city-states became self-governing republics, free from the obligation of servitude to landed dukes and kings. Freedom accelerated the sophistication of urban culture and the growth of manufacturing industry. Poised at the crossroads of Europe, Islam and Byzantium, the merchant aristocracy of these city-states became the bankers of Europe and accumulated great wealth and power, restrained only by the remarkable violence of internal city politics and the fierce competition between the small states for trade, territory and artistic prestige.

The brittle elegance of High Gothic never found a home in central Italy and contact with Byzantine art stimulated a revolutionary realism in the thirteenth century, when art had been dominated by symbol and convention. In the fourteenth century a passionate interest in the literature of ancient Rome led to the rescue of forgotten manuscripts from monastic libraries and a new philosophy, humanism, reconciling Christian and pagan thought. The first home of humanism was the city-state of Florence where the leading families were enthusiastic patrons.

The great artistic revolution, known as the Renaissance, blossomed from this fertile ground in the early fifteenth century. Self-consciously inspired by ancient Rome and rejecting the Gothic, Renaissance artists transformed society in an explosion of creativity. Architects studied the forgotten ruins of Rome to create buildings that served the needs of a society only gradually emerging from the feudalism of the Middle Ages.

The palace of the Medici family (a) was designed by Michelozzo in 1440 to act as a home, business premises and fortress. Protection from the savage vendettas that plagued Italian cities had always set the design of these great city houses but Michelozzo added classical order to the traditional scheme. The walls become progressively smoother in three tiers, each divided by a horizontal band of stone supporting a regular line of arched windows. The whole composition is crowned by huge classical overhanging eaves, the cornice, which take the place of traditional battlements.

When the great scholar and architect Alberti designed the church of S. Andrea in Mantua (b) in 1470 at the end of his life, he had clearer classical examples to follow and drew his inspiration from large Roman vaulted interiors such as the Basilica of Constantine (page 14). He followed the established long church plan, but changed the side-aisles to chapels to support the heavy stone roof. On the exterior he used the design of a Roman triumphal arch for the façade, changing its role from the glorification of an empire to that of the Christian God.

The early Italian Renaissance was an intellectual adventure which launched Europe into the modern world. A fresh consciousness of history was infused with the vigour of originality to create a new classical architecture of great beauty.

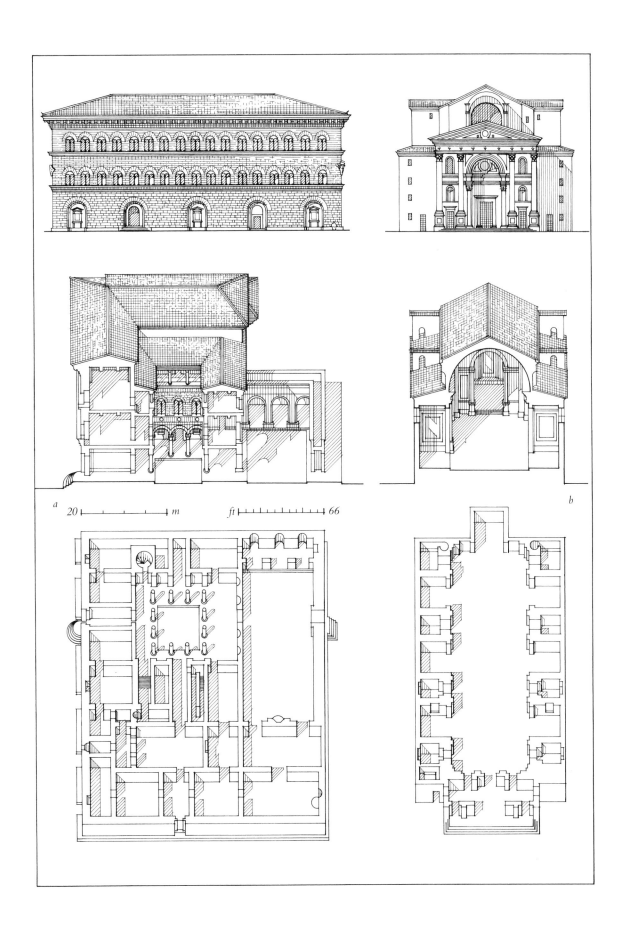

a                20 ├────┼────┤ m          ft ├┼┼┼┼┼┼┤ 66                                    b

# HIGH RENAISSANCE

In 1417 Pope Martin V was elected and three rival popes deposed, thereby ending the Great Schism which had impoverished the Pope's Italian territories and discredited the papacy. Thirty years later Pope Nicholas V moved his residence to the Vatican, signalling a recovery in papal finances and the start of an extensive building campaign. Renaissance artists and architects flocked to Rome which had been reduced to little more than a village among the ruins by centuries of vendettas and battles over papal elections. The new interest in ancient Rome led to the careful study of the many surviving monuments yet, tragically, the search for stone for the new buildings led to their destruction.

Rome became a major cultural focus and the centre of progress in Renaissance architecture and art. The Cancelleria, (a) and (b), designed in 1486 by an unknown architect, introduced a new level of sophistication to the by now familiar Renaissance palace façade. The lower floor has become a heavy base for two layers of flat columns, pilasters, which are not evenly spaced but grouped in pairs. The projecting eaves, or cornice, are in proportion to the top row of columns only, rather than to the total building height. The windows are starting to lose the arches of earlier palaces and flat-topped windows with their own cornice have been cautiously introduced. The whole elevation is completed with very shallow projecting end-wings, or pavilions.

In 1502 the architect Bramante designed a small chapel (c) to mark the place where St Peter was traditionally supposed to have been martyred. Closely based on the remains of surviving circular Roman temples, this tiny building also includes modern features such as railings, or balustrades, and specific Christian symbolism. A jewel of the High Renaissance, it came to be so widely admired that it was soon given the unique privilege of being placed on a level with the buildings of the ancients.

The huge church of S. Maria della Consolazione (d), just outside the small town of Todi in central Italy, was designed by a little-known architect called Cola da Caprarola in 1508. The plan is made up from a series of circles and squares and is one of several similar buildings with one central domed space. Although obviously inspired by ancient buildings, the architects of these rather impractical free-standing churches played with pure geometric shapes with the same sort of academic fascination that led to the recording and classification of the ruins of ancient Rome.

The High Renaissance brought a greater knowledge of antiquity to the Florentine passion for the ancient world. The passage of time brought complete familiarity with the possibilities of classical design and opened up creative possibilities unhindered by the unconscious legacy of the Middle Ages.

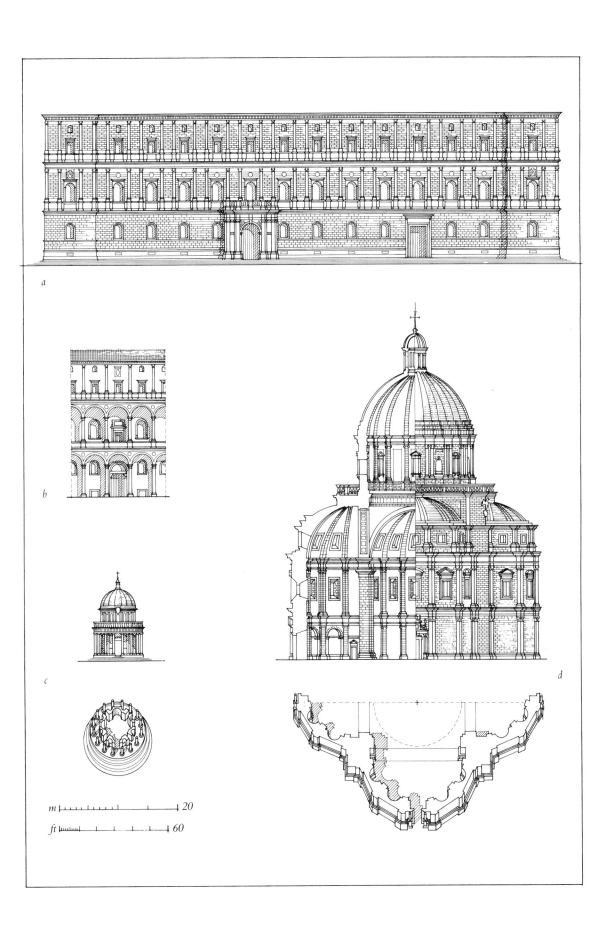

a

b

c

m |⊢⊢⊢⊢⊢⊢⊢⊢⊢⊢⊢⊢⊢⊢⊢⊢⊢⊢⊢⊢| 20

ft |⊢⊢⊢⊢⊢⊢⊢⊢⊢⊢⊢⊢⊢⊢⊢⊢⊢⊢⊢⊢| 60

d

# Mannerism

In 1527 the city of Rome was sacked by the army of the Pope's historic protector, the Holy Roman Emperor, and the Pope became his prisoner. Coming only a few years after Luther's momentous break with the Church, the war in Italy brought the carefree, corrupt, Renaissance papacy to an end. A new wave of spiritualism entered Italy with the Spanish emperor's conquering army. In the arts a century of frantic creativity and scholarship, inspired by the romance of ancient Rome and the worldly reasonableness of humanist thinking, had run out of steam. Weary familiarity with the possibilities of classical art combined with the other-worldly atmosphere of the period to lead architects and artists to seek new inspiration in hidden meaning. A self-conscious, artistic distortion of Renaissance thought, Mannerism, grew out of this introspective climate.

On a doorway in Florence (d), designed by Buontalenti in 1574, almost all the traditional details that surround the door have been distorted. The columns are reduced to a thin profile on the outside of an unusual surround, or architrave; above them, the normal curved top, or pediment, has been cut in half and each half has been turned round, forming an undersized base for an oversized bust which in turn virtually hides an incongruous arched window.

The construction of the Palazzo del Tè, (a) and (b), by Giulio Romano, began a year before the Sack of Rome. Each side of the building was different and had its own peculiar character. Even two sides of the same courtyard had individual quirks. On the north side (a) the three arches are just off-centre and on each side of them the columns are spaced with perverse irregularity. On the west side (b) the door is central and the columns have a regular pattern, but the stones between the columns are out of line and the details themselves seem to come alive. Just below the roof in the spaces between columns a stone appears to be falling out, and above each of the windows underneath, the central stone rises up to meet it, pushing apart the stones overhead.

The great artist Michelangelo more than any other artist freed classical design from rigid conformity. His buildings treated the principles and details so recently reclaimed from the ancient world with an extraordinary artistic licence. His last work, the Gate of Pope Pius IV in Rome (c) of 1561, is little more than a thin façade and yet one door is layered over another and the composition is given a restless drama by using familiar classical details in unfamiliar ways.

Mannerism relied on the knowledgeable familiarity of the onlooker with traditional classical details to create shock and drama. It could not have occurred without the success of the Renaissance and, although some details were too idiosyncratic to be repeated, many of the inventions of the period found a permanent place in the classical tradition.

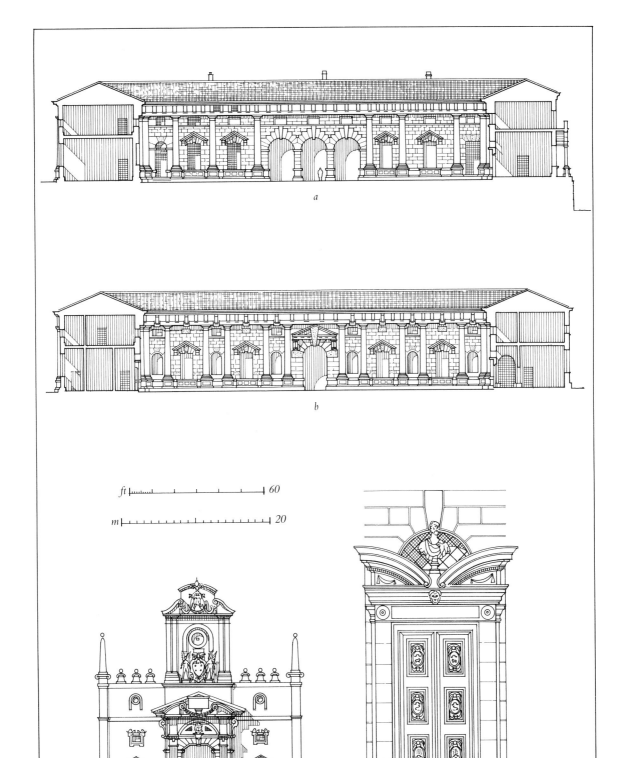

*a*

*b*

ft |‧‧‧‧‧‧‧‧‧‧|‧‧‧‧‧‧‧‧‧‧|‧‧‧‧‧‧‧‧‧‧| 60

m |‧‧‧‧‧‧‧‧‧‧|‧‧‧‧‧‧‧‧‧‧|‧‧‧‧‧‧‧‧‧‧| 20

*c*                                    *d*

# THE RENAISSANCE IN THE NORTH

Architecture founded on the study of the monuments of ancient Rome remained an Italian style for a hundred years. The Church had spread the humanist passion for ancient literature and travelling painters from the north had brought Renaissance realism home with them, but architecture remained firmly Gothic in those countries where its roots ran deep.

France was the first to come under the influence of the new architecture when the invasion of Italy in 1494 drew her into the web of Italian politics. Italian city-states sought advantage in alliance with the invader and their architects visited France. But, without its strong Italian foundations, the new style could be little more than fashionable decoration on long-established Gothic building techniques.

The great Château de Chambord was planned just like a medieval castle with a moat, a ring of buildings for walls and a huge central donjon, or keep (b), but it was designed by an Italian, Domenico da Cortona, in 1519. A dramatic cross-shaped floor plan fits awkwardly into a traditional castle plan and the exterior is a picturesque combination of fine Italian details inventively superimposed on a Gothic jumble of roofs and turrets. It was not long before native architects sought out the Italian origins of the new style, but French custom survived and a distinctive hybrid was developed to become a uniquely French contribution to the classical tradition.

The Protestant break with Rome isolated many of the northern states from their Catholic neighbours. New wealth had been created in the northern countries by the opening up of trading opportunities in the Atlantic. By this time Italian architecture had left behind the purity of the ancient world for the distortions of Mannerism and it was this style that found its way north in printed and illustrated books. In Holland these curiosities were grotesquely magnified and this extravagant form of decoration was exported to her Protestant neighbours.

When Antwerp Town Hall (c) was built by Cornelis Floris in 1561 it established the new classical style as the model for civic buildings in the rich and independently minded cities of the Low Countries. Although Floris had studied in Italy, the steep pitch of the roof, the large areas of window and the richly decorated vertical central gable all come from the Gothic traditions of his native city. So too, when in 1572 Robert Smythson designed a new house for a wealthy courtier at Longleat (a) in the English countryside, he added a thin symmetrical decoration of classical columns and details to the sparse square shape of a late English Gothic building, with its distinctive large windows and flat roof.

In an age of poor communication and emerging divisions in Europe it is in some ways remarkable that classical architecture should have been so universally attractive as to overturn centuries of a much stronger Gothic tradition than had existed in Italy. It is less surprising that it should first appear heavily modified by regional traditions.

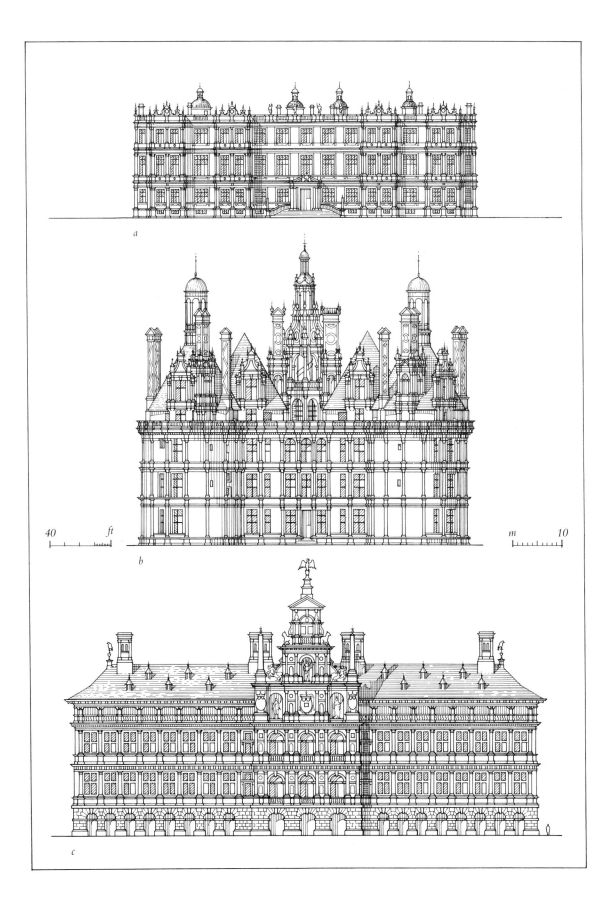

*a*

40     *ft*

*m*     10

*b*

*c*

# INTERNATIONAL BAROQUE

From the middle of the sixteenth century Europe was submerged in a hundred years of virtually continuous warfare, as Protestants and Catholics fought for their beliefs, nations fought for their independence and the trading classes for their freedom. The Roman Church, shocked by the Protestant revolution, purged itself in a savage, Spanish-inspired, militant austerity, the Counter-Reformation, which was designed to turn back the tide of Protestantism. By about 1625 the counter-reformers, confident that Protestantism was checked, if not defeated, abandoned austerity in favour of exuberant and glamorous propaganda. An artistic and architectural style grew up to serve this new spirit of self-indulgence. This, the Baroque style, swept across Europe, in one form or another, as each region recovered from the deprivations of war. By this time classical architecture had made itself felt everywhere and with the universal adoption of the Baroque the whole continent shared one architecture for the first time since the thirteenth century.

One of the most important figures in the development of the Baroque was the Roman sculptor and architect Gianlorenzo Bernini. In his church of S. Andrea al Quirinale in Rome (a) of 1658 the various classical elements and the plan are not separated out in an orderly way, but merged together and moulded to make the building into a vast sculpture which, by enlarging familiar themes and uniting them with a series of sensuous curves, overwhelms the onlooker and allows the building to lift the emotions in a surge of theatrical exhilaration.

The first buildings in France to cast off the remnants of the Gothic tradition used the Italian Mannerist style that had given birth to the Baroque. This early introduction created a more restrained tradition in France which avoided the temptation to indulge in the later extremes of Italy and Spain. The church of the Sorbonne (b) by Jacques Lemercier, begun in 1635, was one of the first examples of this Italian style in France. The rich but scholarly classical decoration, the varied spacing of the screen of columns concentrating on the central door, all crowned by a dramatic dome, resembled buildings in Rome of sixty years before.

The political power of France in the seventeenth century helped to introduce the new style to her northern neighbours. When England emerged from her civil war and the monarchy returned from French exile, Baroque architecture was adopted for a vigorous and enthusiastic rebuilding programme which saw the creation of such great buildings as Blenheim Palace (c) by the architects Vanbrugh and Hawksmoor.

The heavy drama of the Baroque made a major and lasting contribution to the classical tradition. Although it relied for its freedom and inventiveness on the break with Renaissance conformity and the deliberate perversity of Mannerism, in many respects Baroque architecture was closer to the classical freedom of ancient Rome.

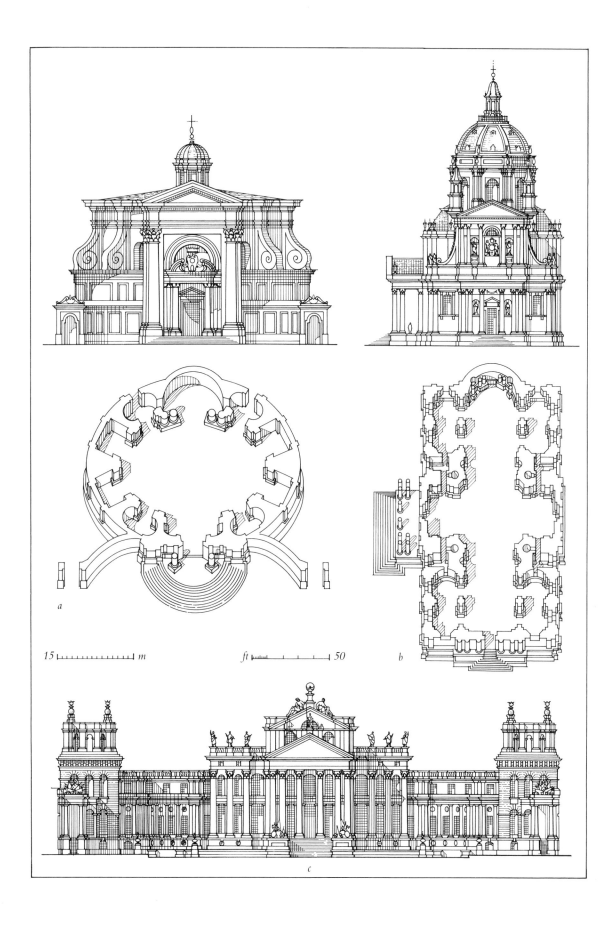

a

15 ⌊ııııııı⌋ m     ft ⌊ıı ı ı ⌋ 50     b

c

# PALLADIO AND HIS LEGACY

The powerful maritime city-state of Venice was skilful enough to escape the ravages of the terrible war that had brought down Rome in 1527 and Florence in 1530. The great armies of the huge kingdoms that had laid waste most of the Italian peninsula convinced the Venetian republic that it should consolidate its wealth within its borders and abandon the perilous course of expansion. There followed a rise in Venetian fortunes when artistic and intellectual exiles sought safety in the neutral republic. The war created a siege mentality and agricultural reforms improved the countryside, encouraging wealthy families to build houses to manage their estates.

The great architect Andrea Palladio flourished in this stimulating atmosphere. His buildings are a unique combination of the freedom of Mannerism and the scholarship of the High Renaissance. Personal study of the ruins of Rome and the artistic licence of the time opened his eyes to the undiscovered liberty of ancient architecture. His Palazzo Chiericati in the Venetian town of Vicenza (b) brings together a traditional application of two layers of columns and a novel inside-out façade where the open courtyard terraces are brought out to the front. This less threatening form of palace perhaps shows the political stability of the Venetian republic, but it also brings the open character of country villa design into the town and it is Palladio's country villas that start a new chapter in classical architecture.

In 1570 Palladio published his *Four Books of Architecture*, which became a standard textbook on classical design. Alongside his studies of ancient buildings were his own designs for churches, palaces and villas. His villas for the Venetian noblemen's management and enjoyment of their improved country estates combined, for the first time since the ancient world, architecture and the total surrounding landscape.

A brief and virtually contemporary adoption of Palladian architecture in England was submerged by civil war and the Baroque, only to re-emerge in 1715 as a sober antidote to the Baroque. The rise of Britain as a major Protestant power gave the new Palladianism a national identity and an enduring international status. Above all, the traditional British country estate with its large house and working farms found Palladio's creation of a simple grandeur in a rural setting irresistible and, in buildings such as Holkham Hall (c) by William Kent, Palladio's Venetian villas became a British tradition.

The translation and lasting fame of Palladio's *Four Books* and Britain's rising position in the world as an imperial power and father of the Industrial Revolution gave Palladianism a remarkably long life and widespread popularity. The style became so generally accepted that, as late as 1796, one of the first colonial revolutionaries to gain independence from Britain, Thomas Jefferson, could regard Palladianism as a natural style for his own house, Monticello (a), in the United States of America.

32

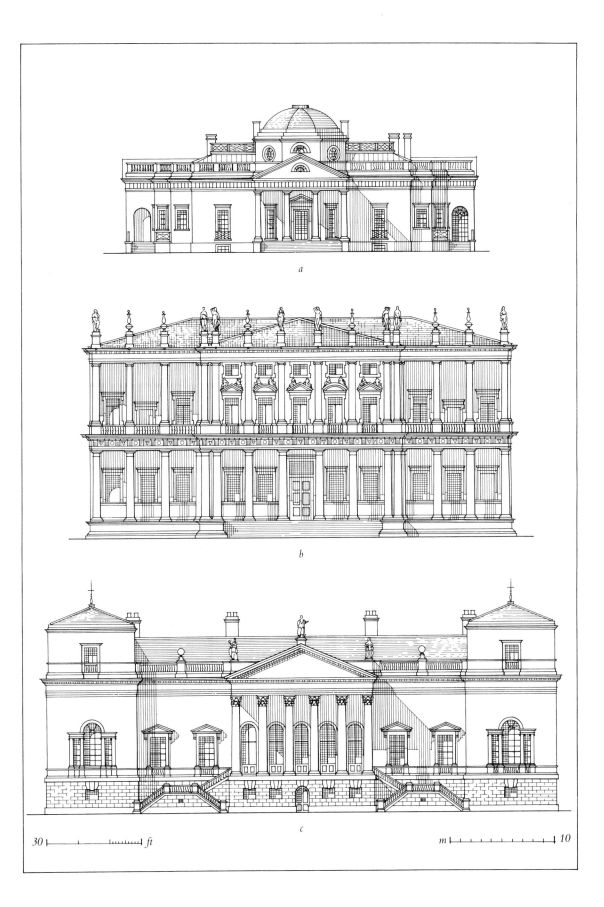

*a*

*b*

*c*

30 |   |   |  |  |  | *ft*                     *m* |  |  |  |  |  | 10

# ROCOCO

While Britain adopted the role of the leading Protestant power and turned its back on the exuberance of the Baroque, the Roman Catholic countries took Baroque design to unsurpassed levels of illusion and extravagance. In the first half of the eighteenth century, in Spain, France, Italy and the states of central Europe, the ponderous drama of the Baroque was transformed by a fragile disintegration of everything that appeared solid and substantial into a riot of surface decoration and visual make-believe. This remarkable outburst of escapism is called Rococo.

The natural home of Rococo seemed to be Spain, where classical architecture in its purer forms had never made anything more than a superficial impression. Eight hundred years of Muslim rule only finally ended in 1494, but the legacy of the sophisticated decoration of the Arabs had, however, preserved a taste for extravagant architecture. A severe style introduced by monkish monarchs in the seventeenth century was abandoned in the eighteenth century and the natural Baroque reappeared, reinforced for the first time by a common direction abroad. The door of the Hospicio Provincial in Madrid (d), designed by Pedro Ribera in 1722, almost submerges the Mannerist classical background in a crust of stone carved in an explosion of decoration representing flowers, jewels, fruit, cascades of drapery and innumerable distortions of traditional classical details. This barely classical, frenzied art was eagerly absorbed by the conquered Indian civilizations in Central and South America who had a native art surprisingly similar in spirit.

As the small states of Germany gradually forgot the horrors of the Thirty Years War and Austria breathed a sigh of relief, having turned back the Turks from the gates of Vienna in 1683, a brilliant society emerged in central Europe where emperors, bishop princes and archdukes competed for artistic prestige. Local architects took over from migrant Italians and a highly sophisticated regional Rococo developed around the church and the palace. This new style was so attuned to the sentiments of the population that it was effortlessly incorporated into the everyday art of the common people. Great buildings such as the Zwinger in Dresden, a ceremonial enclosure with lavish gates (c), by Pöppelmann in 1711, are more fragile and elegant than their Spanish counterparts. Rather than overwhelm the classical forms, the architect has taken the traditional details apart and reconstructed them in a breathtaking composition of curves and double curves, shadows and projecting decoration.

The Rococo was essentially a type of decoration which at its best united with the architecture to which it was applied. It could be used for interior details, furniture and fabrics and in this form, principally by way of France, it found its way into the more austere architectural background of Britain. As the two column capitals (a) and (b) show, in its remarkable freedom and occasional asymmetry it is virtually unique in classical design in paying no regard to the ideals of ancient architecture.

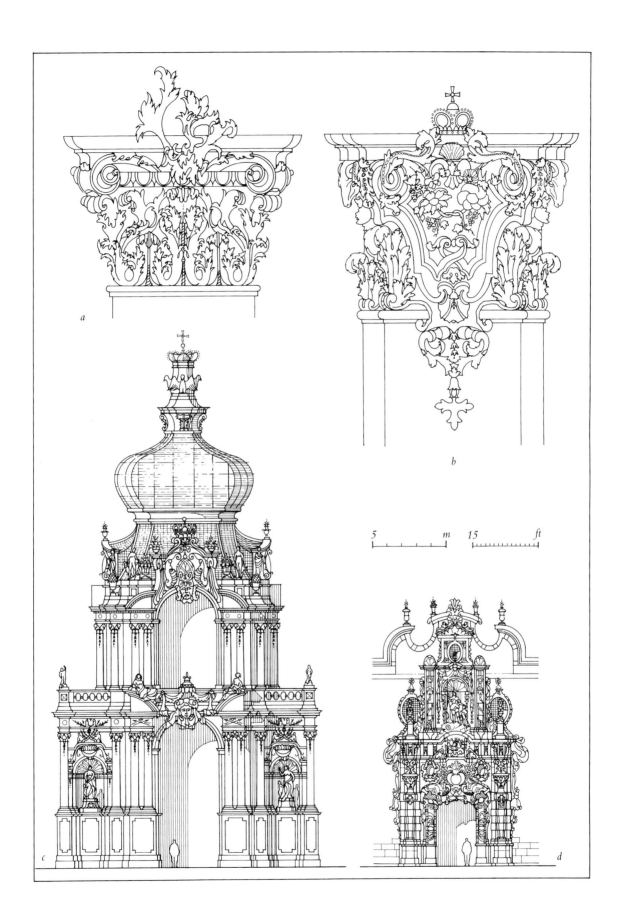

*a*

*b*

*c*

*d*

5        *m*    15        *ft*

# NEO-CLASSICISM

In the eighteenth century, Europe began to cast off its centuries-old systems of government. New philosophies, better education and increased wealth from trade and the Industrial Revolution made the growing middle classes uneasy with the inherited dictatorship of kings and queens. By the middle of the century, a process was under way that would lead to republican revolution in America and France and a weakened monarchy in Britain.

A new way of thinking emerged as people turned from the burden of their accumulated cultural history and sought rejuvenation in the imagined purity and simplicity of their primitive origins. In the search for fundamental truth, philosophers looked to the life and character of the natural man, free from the conventions of society. The study of history for its own sake and the invention of archaeology led artists and architects to seek inspiration in a carefully reconstructed past.

Landowners built mock ruins and English gentlemen travelled to the real ruins of Greece and Rome. The Gothic Revival began and Europe and America entered into a romantic relationship with the past that has lasted to the present day. In 1740, architects at the French Academy at Rome produced designs based on their interpretations of the ancient monuments of the city which were the first examples of a new classical direction, Neo-classicism. A Prussian archaeologist Winckelmann reintroduced Greek art to the west in 1754. Illustrations of the architecture of ancient Greece, published in 1762 by the British architects Stuart and Revett, revealed a simplicity that shocked contemporaries. At the same time, the Scottish architect Robert Adam made his name from books on the more complex buildings of ancient Rome and transformed the Palladian architecture of Britain with elegant interpretations of his studies, such as the Royal Society of Arts (a) of 1772.

The revolutionary leaders at the end of the century saw their spiritual forefathers as the republicans of ancient Greece and Rome, and the new architecture gave eloquent expression to their aspirations. In the revolutionary states of North America, Greece and Rome were embraced with equal enthusiasm and Thomas Jefferson, third president of the new republic, personally designed a new university in Charlottesville, Virginia, in 1817 with a library (b) closely modelled on the Pantheon in Rome.

In France the political and visual revolutions were more violent. Architects such as Boullée and Ledoux anticipated the political revolution with designs of a brutal simplicity inspired by the primitive buildings of ancient Greece and the vast monuments of Rome. Their stark, inventive projects included imaginary schemes for towns and monuments which expressed political theories and symbolic ideals. Designs such as the house illustrated (c) by Ledoux were early expressions of the imposing severity of the last phase of Neo-classicism as it entered the reshaped world of the nineteenth century.

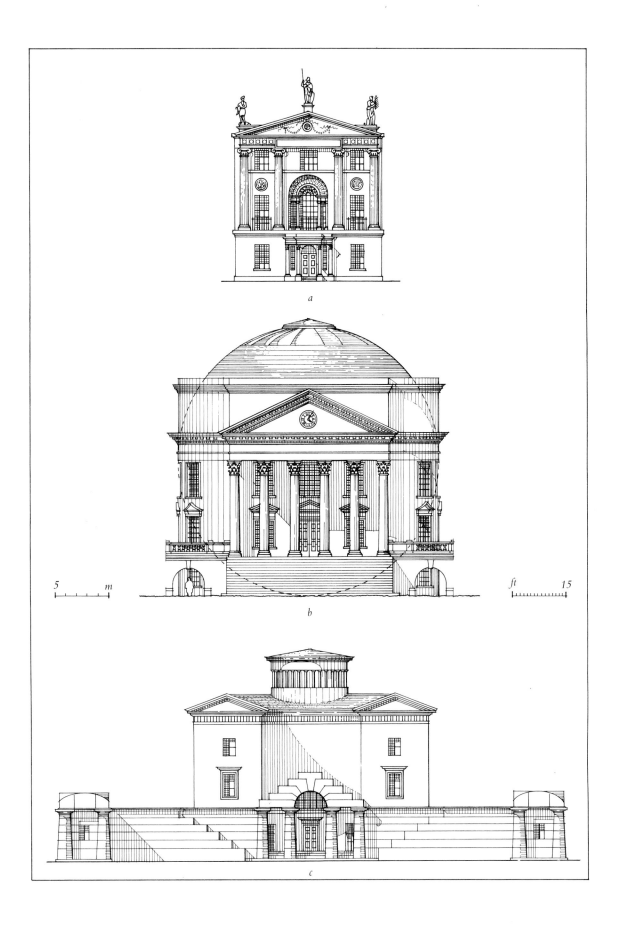

*a*

*b*

*c*

5 _m_

_ft_ 15

# RENAISSANCE REVIVAL

By the middle of the nineteenth century, popular revolt in Austria, Germany, Switzerland, Belgium, Italy and Britain demonstrated that the explosion of the French Revolution could not be contained within national boundaries. Both the wealth and the misery of the Industrial Revolution also broke out of their British home and, together with the democratic consequences of political unrest, created a society with more complicated and varied needs than ever before.

Belief in an underlying rational order in our primitive origins was lost and an irrational interpretation of the past came to the fore. There was a revival of religious faith and literature dwelt on passion and horror. Artists, more interested in self-expression than patrons, starved in their garrets and architects tired of the bare orderliness of neo-classical buildings. The Gothic Revivalists allied themselves with religion and decisively spurned their frivolous association with classical architecture. The busy decorative elegance of Gothic, and the freedom it allowed in designing for the more complex demands of an industrial society, were in tune with the taste and needs of the century.

Neo-classical architects continued to design throughout the century, but by dogmatically adhering to the forms of the ancient world made the accommodation of new functions difficult. The revival of the Renaissance solved the problems of the new age: its elegant proportions and use of decoration contrasted with old-fashioned neo-classical buildings. The large range of building types, and the freedom to create more, answered the need for complicated plans. The ambiguous relationship between early Renaissance and Gothic architecture, and the varied development of the Renaissance, were behind a free mixing of styles and details that became characteristic of the nineteenth century.

The influence of the Renaissance first appears in Paris in the first decade of the century. In 1828 the remarkable Prussian neo-classical architect Schinkel designed a house in Berlin (a), for a manufacturer of terracotta, which displays his client's decorative products on a simple Renaissance façade. In the following decade the revival became established and with his Reform Club (b) of 1837 Charles Barry became a pioneer in Britain. Barry's simple High Renaissance exterior has a functional interior which skilfully organizes the varied accommodation required for a gentleman's club around an Italian courtyard with a glass roof to keep out the English weather. The Henry G. Villard houses (c) by McKim, Mead and White in New York City, bring together six houses around a courtyard, opening on one side to the street. This distinguished urban design was built in 1882. Its late date is a witness to the great success of the Renaissance revival in meeting the functional and visual needs of the nineteenth century.

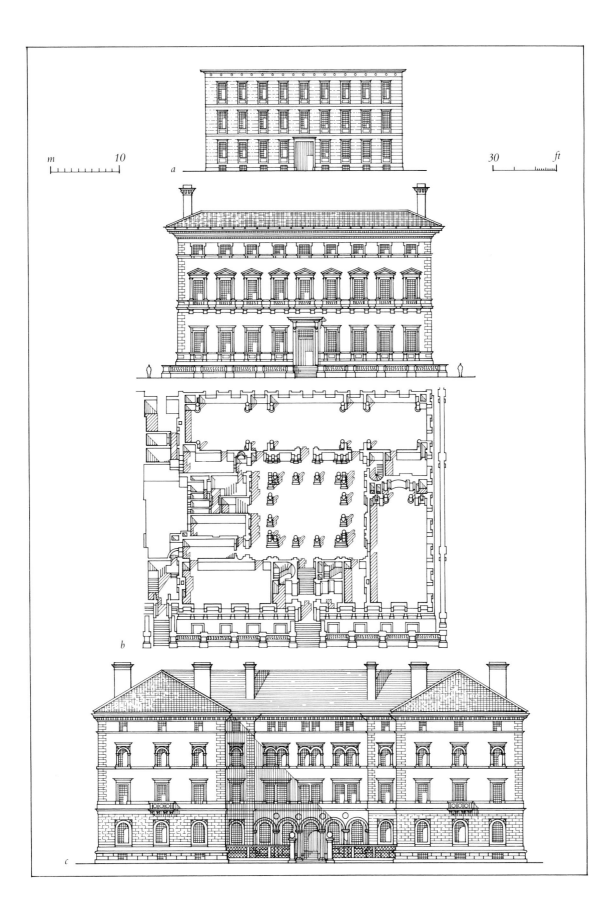

m   10                                          30   ft

b

c

# THE ARTS AND CRAFTS MOVEMENT

The Industrial Revolution brought Britain early power and wealth, but was also a source of squalor and exploitation. As manufacturing industry was the cause of the bad living conditions, a reform of the manufacturing process seemed to some philanthropists to be the solution to the problem. At the same time the Gothic Revival was not only considered to be uniquely Christian and English, but the Middle Ages were idealized as a moral age where anonymous but contented workers hand-made products of great beauty.

In the 1860s the writings of Ruskin and the writings, products and influence of William Morris brought socialism and art together, creating the Arts and Crafts Movement. Pioneers of the movement made furniture, pottery, textiles and metal-work of the highest quality. The practical features of these pieces were embellished with restrained decoration applied according to moral rules. Although the movement failed to reform industry, its products were much admired by discerning buyers.

In architecture early Arts and Crafts buildings were few. These were mostly individual houses which tried to create a native Gothic domestic character. The movement did not really start to have a major architectural impact until the foundation of the Art Workers Guild in 1884.

All the founding architects were from the office of Norman Shaw and, as his Swan House in London (a) of 1875 shows, by this time progressive architects were starting to move away from the Gothic to a similarly free and distinctly British style, classical in spirit and inspired by early-eighteenth-century domestic architecture in the reign of Queen Anne.

This style was readily copied and quickly spread to the United States in buildings such as the Baltimore house (b) by Wilson in 1879 for Mrs McKim. This classical direction did not dominate Arts and Crafts architecture, but free classical elements are often to be found mixed with Gothic planning and some of the distinctive features of the movement. Some of the architects continued to observe the strict Gothic ideals of Morris, but this purity was generally short-lived. By the turn of the century, distinctly classical buildings such as Luckley at Wokingham (c) by Ernest Newton were being designed by most of the old Arts and Crafts architects. Most of these buildings remained true to the principles of the movement in the support of the craftsmanship, the use of local materials and the creation of a distinctly regional character.

The Arts and Crafts Movement had an influence out of proportion to the small quantity of its products. The movement was paradoxically to influence both those who sought the end of the classical tradition in the Modern Movement and, through its own architects, the course of twentieth-century classical architecture.

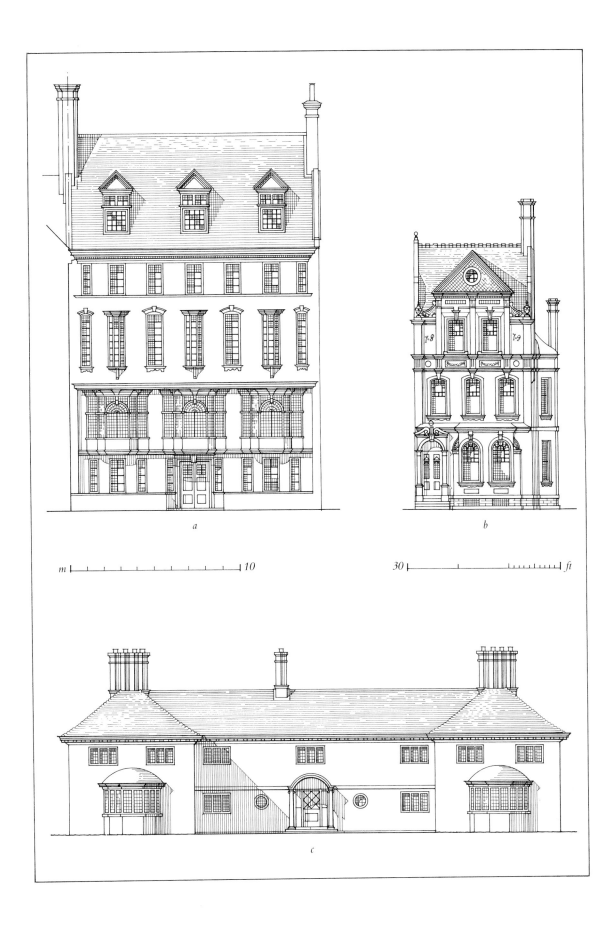

a

b

m ⊢──┴──┴──┴──┴──┴──┴──┴──┴──┴──┤ 10          30 ⊢──┴──┴──┴──┴──┴┴┴┴┴┴┤ ft

c

# BAROQUE REVIVAL AND THE
# BEAUX ARTS

Eighteen hundred and seventy-one saw the unification of two major European powers, Italy and Germany. A period of fierce competition ensued, new and old nations struggled to maintain markets for their products, the late starters tried to carve out overseas territories for themselves and an atmosphere of militant nationalism prevailed. As the United States recovered from the Civil War, she too entered the imperial arena while Japan started to flex her muscles in the east. The relaxed, free-market days of the middle of the nineteenth century were over and the major nations of the world set in motion a propaganda campaign for their empires.

Establishment art and literature inflated imperial ideals and dwelt on the glories of Imperial Rome. Throughout the western world the prosperity gained from expanding economies and captive imperial markets was lavished on grandiose building projects. Both England and France turned to their own seventeenth-century architects, who combined the ostentatious inventiveness of the Baroque with a national individuality, allowing new buildings to be creative and prestigious without being restricted by archaeological correctness.

In France the classical tradition had been vigorously maintained throughout the nineteenth century by a unique official architectural education system which trained architects in the design of grand public buildings and included study at the French Academy at Rome. By the end of the century the style came to be called Beaux Arts, after the architectural school in Paris. Buildings such as Girault's Petit Palais, (b) and (c), built for the Paris Exhibition of 1900, show the characteristic, complex, majestic axial plan and the rich and imposing elevations of the style. This was particularly influential in the United States where a new self-confident wealth was stimulating the construction of a large number of impressive public and commercial buildings such as the New York Public Library (a) of 1911, by Carrére and Hastings.

In Britain the Baroque revival was taken over by architects of the Arts and Crafts Movement, who imbued it with their own brand of originality and nationalism. Both the Arts and Crafts Movement and the Gothic Revival were to decline in the face of the exuberant, ostentatious classical architecture of buildings like the huge Ashton Memorial (d) by Belcher and Joass, built in 1907 to celebrate the public spirit of the principal industrialist in the town of Lancaster.

Imperial nationalism was one of the contributing causes of the First World War and of the rise of international revolutionary socialism. The new sumptuous classical style and the demise of the rational and moral Gothic Revival helped to fuel the Modern Movement, a revolutionary artistic undercurrent which rejected all that the past represented and sought to create a new socialist world served by an art that looked to the new technologies of the coming century.

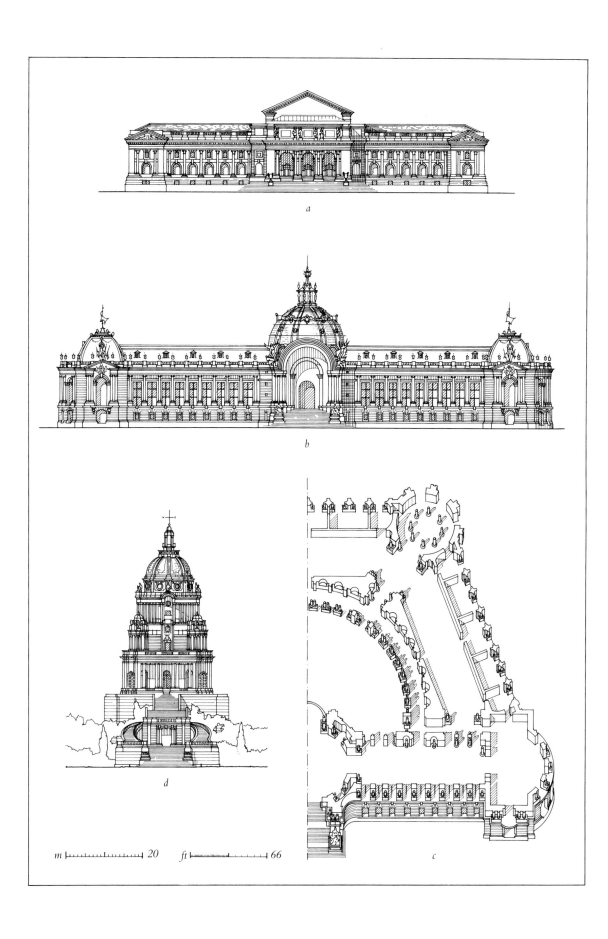

a

b

d

c

m |⊢⊢⊢⊢⊢⊢⊢⊢⊢| 20    ft |⊢⊢⊢⊢⊢⊢⊢⊢⊢| 66

# BETWEEN THE WARS

The aftermath of the First World War threw the western nations into a decade of confusion and revolution out of which emerged the ingredients for a further bloody collision of interests. Before the war a series of imperial monarchies with different levels of democracy were competing for trade and influence. After the war the political complexion of the west changed dramatically and national governments of quite different and opposing political ideals viewed each other with increasing unease.

Among the victors, the United States, Britain and France retained their historic democracies, although the French government was notoriously unstable and the European empires began to break up. Italy, one of the victors, invented fascism as an authoritarian way out of the financial and social chaos caused by the war. Fascism was taken up with enthusiasm by the losers, Germany and Austria, and emerged triumphant out of a civil war in Spain. The communist revolution that had taken Russia out of the war was responsible for much of the political instability of the period, as international socialism seemed to threaten the stability of other countries. Neutral nations such as Switzerland and Sweden, unaffected by these major upheavals, maintained their own democratic systems.

In the years after the First World War in Russia and, in particular, in Germany, artistic and architectural innovators of the Modern Movement tried to create a new artistic direction by abandoning tradition. This was abruptly halted in both countries by unsympathetic dictators who insisted on retaining the classical tradition that was the principal form of architecture in the other western nations. The Modern Movement continued as a minority style in the democracies.

Classical architecture in these two decades represented all the differing political systems in the west. In Germany, Hitler had an interest in architecture both personally and as a medium in the propaganda that sustained his power. His architect Speer designed monumental schemes, influenced by the Prussian neo-classical architect Schinkel, to glorify the regime, and a number of official buildings such as the Chancellery building in Berlin (a) were constructed. In Britain, the empire teetered on and the country experienced no political discontinuity. Architects such as Lutyens continued to build in a more subdued version of the pre-war Baroque, such as in the new offices of the Anglo-Iranian Oil Company in London (c). A new air of restrained simplicity was emerging. In Britain it was called neo-Georgian, but it was most influential in the pioneering welfare states of Scandinavia. The Swedish architect Asplund was one of the principal exponents of this Nordic classicism, which can be seen in buildings such as his Stockholm City Library (b). The simplicity of this style of classicism allowed the Modern Movement to develop a less contradictory relationship with classical architecture in the Scandinavian countries.

*a*

*b*

*c*

*m*         20         70         *ft*

# A NEW BEGINNING

The end of the Second World War brought democratic unity to the nations outside the influence of Russia, and the election of left-of-centre governments in western Europe. The task of rebuilding was accompanied by a determination to create a better society. The technical advances made under the pressure of war instilled a great confidence in the possibilities of new industrial solutions to inadequate housing and war damage. The exhilaration of victory inspired a belief in the feasibility of making a better society through social engineering. The upheavals of war and an erosion of the rigid European social hierarchy prepared the population of Europe for the introduction of radical change.

This was the perfect climate for the Modern Movement whose exponents were radically opposed to the retention of tradition and were optimistic enough to believe that the movement's artistic superiority was so self-evident as to merit universal adoption. Modernist architects had long been developing schemes for social engineering and their designs were based on the exploitation of all that was new in technology. The movement also enjoyed the psychological advantage of having been banned by Hitler. The result was the complete takeover of all artistic and architectural institutions and the suppression of all remnants of the classical tradition.

After twenty-five years of the total dominance of the Modern Movement, its social assumptions were increasingly called into question and the population, far from learning to appreciate it, had developed a strong distaste for its aesthetic. When the oil crisis of 1974 undermined confidence in technology, some artists and architects began to look for more sympathetic means of expression. This led to a rebirth of the classical tradition.

The influence of the Modern Movement remains in the most widespread form of the new classical architecture, the Post-Modern. The huge housing complex outside Paris, Espaces d'Abraxas (a) by the Spanish architect Bofill, while obviously classical in form, relies on a display of new materials for their own sake and a shocking novelty of distortion that is typical of the Modern Movement. Another direction has been the denial of not only the Modern Movement but much of the nineteenth century in careful recreations of a complete historic style such as the United States architect Greenberg's new farmhouse in Connecticut (b). Between these two extremes are buildings such as the new office building in Hampshire (c) by the author which seek to continue the classical tradition without denying the existence of new technology or the possibilities of progress within the classical tradition.

A small but growing number of architects have returned to the classical tradition, but the Modern Movement still dominates the artistic and architectural establishment. The weight of three thousand years of popular artistic tradition has, however, sufficient energy to overcome fifty years of cultural dictatorship.

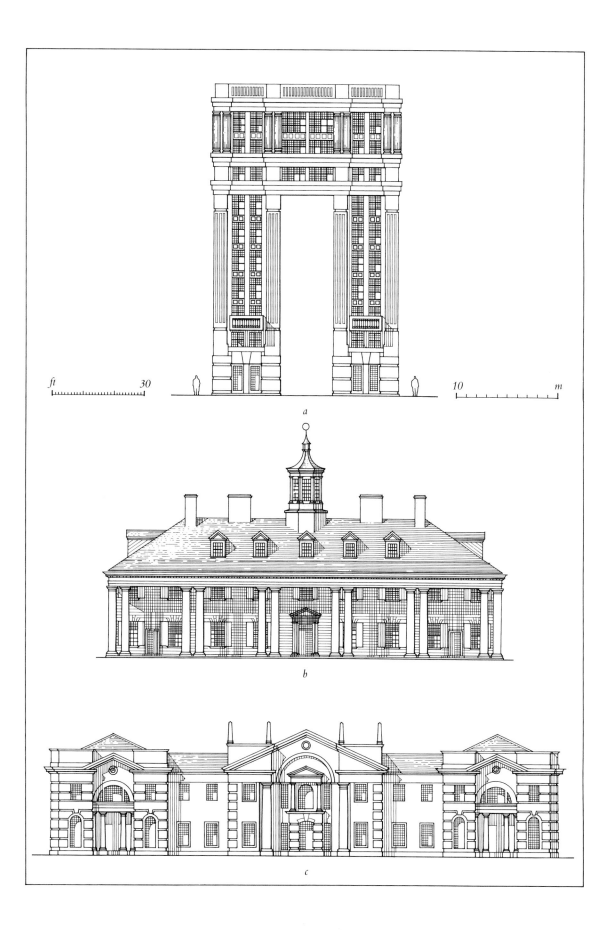

ft 30    10 m

a

b

c

# 2. THE CLASSICAL BUILDING

## THE TEMPLE

Over the centuries certain types of classical building have evolved through the contribution of successive generations of architects. Sometimes building types are chosen for practical reasons, sometimes for their associations. Often, a combination of these reasons lies behind the choice. The history of a building type can always inspire the architect to make creative use of the relationship between a new building and its predecessors.

Above all others the building type that has come to symbolize the classical tradition is the temple. On pages 6, 7 and 8 we have seen how its development set the pattern for the progression of classical architecture. This has led many architects to design temple-like buildings.

As a building originally intended for worship, the temple has often been adopted as the pattern for churches, synagogues and buildings that glorify the state. La Madeleine in Paris (c), designed by Pierre Vignon in 1807 to celebrate the secular glory of Napoleon's army, has the outward appearance of a large Roman temple. Eighteen years later the interior was redesigned as a church by Huvé, in a style derived from Roman baths.

The Grange in Hampshire, England (a) was remodelled by William Wilkins in 1809 from an older house to resemble an early Greek temple. The drama of the open columns and the deep porch, positioned high on a ridge overlooking a river, was more important than the convenience of the occupants. Uncompromising designs of this kind were not often repeated.

In 1866 the architects Heinrich Strack and Friedrich August Stüler skilfully designed the National Gallery in Berlin (d) to fit into a temple of a Roman type. The height of the building, the impressive flight of steps and statue of the Kaiser indicate that the expression of national pride in the design was of great significance.

The Lincoln Memorial in Washington DC (b) is a monument to a national hero which successfully fulfils a function similar to that of an ancient temple. It was designed by Henry Bacon in 1911 to house a huge statue of the former president and includes symbolic references to the state and presidency. It is loosely based on the Parthenon in Athens but the plan is modified to provide an entrance on the long side.

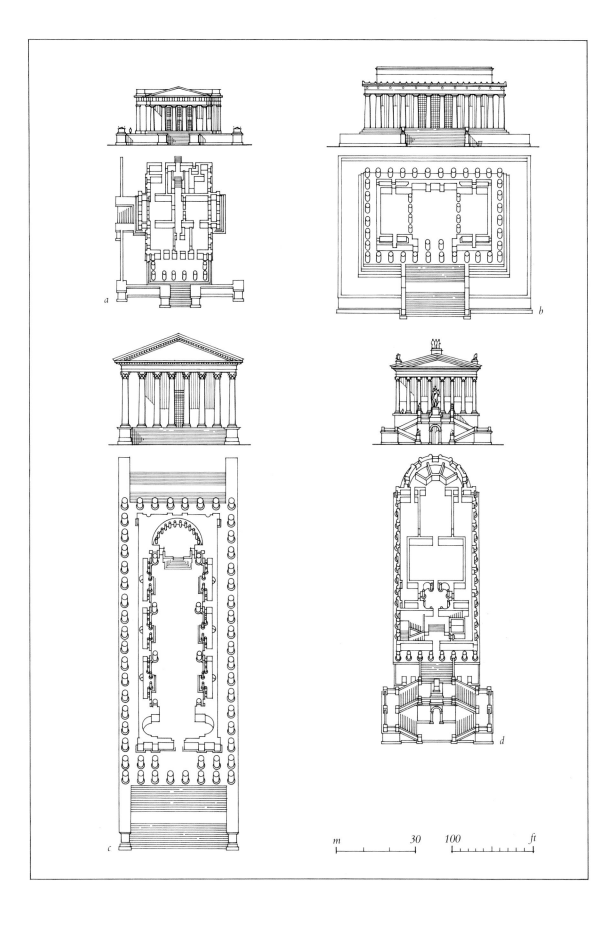

*a*

*b*

*c*

*d*

m       30     100       *ft*

# BASILICAS AND ROUND TEMPLES

The legal and commercial functions of Roman cities were answered by the construction of large covered halls, or basilicas, which became a characteristic feature of Roman communities throughout the empire. Although its name suggests the hall of a Greek king, the basilica was developed to a universal form by the Romans. It generally housed both a court and a public hall. The court, or tribunal, sat in one or both ends of the building in a space, often identified by a semicircular plan, that contained a raised platform for a judge. In front of the tribunal was a public hall which could be used for assembly or trade. The sizes of these halls varied, but the limited width allowed by the roof structures of the time meant that an enlargement to the sides of the open central hall, the nave, could only be achieved by supporting the main walls on columns, or piers, and adding narrower passages, aisles, around the perimeter. This arrangement made it possible to elevate the central roof above the roofs of the side-aisles and so to admit light to the centre of the building through high-level, clerestory windows.

The basilica became one of the great architectural achievements of the ancient Roman civilization. Huge and prestigious examples such as the Basilica Ulpia (a), built by the Emperor Trajan in his new Forum in Rome in about 100 BC, were famous throughout the empire. The Basilica Ulpia had two rows of aisles, an internal and external upper gallery and, unusually, two tribunals.

The basilican layout was also used for small meeting or dining halls and, when near-eastern mystery religions became popular in the empire, some of their secret rites were practised in these small halls with the cult figure or altar in a semicircular apse at one end. When Christianity rose from among these cults to become the official religion of the late empire, its architects developed this early association with the basilica. Great basilicas such as S. Paolo fuori le Mura in Rome (d) were erected on sacred sites to a size and design that was not only intended to associate the new religion with the greatest buildings of the old empire but also performed a similar function of public assembly. These early Christian buildings have set the pattern for the design of churches to this day.

The Roman circular temple also found its way into the architecture of Christianity. Circular temples, such as the Temple of the Sibyl at Tivoli outside Rome (b) from the first century BC, were probably derived from primitive Italian circular huts. Simple round buildings of this type were often used for tombs. Early examples did not have an outer ring of columns. Early Christian baptistries, such as that of Constantine in Rome (c) of AD 430, were often of a circular or near-circular plan. By adopting the architecture of the circular temple, associated as it was with death, and introducing the symbolism of baptism as a release from death, the designers of these buildings preserved an ancient Roman form in a new Christian tradition.

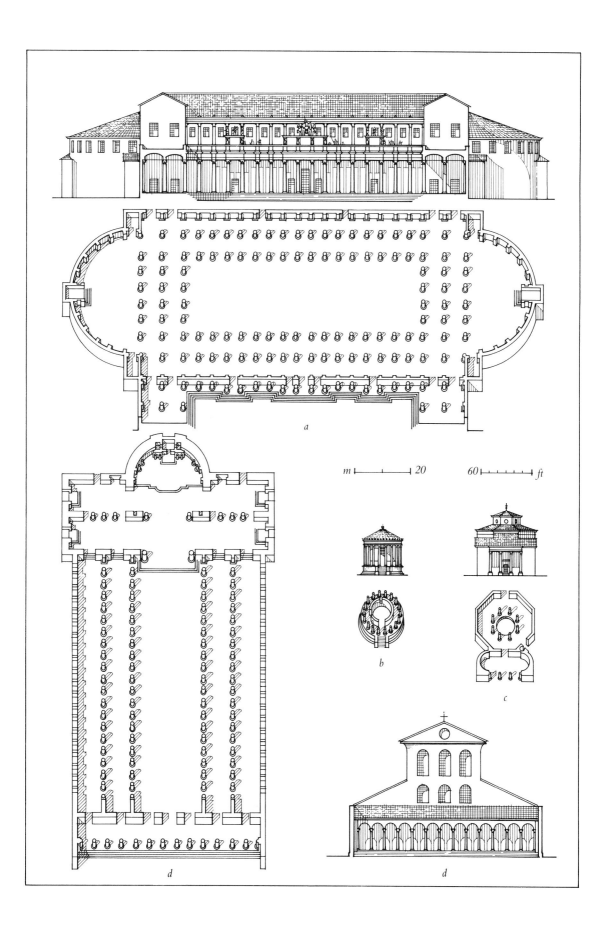

*a*

*m* ⊢——┼——┤ *20*     *60* ⊢—┼—┼—┼—┤ *ft*

*b*

*c*

*d*

*d*

# RENAISSANCE AND BAROQUE CHURCHES

Western Christians continued to worship in churches that retained the form of the basilica. The basilican plan became a firm tradition in church design as the rituals of religious service became established through customary use of the building as a place of worship. When Renaissance architects began to change the Gothic inheritance of church architecture, at first they only rationalized the basilican plan of the medieval church and changed the decorative vocabulary to accord with their new interest in the architecture of the ancient world.

The church of S. Lorenzo in Florence (a) by Filippo Brunelleschi, designed in 1419, was the first complete classical church since antiquity. The plan of the building is very similar to local Gothic churches but displays a new interest in geometric purity. The central nave is exactly twice the width of each of the side-aisles and each division in the aisles is a square. These square divisions, or bays, are repeated for each of ten chapels around the altar. The ceiling of the nave is flat and is decorated with small square panels, or coffers. The ceiling of each division in the aisles and of each chapel has an identical dome in a square. A large dome, four times their size, sits in the centre of the crossing, where the nave and the transept cross. This precise geometry combines with classical details to give to the interior an ordered and rational atmosphere quite unlike that of earlier Gothic churches.

The search for perfection in ideal geometric forms led Renaissance architects to look at ancient circular buildings and at the domed, cross-shaped plans of the Byzantine Greeks (see page 16). These plans by their intellectual purity seemed to reflect the purity of God. The Madonna di S. Biagio at Montepulciano (b) of 1518, by Antonio da Sangallo the Elder, was one of a large number of churches designed in Italy that centred on large domes and had plans that were circular, cross-shaped or cross-shaped inside a square. The equal arms of the Greek cross eliminate the traditional nave of the basilica and the lack of a processional route emphasizes the importance of the altar. The central space dominates the building both inside and out while the huge dome, sitting on the windows of its tall drum, owes more to Byzantium than to antiquity.

While these ideal plans continued to be used for memorial chapels and other specialized churches, they were impractical for the everyday requirements of parish churches and cathedrals. As Baroque architecture moved away from the rarefied atmosphere of the Renaissance back to a passion more akin to the Gothic, the drama of the domed central space was unified with the traditional progressive approach down the nave to the altar. The Baroque sculptural treatment of the supporting walls allowed buildings such as St Paul's Cathedral in London (c) of 1675, by Christopher Wren, effortlessly to combine the Greek cross of the Renaissance with the traditional nave and choir layout of the English Gothic cathedral.

a

b

m            40       ft          100

c

# HOUSES OF ANTIQUITY

In antiquity people lived in many different types of house. Peasants lived in huts and in Imperial Rome much of the population lived in large apartment buildings. Classical civilization was, however, characterized by its widespread urban communities, dominated by powerful local élites. Their substantial town houses have been regarded as the typical houses of antiquity.

These houses looked inward to their own enclosed courts. There were few windows to the outside, so light and ventilation were gained from these central openings. The construction of the courts, and the way the rooms were organized around them, gave the houses of each period and locality their distinctive characteristics.

The primitive Greek house consisted of a single rectangular room with an entrance porch supported on columns. This building, the megaron, is the same as the simple temple illustrated on page 3. By the fifth century BC, however, Greek houses were built around courtyards. In the Greek communities in Europe these courts were informally planned, sometimes on two storeys, with open porches supported on columns around two, three or all four sides. In Greek Asia Minor the megaron survived as a distinctive higher element in the assembly of rooms, containing the principal accommodation. These megarons were surrounded by courtyards of varying design (b). By the first century BC the courtyard had developed throughout the Greek world into a more formal design known as a peristyle.

Roman houses from their Etruscan origins onwards were built around a special kind of court, the atrium, which was the heart of the house. The atrium had a central opening supported on beams or columns which allowed rain-water to fall into a central rectangular pool. It was entered from the street by a small lobby and contained important furnishings such as the family shrine and the strong-box. On either side, in early Roman houses, lay the bedrooms and at the far end a dining-room and a principal reception room faced the atrium, but could be closed off by folding doors.

Exposure to the luxurious lifestyle of the Greeks in southern Italy in the first century BC introduced the peristyle to the Romans. This colonnaded courtyard contained a central garden and had its own special reception room. At first the peristyle was just put behind the principal reception room, but in time, as in illustration (a), most of the reception rooms came to be placed around it and it was linked directly with the atrium.

The Romans did not spend all their time in their town houses but enjoyed the seaside and natural scenery. Wealthy Romans usually had a country house, or villa, and some of these villas also operated as working farms. In many of the surviving wall paintings in Pompeii are pictures of the seaside villas that spread along the bay of Naples. Illustration (c) is an interpretation of one of these paintings showing a curved façade facing the sea, a central viewing tower and jetties at the water's edge.

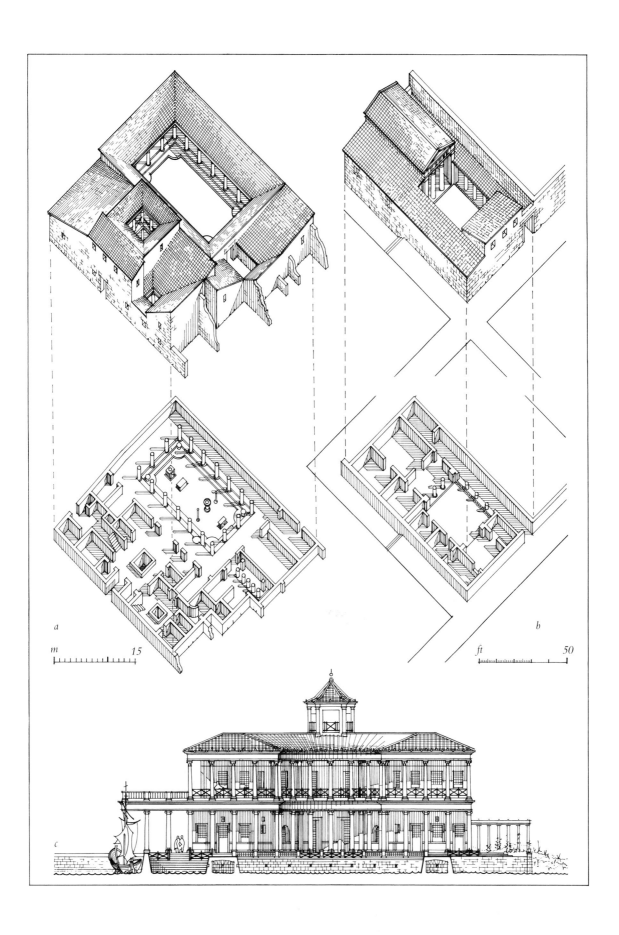

a

m                    15

ft                    50

b

c

# RENAISSANCE AND BAROQUE PALACES
# AND VILLAS

The nobility of medieval Europe generally lived in fortified buildings for security. In Italy, a long tradition of urban life led the merchant nobility to construct urban fortresses or palaces rather than isolated castles. Facing inwards to a courtyard, which acted as the principal means of internal circulation, these large houses had a tradition of elegance and spaciousness long before the Renaissance. The new concern for classical antiquity and proportion in the fifteenth century did not remove the need for protection. Renaissance architects, such as Benedetto da Maiano, designer of the Palazzo Strozzi in Florence (a) in 1489, concentrated on creating precise classical details and proportions on the forbidding façades and hidden courts, and organized the overall plan into a rational and symmetrical composition.

During the sixteenth century a more settled political life often allowed the nobility to move out of their castles to more comfortable accommodation. In northern Europe the aristocracy maintained their major residences at the centre of their rural territories. In France the castle, or château, was still surrounded by a moat and fronted by its customary wide court, but the principal range of buildings no longer had to serve a defensive function. Architects could now concentrate on the grandeur of the approach and interiors, and the outlook on to carefully designed views across the immediate landscape. The unrestricted space, and the contemporary Baroque preoccupation with the creation of impressive sculptural effects, allowed architects, such as Louis Le Vau in the principal buildings of the Château de Vaux-le-Vicomte (c) of 1657, to produce dynamic compositions and interior volumes that would have a profound influence on all subsequent architectural planning.

In Italy the urban tradition continued but, inspired by accounts of the villas of the ancients, the nobility built pleasure pavilions for themselves just outside the town. One of the most influential of these was the Villa Giulia (b), built outside Rome by Vignola, Ammanati and others for Pope Julius III in 1550. The outside world has no part in this design as the building looks inwards to carefully controlled views of its own internal landscape. An unadorned garden court is surrounded by an open curved façade decorated with painted ceilings and delicately sculpted arcades containing ancient sculptures of gods. This composition ends with a small arch leading to a sunken garden with fountains, known as a nymphaeum, and a walled garden beyond.

At about the same time, the aristocracy in the Venetian republic were building villas for their country estates. These often quite modest houses combined rooms for pleasure and entertainment with cellars, lofts and outbuildings for the agricultural functions of the estate. Buildings such as the Villa Badoer (d) by Palladio combined business with pleasure and grandeur with practicality. Their outward perspective on the working landscape set a new standard for countless rural buildings.

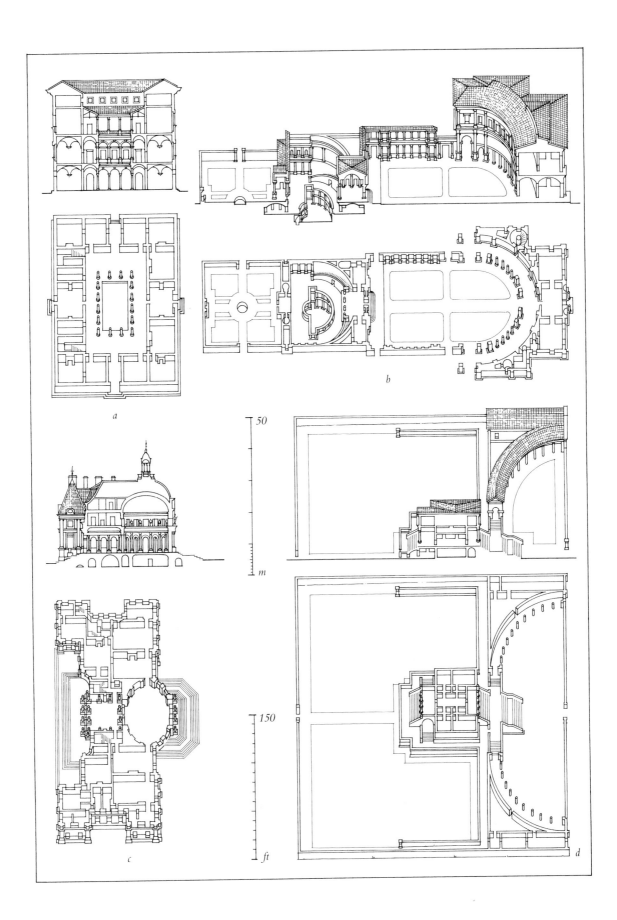

a

b

c

50

m

150

ft

d

# THE SMALL TOWN HOUSE

In towns, the width of buildings is often limited by the high value of the land that faces on to the streets. This restricts the design of houses as daylight can often only be obtained from the back and the front, the stairs can be awkward and, if the front room is to be separated from access to the rest of the house, the main entrance and its passageway must be located to one side.

Illustrated (a) is a house in Rome built in 1500. It is a tradition in Italian towns that even imposing dwellings often have shops on their ground floor. This has allowed the architect to produce a balanced design by creating three vertical divisions, or bays, thereby disguising the off-centre entrance for the accommodation above.

The next example (b), from the sixteenth century in the Hungarian town of Bistrita, includes the common combination of business premises with substantial residential accommodation for the same family. The façade is dominated by the large door for heavy goods deliveries to the workshop and shop on the ground floor. The design is rationalized by a row of symmetrical windows on the upper floor unrelated to the openings below.

A French design (c), by Pierre Le Muet in 1647, is a simple plan including stables beyond an internal courtyard. This became a common feature of larger town houses, where the occupants could afford horses, and was extensively used in later houses in London. The façade is given a strong central emphasis by the roof and windows. This lessens the imbalance created by the asymmetrical position of the door.

The Low Countries had a long tradition of narrow houses jostling for valuable trading frontage on their streets and canals. Example (e), from seventeenth-century Amsterdam, shows the distinctive Baroque gables that were created as architects tried to reconcile classical discipline with the traditional Gothic gables. Other northern countries abandoned these gables in favour of roofs pitched in the opposite direction.

In England, more than any other country, the development of rows of virtually identical houses, grouped according to status, became widespread for all social classes. Illustrations (d) and (f) from 1823 show the highest and lowest standards respectively. The larger house could have an aristocratic occupant, but has a virtually identical plan to the small house intended for an artisan. The houses are distinguished by their size and by the quantity of internal and external decoration.

The problems of designing small town houses in the twentieth century have been changed principally by the widespread ownership of motor cars. Where only one street front exists, sometimes the cars have to be accommodated within the house. The large opening required is seen in illustration (g) and poses similar problems to those of the shop or workshop in (a) and (b). In this example the garage door and entrance are united by a horizontal band and the square of the garage opening is repeated in diminishing proportions vertically.

a

b

c

d

e

f

g

m       11     35       ft

# THE SMALL COUNTRY HOUSE

The small country house can as a type be in a town or suburb as well as in the countryside. All of the designs illustrated here have front doors in the centre and one room on each side of a hall but, despite their apparent similarities, there are significant differences between them.

The small sixteenth-century house on the outskirts of Rome, illustrated (a), has a simple plan with an open porch, or loggia, at the back which gives access to the ground-floor rooms and the stairs. The equally simple elevation gives more importance to the relationship between the upper and lower windows than to the balance of windows inside the ground-floor rooms.

Wick House in Richmond, on the outskirts of London (b), was designed by Robert Mylne in 1775. The plan is sophisticated and creates the maximum effect within the limited space available. The stair has been moved to one side and the passage from the entrance leads straight to an oval salon. Both of the front rooms have windows placed centrally on the interior and the façade is simple and balanced. Service rooms are inconspicuously fitted into each side of the salon and a quadrant stair fits neatly behind the oval.

The eighteenth-century Swedish house in illustration (c) has a symmetrical façade that conceals an irregular collection of rooms. Although the design of individual rooms attempts to rationalize the arbitrary positions of the doors and windows, there is no underlying theme in the layout. There is a large entrance hall containing a grand stair to one side of the front door and the consequent loss of symmetry has been disguised with a false wall.

The mid-nineteenth-century French farmhouse (d) has an austere and utilitarian plan. A narrow hall is just large enough for the stair and leads to a large kitchen on one side and a living-room on the other with a washroom behind. Only the sparse exterior features identify the design as French – minor variations of this plan could be found in almost any European country.

A villa in Aachen in Germany (e), built early this century, shows a less rigid separation of rooms. The hall, the back rooms and one of the front rooms have no rigid divisions between them. The stairs are symmetrically positioned in relation to the front door and the hall by bringing the entrance through a small lobby under a half-landing. The plan is not contained in the simple rectangle suggested by the façade but is modified by ground-floor extensions.

The late-nineteenth-century Californian house (f) has a plan that might be found in any European country. The distinctive American appearance is created by the characteristic porch across the main façade, the deep cornice below the eaves and the low roof, which is largely flat but is intended to give the impression of a French double-pitched, or mansard, roof.

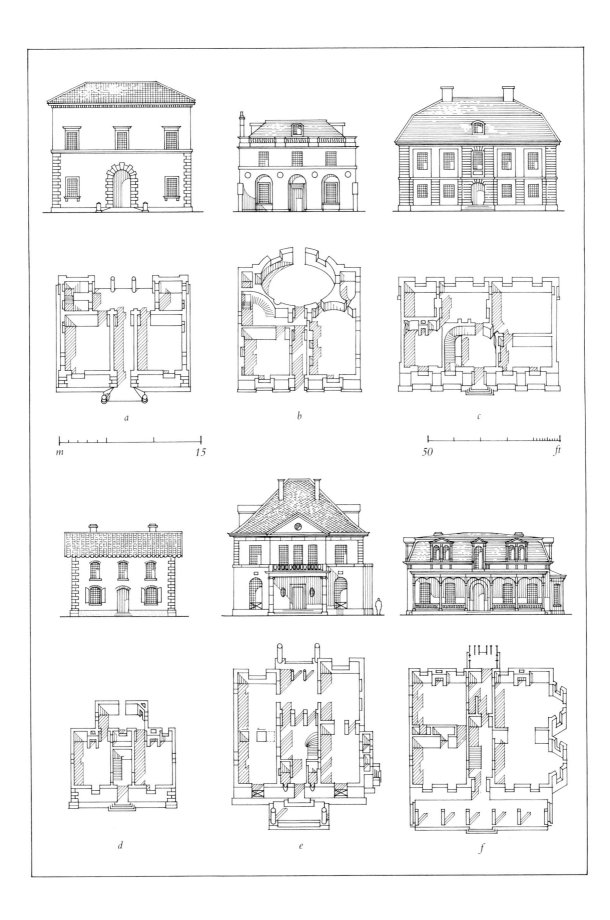

a

b

c

m                15          50          ft

d

e

f

# New Uses, New Interpretations

As times have changed, buildings have had to change. In recent times, as in the past, the classical tradition has been adapted and developed to provide accommodation for uses quite unlike anything that has come before. Sometimes an ancient building type provides such a direct source of inspiration that the new building can serve its different purpose well, yet still closely resemble the original. At other times the needs of the new use are so particular or unprecedented that architects have taken the principles of classical design to create a new building type which, if it is successful, becomes in its turn a part of the classical tradition.

Pennsylvania Railway Station in New York (a) was designed by McKim, Mead and White in 1904 for electric trains crossing the busy business centre of Manhattan Island. This vast building managed the complex meeting of people, motor cars and trains within an ordered classical design incorporating major elements inspired by Roman bath buildings. Free from the smoke of steam trains, changing levels were used to separate the different forms of transport. The railway lines and platforms were all on the lowest level. Pedestrians entered principally through a grand entrance at street level and walked along a shopping arcade to waiting-rooms and ticket-offices grouped around a high and impressive central hall resembling the central hall of the Baths of Caracalla in Rome. Beyond this hall the main concourse was covered with a large iron and glass canopy and led, by way of staircases, to the platforms below. Pedestrians could also enter from the sides on bridges over covered ramps for motor vehicles which, together with ranges of offices to the rear, gave the station an enclosure like those of Roman baths.

The Town Hall in Leeds, England (b) was designed by Cuthbert Broderick in 1853 to satisfy both the public and administrative needs of the newly rich industrial town, and as an expression of civic pride. The freely designed classical building was raised on a high platform and contains at its centre a public assembly room and concert hall to seat 8000 – the largest in its time. Around this are ranged the law courts, committee rooms and offices required for the increasingly complex administration of an industrial community. A huge, wholly decorative and unorthodox tower, paid for by public subscription, rises over the building.

In 1839, in the university city of Oxford, C. R. Cockerell combined a purpose-built museum with a language institute in a single building, the Ashmolean Museum and Taylorian Institute (c). It was one of a number of specially designed museums of the period, which saw a new concern for public access to the arts and an expansion in public education. Behind a strongly sculptured façade, the varying needs of galleries, lecture rooms and libraries are brought together with an inventive combination of Greek Revival and Renaissance details to create a highly original and sophisticated building.

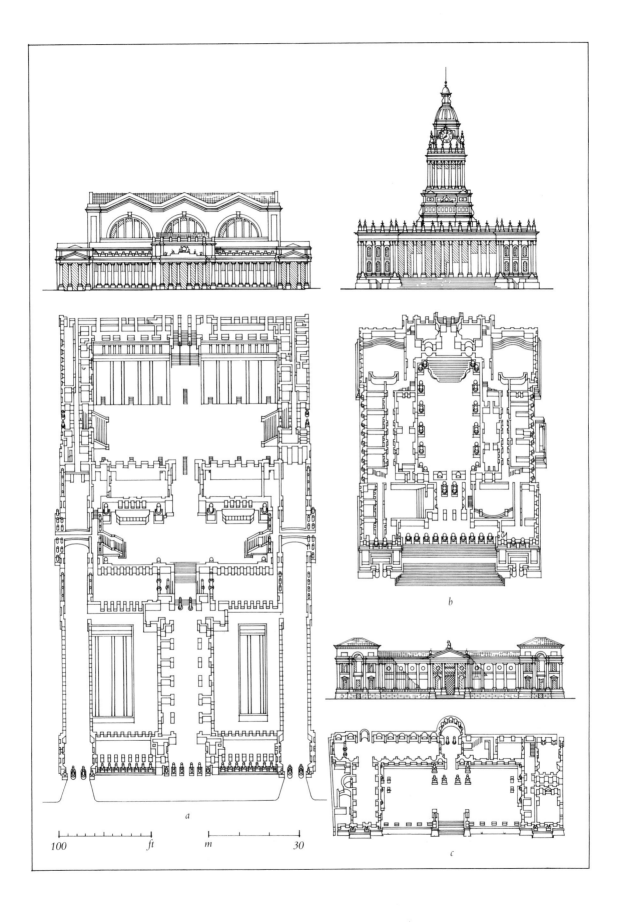

*a*

100       *ft*      *m*       30

*b*

*c*

# New Technologies

Throughout history new methods of building and new materials have been invented. Classical architects have taken these innovations and made them familiar by developing the classical tradition to make room for new technologies. The ancient Greeks changed their timber buildings to stone; the Romans made the arch and the baked brick part of the vocabulary of classical architecture.

In the nineteenth and twentieth centuries the pace of change has been particularly fast and industrial invention has gone hand in hand with the growth of a more complex and crowded society. New building materials have become available, enabling designers to mass produce features that in an earlier age would have been made individually at great expense. The mass production of architectural decoration in fired clay goes back to ancient Greece, but in the eighteenth and nineteenth centuries much larger and stronger building components could be made by using new industrial processes in the casting of iron. This made it possible to produce whole façades and even buildings in a factory, and then transport the components to the site for assembly. Cast-iron buildings such as the Haughwout Building in New York City (d), by John P. Gaynor in 1856, combined an intricacy of classical decoration with the latest opportunities offered by new manufacturing techniques.

New methods of steel production and the invention of Portland cement enabled engineers to design foundations and frameworks to carry buildings of unprecedented height. The development of the safety lift allowed easy access to these heights. In the crowded island of Manhattan, in New York, a new architecture of tall buildings evolved in the early twentieth century. The scale of these towers was so new that architects struggled in an age of stylistic uncertainty to create an appropriate architecture. Great advances were made in the development of the classical tradition to take advantage of the opportunities of increased height. The US Courthouse in New York (a) by Cass Gilbert Jr, completed in 1936, is one of the last of these pioneering buildings.

New building types were also required to house new machinery and accommodate its users. Railways, motor cars and aeroplanes in their turn have required their own buildings. Although the machinery is new, the underlying needs of the users or the machines are often familiar and, as with many new uses of the nineteenth and twentieth centuries, classical buildings have been designed to service them. The famous Morris Garage in Oxford (b), which gave its name to the MG sports car, was designed by Harvey Smith in 1932 and the world's first purpose-built airport at Croydon, south of London (c), was designed by government architects in 1928.

Classical architecture has always responded to the changing needs of society. The opportunities offered by technological innovation and construction techniques are just some of the new demands that bring about changes in a living tradition.

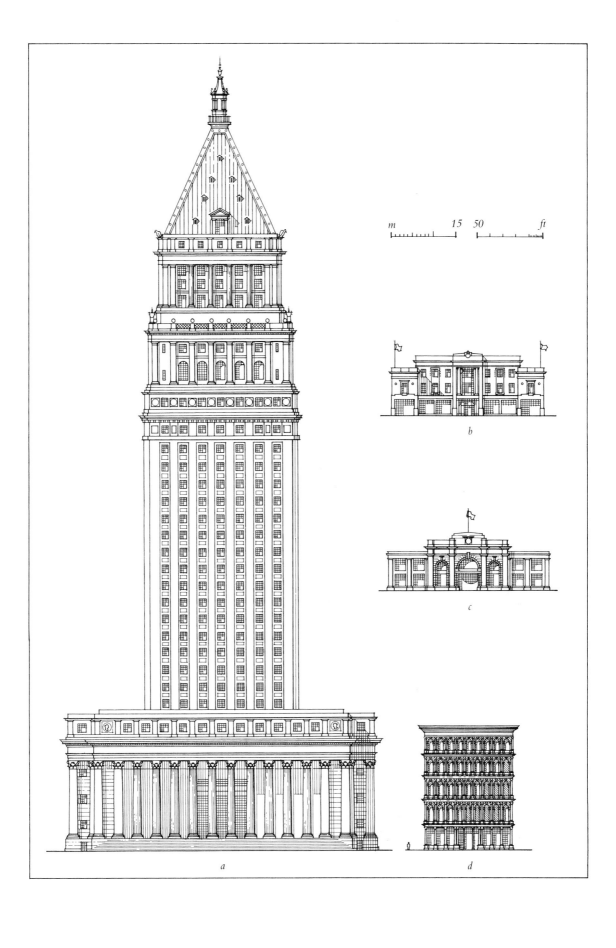

m                15   50              ft

b

c

a                                    d

# CURIOSITIES

Classical architecture does not have to be serious, constrained or inflexible. Experiments and extravagances of the past have become permanent additions to the tradition.

Single columns were often erected in antiquity for commemorative or ritual purposes and supported gifts to the gods, trophies and statues. As free-standing monuments, single columns were often more inventive than those used for buildings. One of the most famous was the tall column (d) that the Emperor Trajan put up in AD 113 as a part of his Forum in the centre of Rome. A continuous strip of sculpture is wrapped around the column in a spiral, like a huge scroll, telling the story of Trajan's conquest of Dacia (Romania). On the top, 41 metres above the ground, stood a statue of the emperor. While the rest of Trajan's Forum was destroyed, the column has been preserved to this day and in the succeeding centuries has become the model for many designs, from candlesticks to full-size copies.

The Romans were very imaginative in the design of their tombs. Strict laws required that graves, and their often large commemorative structures, be located on sites outside the city walls. This isolation often ensured their preservation. The Tomb of Gaius Cestius (e) of 12 BC is a 29-metre-high concrete pyramid faced in white stone, built just outside the city of Rome and later incorporated into the enlarged city walls. It must have reflected some personal interest or involvement in the recent conquest of Egypt and is an early example of the Egyptian taste that the Romans added to the classical tradition. The Tomb of the Julii near Arles in France (c) was built in 40 BC and is an example of a particular type of tower-shaped monument. It has a sculptured base with an open, square, second level and a circular top containing statues of the deceased. This is just one of many styles of tomb whose influence can be seen in buildings from the Middle Ages to this century.

The gates on the entrance drives of large houses from the seventeenth century onwards often included small houses, or lodges, to be occupied by employees. As the approach to an important building and the roadside expression of the status of the occupier, a great deal of attention and originality could be devoted to their design. In Hampshire in England one of the gates to Stratton Park (a) was designed by Charles Dance. Two small Greek Revival lodges are joined by curved walls to a curious gate, almost medieval at first sight, but decorated with ancient Greek features.

The variety of these curiosities is endless and even includes artificial classical ruins (b) to enhance the romantic atmosphere of an eighteenth-century English garden. Although it is possible to divide these curiosities and all classical building types into categories, there is no limit to the opportunities to serve different functions with inventive classical designs.

*a*

*b*

m          5  20          ft

*c*

*d*

G·CESTIVS·L·F·POB·EPVLO·PR·T·B·PL
VII·VIB·EPVI ONVM

*e*

# 3. THE ORDERS

## The Orders

At the heart of all classical architecture lie the orders. It is impossible to understand classical design in any depth without a knowledge of the five distinct and formalized systems of columns and horizontal supports, called the orders, that have guided classical architects from antiquity to the present.

The three principal orders are illustrated here; these are the Doric, Ionic and Corinthian. There are two others which are discussed later in this chapter, Tuscan and Composite, but these are derivatives of the Doric and Corinthian orders respectively.

Each order is most readily identified by the decoration at the top of the column – the capital. Doric has a plain cushion-shaped detail, or echinus, below a square plate, or abacus. Ionic has two spiral curls, or volutes, below a square but modelled abacus. Corinthian has a three-tiered capital of stylized leaves from a Mediterranean plant, the acanthus, gathered around a vase-shaped core below a modelled abacus that curves inwards on all four sides.

The capital is, however, only the most elementary way of identifying each order. All the orders are divided into parts, each of which has its own name. These are noted on the illustration opposite. The same names and divisions apply to each order. Each part differs in each order and it is often possible to identify an order from any one of them.

The orders are essentially a proportioning system and the proportion of each part is different for each order. For convenience it has been accepted for two thousand years that the proportions of the orders should be measured in multiples or divisions of the diameter of the lowest part of the relevant tapering column shaft. This is called the module.

For centuries authors have published ideal proportions and details for each order. The three illustrated are from Palladio's *Four Books of Architecture* of 1570. These publications have tended to disguise both the common variation of proportions, according to the size of building and visual context, and the variety of details and proportions to be found historically. Authors such as Palladio have provided a useful and authoritative basis for classical design where a lack of familiarity makes successful variation unlikely, but they can give the misleading impression that classical architecture is merely the application of old rules and devoid of creative potential.

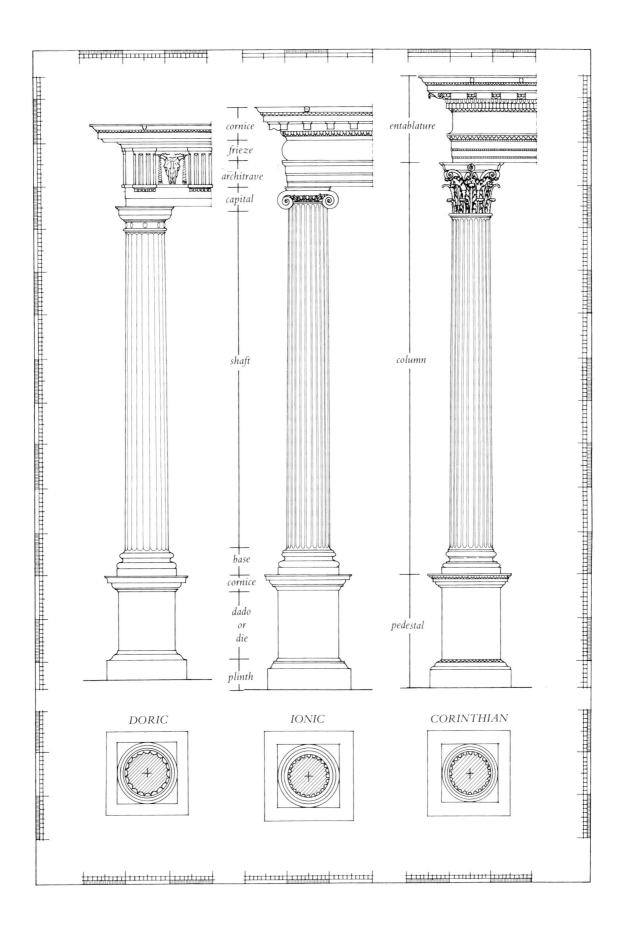

cornice
frieze
architrave
capital

entablature

shaft

column

base
cornice

dado
or
die

pedestal

plinth

DORIC                    IONIC                    CORINTHIAN

# THE DORIC ORDER: ORIGINS

The Doric order is the foundation of all the orders. Its origins are obscure, but there are some aspects of its early history that we can identify with reasonable certainty.

Much of the characteristic stone decoration of Doric is clearly derived from timber construction. This was recognized in antiquity at a time when some examples of timber temples survived. Illustration (b) is reconstructed from a painting on the François Vase from the sixth century BC and shows an early temple with a mud roof. The temple almost certainly had mud-brick walls and two timber columns supporting timber beams. This building features most of the details of the later Doric order, but significantly some details do not correspond to the requirements of a rational timber structure. The apparently simple picture of the timber origin of Doric in the seventh century BC in Greece is further complicated by illustration (a) which shows part of a colonnade from the funerary temple of Queen Hatshepsut in Egypt from 1480 BC. This has such a remarkable resemblance to Greek Doric that it cannot be accidental. These examples demonstrate that attempts to explain the fine details of the Doric order strictly according to a timber origin are futile. Even in the original timber structures there may have been the influence of a much older Egyptian translation of timber to stone.

It is dangerous to assume that these people saw structure and its decoration in a modern sense as separate; they are more likely to have decorated their timber buildings with aesthetic caprice. Illustration (c) must not, therefore, be taken too literally. It is one of many attempts to reconstruct a timber Doric building rationally and includes a certain amount of guesswork for which there is no direct evidence. It does, none the less, help to explain not just the Doric order, but the way the parts of all the orders relate to one another.

The wooden columns are capped by a board or stone slab, the abacus. Spanning them are beams which are bound together by a short board, or regula, and over the regula is a small projection, the tenia, which seems to be the edge of a continuous flat board. These beams and their connecting boards make up the architrave. The roof beams rest on the architrave and are fixed to it from below by pegs, called guttae. The exposed ends of these beams are triglyphs and together with the gaps between them, the metopes, make up the frieze. Over the frieze a timber plate supports the rafters, or mutules, which are laid flat and are firmly secured to overhanging wooden eaves, the corona, by more pegs. This corona must be fixed to the last of the large clay tiles in order to prevent the rest of them slipping off the shallow roof. This final tile sometimes takes the form of a gutter called the cyma, or wave, after its shape. The plate, rafters and gutter are together called the cornice.

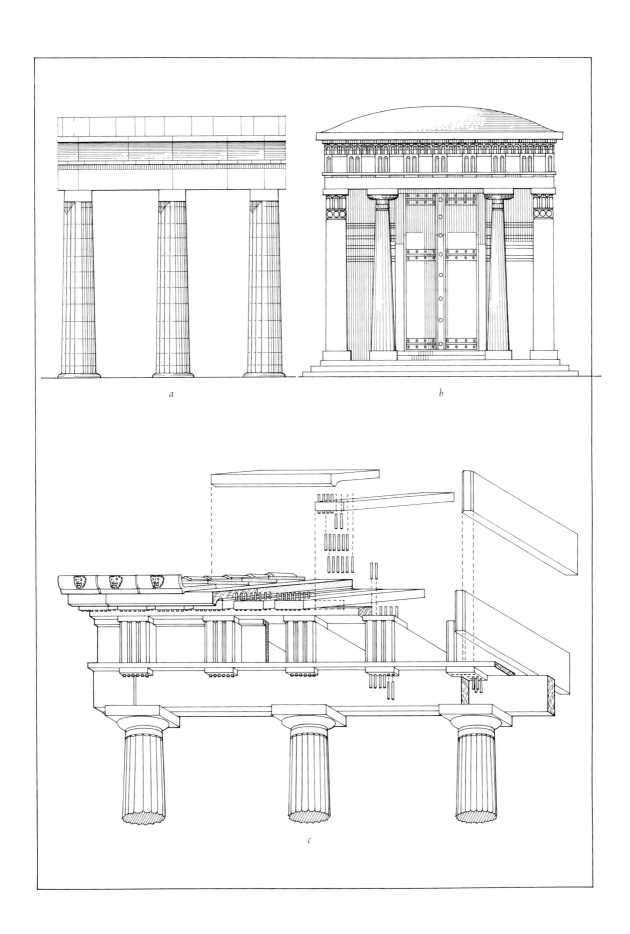

*a*                                    *b*

*c*

# The Greek Doric Order

Early Greek architects built their first stone buildings cautiously in imitation of their timber buildings, modifying the proportions to allow for the heavier weight and poorer structural qualities of stone. This same caution is evident in the visual development of the Doric order. There were a number of experiments with different details and arrangements, particularly in the earlier buildings, but all such variations took place within a very clearly established traditional composition of elements. Minor successful modifications were adopted and unsatisfactory ideas rejected, but the general tendency over the centuries was to make the order more slender, perhaps encouraged by a greater confidence in the strength of stone.

The Temple of Poseidon in the Italian colony of Paestum, south of Naples (b), dates from about 460 BC and shows the stout proportions of the early stone temples. The columns are broad and 4.25 diameters, or modules, high, and the entablature 1.75 diameters high. This can be contrasted with a building from the island of Delos (c) of about 95 BC where the column is 7.25 diameters and the entablature 1.85 diameters.

The Parthenon in Athens, (a) and (d), was highly respected in antiquity and since the middle of the eighteenth century has been generally regarded as the finest of the Greek Doric, if not of all Greek, buildings. It was designed in a particularly prosperous and creative period of Athenian history and is often considered to be the model example of a refined study of proportions made possible in part by the continued adherence to the traditional arrangement of the order. The column is 5.5 diameters high and the entablature 2 diameters high. The architrave and frieze are of approximately equal height and the cornice a little over 0.5 diameters high.

The Greek Doric order is consistently faithful to its timber origins, probably because of the parallel existence of significant numbers of surviving wooden buildings. The mutules under the eaves in the cornice always slope to match the pitch of the roof and the use of triglyph beam-ends is universal. Columns almost always have the shallow fluting characteristic of the order which seems to derive either from the timber grain or more likely from the cuts of the metal tool used to trim the log. The last triglyph on a corner is always moved to the corner of the entablature away from its usual position on the centre of the column, perhaps following a timber detail, thereby making the last metope rather longer than those on the rest of the frieze.

In the Greek world, the similarity between timber and stone buildings was heightened by the bright painted decorations they shared. Sculptural decoration in relief was limited to individual projecting mouldings and places such as the metopes where there would have been no essential timber structure. Recognition of the history of such classical details as these has always given their knowledgeable use a satisfying consistency.

*a*　　　　*b*　　　　*c*　　　　*d*

# ROMAN AND RENAISSANCE DORIC

There was no break between the Greek use of the orders and their adoption by the Romans. Rome's Etruscan ancestors had used provincial versions of the Greek orders long before the Roman conquest of the Greek colonies of southern Italy eclipsed Rome's native architectural traditions. But more than four centuries of Roman use did bring about some changes and none was so significant as the modifications to the Doric, the oldest and most conservative of the Greek orders.

The Romans continued the later Greek tendency to make the column more slender and on the Theatre of Marcellus in Rome (d) of 13 BC the column is 7.65 diameters high. The eccentric position of the Greek corner triglyph was thought to be irrational and it was brought back to the centre of the column to match the others on the frieze. Influenced by local traditions, the Romans introduced other modifications. Occasionally a moulded base was added to the column and more commonly the complex Greek system of rings below the capital was simplified by the addition of a small, round, astragal moulding which marked the end of the now optional fluting. The entablature was often quite different from that of traditional Greek timber buildings, which were by now rare and historic. The Theatre of Marcellus has an entablature of about 2 diameters with a reduced architrave. There are small tooth-like projections, or dentils, in the cornice and the mutules are concealed under the corona. On later examples, such as the Baths of Diocletian (b) of AD 305, the mutules on the entablature (not illustrated) are omitted altogether and the whole order takes on a typically Roman opulence with rich carving applied to all the details.

The Renaissance rediscovered Rome but knew little of Greece. Fifteenth- and sixteenth-century Italian architects studied the diverse ruins of Rome but, above all, they were interested in fitting ancient architecture into new theories of design. The invention of printing brought these theories to a wide audience.

Many Renaissance authors published their own versions of the orders. This resulted in the universal addition of a Roman base (a) or an Ionic base (c) and the creation of a plinth in order to match Doric with the other orders as in the Doric order of Scamozzi (c). Almost all publications made the column 8 diameters high, but details of the base, capital and entablature varied according to the author. Some books offered dentils in the cornice or an Ionic style of base. Where mutules were included the pegs, or guttae, either became a shallow decoration on the underside of the projecting corona or, as in Vignola's Doric (a) of 1562, they ceased to be rafters and became decorative horizontal brackets.

Until the rediscovery of Greek architecture in about 1750 these rationalized versions of Roman Doric were almost universal. Since the Renaissance they have been used regularly, both as an established variation in the classical tradition and as a consequence of the continued influence of the Renaissance publications.

74

# THE USE OF THE DORIC ORDER

The Doric order is so called because it was the architectural style of the Dorian Greeks who occupied the Greek mainland and its colonies. In the early Greek republics the use of this order signified a building associated with the Dorians. We also know from the Roman architectural author Vitruvius that the proportions of the column, and hence the order, were traditionally thought to be derived from the proportions of a man. The broader proportions of the column in comparison with the other orders and the more rugged reputation of the Dorians in relation to the Asian Greeks lend weight to this tradition, but Vitruvius' suggestion that a temple order was chosen to match the sex of the god does not seem to have been followed.

The male association of the order has remained and it is here illustrated by a sixth-century-BC column from Selinus in Sicily and a statue of an athlete from about the same period.

In succeeding centuries the order has come to take on other connotations. As the least decorative of the orders it has been associated both in later antiquity and in more recent times with inexpensive and utilitarian buildings. When this is combined with the masculinity of the order it can be seen as particularly suitable for military architecture, prisons or other buildings that are deliberately robust or aggressive.

As the lowest of an ascending tier of orders (see page 128) these characteristics can simultaneously express, for example, the defensive character and the service functions of the lower floor of a Renaissance palace. In this context and as a reinforcement to its robust character, the order is often accompanied by rustication.

Doric can, however, also express elegance and sophistication unconnected with any allusion to practicality or sturdiness. William Chambers' Casino, at Marino in Ireland (a), built in 1761, employs a Roman Doric in emulation of ancient Rome to create a small building of surprising grace and complexity.

The Greek Revival of the eighteenth century introduced a new range of interpretations of the order. Chambers' Casino can be contrasted with the design by Claude Ledoux for a Paris gateway (b) of about the same date, where the use of a Greek Doric order and the bold design represent a deliberate return to a primitive purity. New studies of Greek monuments engendered a profound respect for the proportional mastery of the ancient Greeks and the use of the Greek Doric order went beyond an association with fundamental origins to allow designs such as Schinkel's early-nineteenth-century church design (c) to express an air of calculated elegance. Concentration on the proportions of the least decorated order led, in the first part of this century, to an attempt to show underlying classical proportions stripped of much of their historic decoration. Twentieth-century Doric buildings such as Aalto's Worker's Club in Jyvaskyla in Finland (d) of 1924 suggest a new abstract purity.

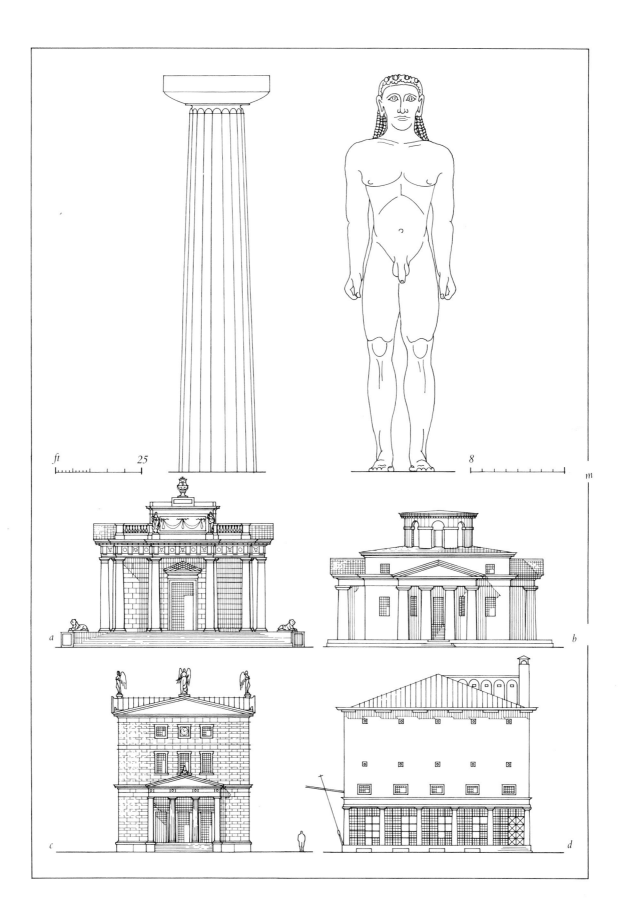

ft          25                              8

a                                    b

c                                    d

m

# THE TUSCAN ORDER

In the usual sequence of orders the Tuscan is placed first because it has the widest column. This can give a misleading impression as the Tuscan order is, in fact, a provincial form of the Doric. It was used in the early years of the Roman republic before closer contact with Greek colonies to the south brought Roman architecture into the mainstream of the classical tradition. Archaeologically there is little evidence of the way the columns and other elements of Tuscan or Etruscan temples were assembled. Remains of native Italian Doric or Tuscan columns have been found from these buildings but the Doric order can be traced to at least a century before anything similar appears in central Italy.

The Tuscan order is first mentioned by Vitruvius in the first century BC as an addendum to a description of the Doric, Ionic and Corinthian orders, more or less copied from Greek authors. There can be little doubt that this description was a patriotic attempt to give the architecture of ancient and revered native temples the same intellectual and mythological respectability as was attached to the Greek orders. We can reconstruct one of these early Roman or Etruscan temples (b), from about 150 BC, from archaeological evidence. These buildings were raised on a stone podium but the walls were probably made of timber and mud, and the roof was timber with terracotta decoration. They had very deep projecting eaves, probably to protect the mud walls, and the example illustrated has a clay tile roof. Thatched temples, which must have had steeper roofs, did, however, survive until the first century AD.

No Tuscan order was formalized in Roman imperial architecture. The principal legacy of this indigenous style has been the Roman development of the Doric order, which incorporated some features of Etruscan columns such as the base, smooth shaft and more complicated capital. When native temples fell into disrepair they were rebuilt in the up-to-date Doric order although the traditional plans were retained to create a distinct Roman temple type. The ease with which the old buildings were so redesigned is witness not just to respect for orders of Greek ancestry, but to the derivative nature of the original style and its lack of a systematic tradition.

The Tuscan order as we now know it is the result both of sixteenth-century theorists drawing their evidence from Vitruvius' description and of the need to reduce the Doric order to make their description of the Tuscan order fit in with a logical sequence. In this form it has become established for nearly five hundred years as a part of the classical tradition.

The Tuscan order shown, (a) and (c), is from Palladio and, in common with all other versions, follows Vitruvius in giving a column height of 7 diameters. The base is also of a consistent pattern, resembling the simple Roman Doric type, although to accord both with Vitruvius and archaeological evidence it should be totally circular. A pedestal has been added to match the other orders.

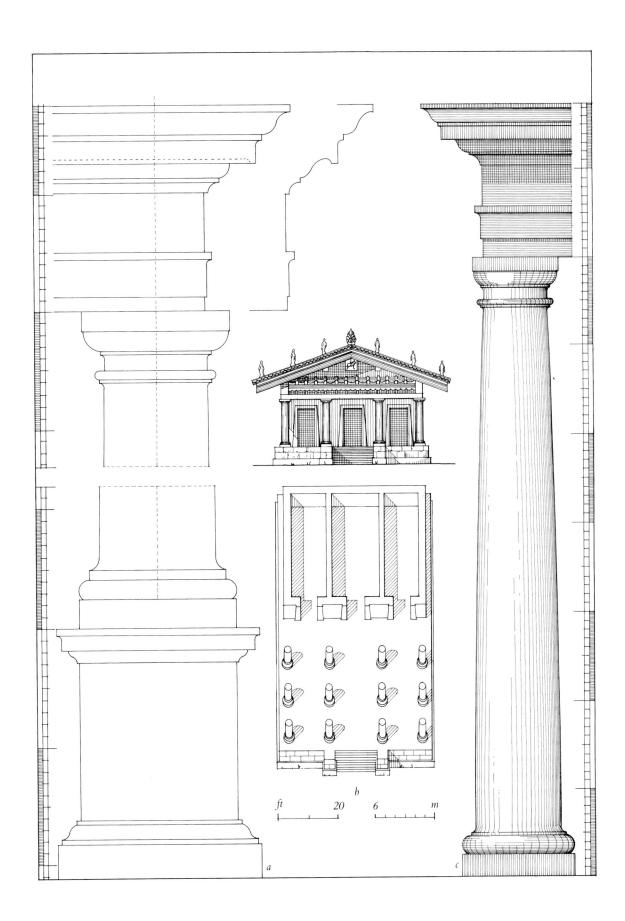

*ft*       20     6      *m*

*a*    *b*    *c*

# THE USE OF THE TUSCAN ORDER

The Tuscan order owes its continued use and the form it took after the Renaissance to the first-century writings of Vitruvius. The Etruscan architecture that Vitruvius tried to make into a formal order would have been identified immediately by his contemporaries as the native style of the Latin and Etruscan communities of central Italy. The Tuscan order formulated by sixteenth-century theorists would probably have been regarded in antiquity as a variant of Doric rather than as a separate order, and even today the similarity of proportions and details on Tuscan and Doric columns and the freedom of design often used on Doric entablatures can make identification difficult. Both in antiquity and after the Renaissance there has, none the less, been a style, or order, which has a separate identity.

There is no ancient tradition associating the Tuscan order with a specific human form, but in publications after the Renaissance some authors chose to give the order a human character in line with the range of characters given to the three principal orders. Therefore, due to the Tuscan column's breadth and its more native and apparently less sophisticated origin, the order was sometimes given the character of a thickset rustic man. In the interests of consistency and in recognition of the tradition of the attribution of a character by past authors, the Tuscan order is here represented by the figure of an Etruscan athlete. His beard gives him something of a rustic character in contrast to the clean-shaven Doric figure; the more advanced representation of the sculpture in relation to the Doric man indicates that the origin of the Tuscan order post-dates the Doric and, as both the Doric man and the Tuscan man are athletes, there is a reminder of the association of the two orders.

The Tuscan order shares many of the attributes of the Doric. It is even more economical than Doric to use, due to its very simple detailing. St Paul's in Covent Garden in London (d), by Inigo Jones in 1631, was specifically designed to be economic to construct and is also a rare attempt to represent literally Vitruvius' description of the order.

The proportions of the order and its primitive associations make for a particularly suitable relationship with rustication. Both York Water Gate in London (a) of 1626, probably by Gerbier, and Hawksmoor's gate to Queen's College, Oxford (c) of 1709 have heavily rusticated orders. The open dome on Queen's College shows an elegance unusual on Tuscan buildings and indicates that the order can be used to exploit its proportions but otherwise be treated with the same finesse as the other orders.

Above all, the Tuscan order expresses simplicity. The simplicity can be a consequence of the function of the building or, as with the mausoleum design (b) by William Thomas, of 1781, can intentionally create an atmosphere of sombre severity or geometric solidity.

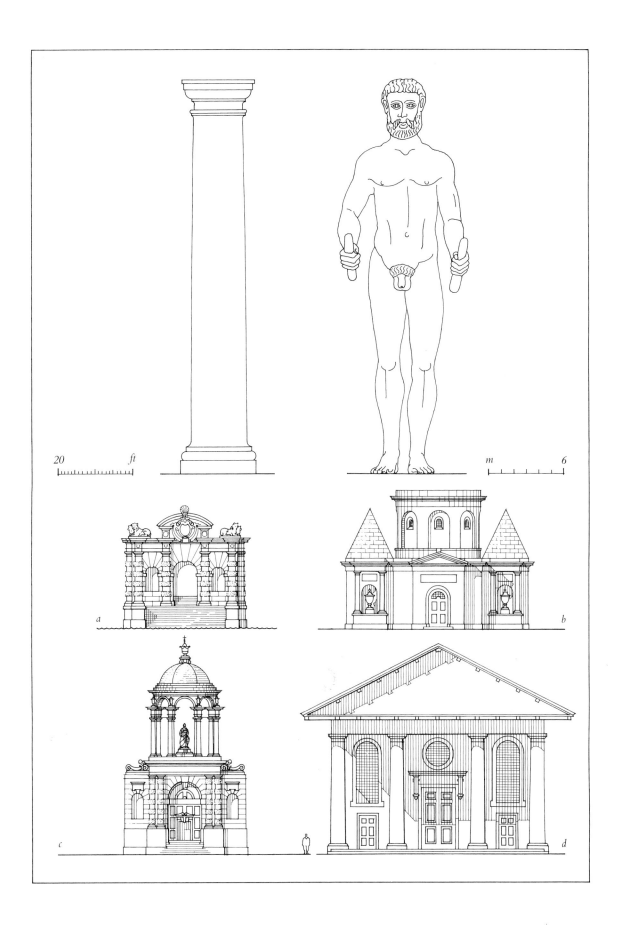

20 *ft*

*m* 6

*a*

*b*

*c*

*d*

# THE IONIC ORDER: ORIGINS

The Ionic order originated in the Greek communities of Ionia, which is today the west coast of Turkey and the adjacent Greek islands. The order is almost certainly a later development than Doric as the first evidence of architecture of this distinctive type dates from about the middle of the sixth century BC.

The details of the order differ noticeably from the Doric, the most apparent differences being the slender column and the distinctive curls, the volutes, on the capital. According to the ancient author Vitruvius these volutes had a legendary association with curls of female hair and the column itself was similarly thought to have derived from the proportions of a female figure. Such association of columns and figures was common in antiquity and the Egyptians particularly gave temple columns some of the personality of the relevant deity, as can be seen in the column from a temple to the goddess Hathor, illustrated (a). Early Ionian buildings also had such literal column figures, or caryatids, on sixth-century treasuries (c) built to represent individual Greek communities at the sacred site of Delphi. It is not hard to understand that the first Ionic columns, which were built to the goddesses Hera, on the island of Samos, and Artemis, in the mainland city of Ephesus (b), could have been seen to represent the goddesses themselves.

The origins of the capital itself are more confusing. There were column capitals with spiral decoration on near-eastern buildings in the tenth century BC and similar designs were used on Phoenician and Syrian ivory and metalwork. Buildings of the seventh century BC in Ionia used a distinctive capital, (d) and (e), that was probably influenced by these older examples and is likely to have been the source of the first Ionic capitals (g). This theory of evolution does not necessarily contradict the legend of the curls as such an association could have been suggested simultaneously by the dedication of the temple.

The order differs in other respects from Doric. The column base was first introduced to the classical vocabulary through this order, probably for purely decorative effect. The architrave is made up of overlapping sections, perhaps imitating overlapping boards. In early examples a series of large rectangular projections below the cornice, called dentils due to their resemblance to teeth, are likely to represent the exposed ends of closely spaced beams. This origin for the dentils is further supported by the early absence of a frieze and the consequently shallower entablature (f).

The Ionic order was rationalized to relate more directly to the Doric order when it was introduced to the Doric builders on the Greek mainland in the middle of the fifth century. The Temple on the Ilissus in Athens (h) includes a deep frieze of Doric proportions and a simplified base. Later builders reintroduced the dentils and stepped architrave. The proportions and details of the Ionic order now became established, retaining the distinctive, elegant and decorative character of the early order.

a

b

c

d

e

f

g

h

# THE IONIC ORDER

The arrangement of the parts and proportions of the Ionic order became relatively consistent in the fifth century BC. The column, with few exceptions, has remained between 8 and 9.5 diameters high from Greek republican examples to the present day. Although Roman architects sometimes reduced this to 7, since the Renaissance a height of between 8 and 9 diameters has been the general rule.

Vertical fluting on the column shaft seems always to have been intended, if not always executed, on early examples of the order. The earliest examples of columns from Samos and Ephesus have forty flutes, with the same shallow profile as Doric columns. These flutes soon reduced in number to twenty-four and became deeper, semicircular grooves with narrow vertical bands, or fillets, between them. Some Roman and Renaissance columns have no fluting and the occasional Roman building has only twenty flutes, but it is generally accepted that the Ionic column is fluted twenty-four times.

The column base has a complicated history. At first it was a swollen disc joined to the lower end of the shaft by a small concave moulding. This sometimes sat on a square slab and was usually decorated with a complex series of horizontal grooves which either left the outline of the outward swelling visible as a simple curve or divided it up into a series of deep concave grooves and convex curves. Bases of this type, such as on the Temple of Athena Polias at Priene (d) of 334 BC are called Ephesian. Extant examples show considerable variety. When Ionic buildings came to be constructed on the Greek mainland this arrangement was simplified, two or more swollen torus discs being clearly separated by concave scotia mouldings. The torus discs could be decorated with the traditional horizontal grooves or in other ways. This is known as the Attic base. It is found on the Erechtheion in Athens (c) of the late fifth century BC. This base became the standard type in Rome and then in the Renaissance when, characteristically, an optional pedestal (a) was added.

The entablature has remained quite constant. The early omission of a frieze, which may have been absent at Priene (d), did not survive into the Roman period. As an addition without any structural origin, the frieze was often decorated in its entirety with relief sculpture. The architrave generally has three, but occasionally two, divisions stepping progressively outwards and sometimes decorated at each step. The cornice usually has a row of projecting dentils which, although they were omitted on the Erechtheion, are generally found on both Roman and Renaissance buildings. In the sixteenth century both Palladio and Scamozzi (b) suggested a variation which puts a row of small brackets in place of the dentils.

The capital is, more than any other element, the defining feature of the order and, in spite of the universal use of the volute, there is great variety in its design. The complex geometry of the volute and these variations require their own description.

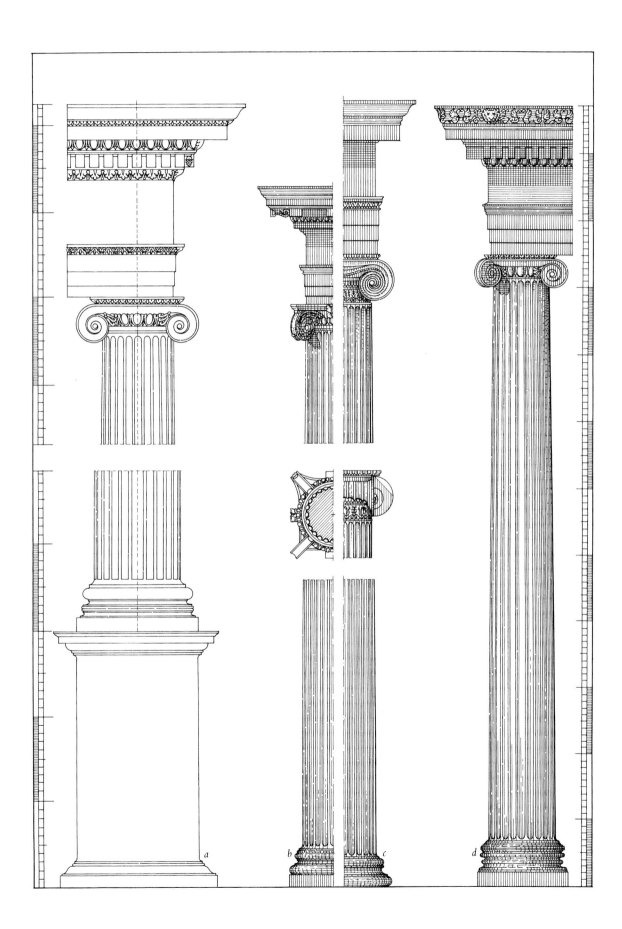

*a*      *b*      *c*      *d*

# THE IONIC CAPITAL

Volutes, which are the distinguishing feature of the Ionic capital, appear frequently in various forms on classical decoration. They are found in a number of natural forms, but when they are reproduced they require the application of a precise geometry based on circles and squares.

Although we have evidence of how volutes were originally calculated, since the Renaissance several simple methods have been developed. They all share one essential characteristic: the spiral is created by drawing a series of quarter-circles and gradually diminishing their size by moving the centres of the circles progressively around a small central square. Goldman's method for drawing a volute is illustrated opposite.

The centre of the eye of the volute is half a diameter out from the centre of the column and a quarter of a diameter down from the top of the volute. The eye itself is 0.045 diameters. The square for setting up the spiral has sides half the length of the diameter of the eye. One side of the square, the line 1 to 4, is centrally placed on the vertical diameter of the eye. Two smaller internal squares are created by joining the two outer corners 2 and 3 to the centre of the eye, dividing the side of the square on the centre of the volute into six equal parts to give points 1, 5, 9, X, 12, 8 and 4 and then extending these points horizontally to meet the lines 2X and 3X. The spiral can now be drawn by moving the centre point of a series of quadrants progressively round the diminishing squares in the numbered order shown. The circumference of the first quadrant starts vertically above its centre at point A below the abacus and stops at point B on the horizontal extension of line 1, 2. The centre is moved to point 2 and the radius reduced to meet point B and the next quadrant drawn to point C, and so on until the quadrant centred on point 12 finally merges into the eye. When the volute line has two edges these should gradually converge by repeating the process but moving each point slightly inwards.

The design of Ionic capitals, while sharing this geometry, can vary considerably. Example (a) is from the fifth-century-BC Erechtheion in Athens. Examples (b), (c) and (d) are all from Rome and show the variety of Roman interpretations. The simplified version (d) is from the Colosseum and (c) is of particular importance as an example of how the Romans rationalized the capital to overcome the problem that occurred on a corner column where one volute of the capital had to be twisted round to face both ways. The Romans invented a capital where all four sides were identical and all volutes twisted round on every column. Finally, example (e) by Michelangelo from the Palazzo dei Conservatori in Rome, built in 1568, shows the inventive embellishment of the order that became popular in Baroque architecture.

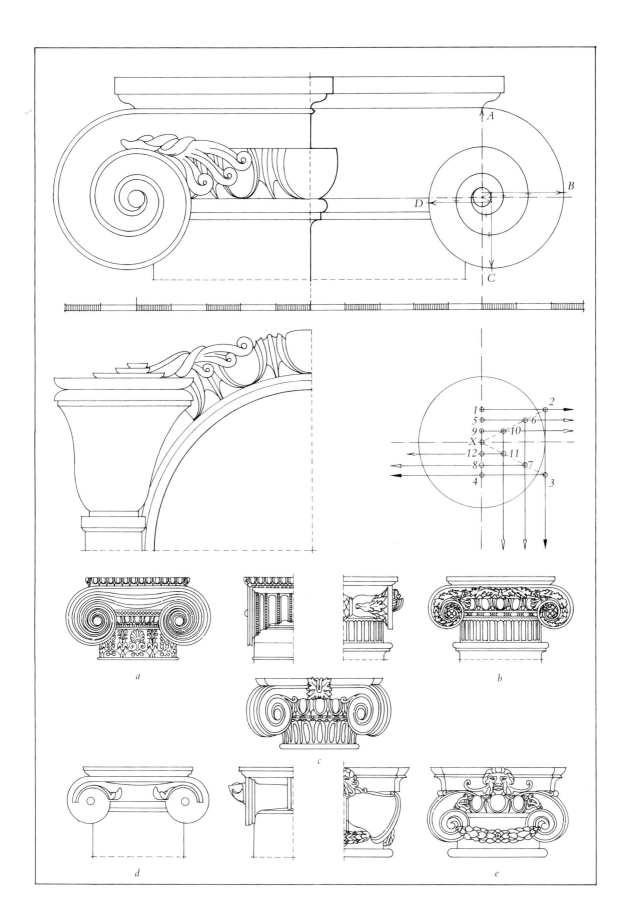

a

b

c

d

e

# THE USE OF THE IONIC ORDER

The early Greek city-states identified the Ionic order with the peoples of what is today western Turkey and with their colonies. The column and its decoration are said to be derived from the proportions and features of a mature woman, in contrast to the masculine order of the Dorians. In antiquity the Ionians were, indeed, contrasted with the more vigorous Dorians by a luxurious and leisurely lifestyle that was then associated with femininity. Statues from the island of Samos in the sixth century BC, one of the places of origin of the Ionic order, further support the myth. The column was said to have curls like those of a woman's hair and the vertical fluting was said to represent the folds of a woman's dress, like the dress of the statue of the worshipper illustrated.

The Ionic order has neither the simplicity of the Doric nor the versatility of the Corinthian. Its use seems consequently to have been limited both in antiquity and since the Renaissance. Although used by the Romans, it was less favoured than the Corinthian order or their own Composite order. In the early Renaissance, Ionic capitals were used on parts of buildings to express the various interpretations of the order current at the time, but there were few examples of wholly Ionic architecture.

The influence of Vitruvius' story of the female origin of the order seems to have persisted and Ionic continues to be associated with the female sex. It is thought suitable for sedentary activities or individuals of an inactive nature. The establishment in the sixteenth century of a tradition of placing the five orders in an ascending sequence gave Ionic a new respectability and an intermediate position between Doric and Corinthian. It may be nothing more than an interest in an intermediate set of proportions that led Palladio to make the Villa Foscari near Venice (c) of 1559 an Ionic building.

Baroque architects seemed to find the Ionic order particularly interesting and in the seventeenth century, and subsequently at the turn of this century, it was widely used. Baroque distortion gave the order a new significance in the return to classical purity in the eighteenth century. John Soane's use of an historically accurate Greek Ionic order at Pitzhanger Manor outside London (a) in 1800 could be seen to evoke an archaic simplicity. In the USA the rigid reproduction of a Greek Ionic temple for the Montgomery County Courthouse, Dayton, Ohio (b) of 1847 uses this new archaeological knowledge to represent a belief in the quality of justice in an heroic democracy. Carrére and Hastings chose an elaborate Baroque Ionic for the Sloane House in New York (d) of 1894. This form of Ionic offered greater opportunities for creative embellishment than archaeologically derived examples, or even the already rich Corinthian and Composite forms.

20     *ft*

*m*     6

*a*

*b*

*c*

*d*

# THE CORINTHIAN ORDER: ORIGINS

By comparison with the Doric and Ionic orders, the Corinthian order is a relative newcomer. It is named after the city of Corinth, but its origin and significance are shrouded in mystery and myth. The first example dates from about 400 BC.

The Roman author Vitruvius, probably repeating an earlier Greek legend, tells a story of the origin of the order. The famous Athenian sculptor Callimachus is said to have passed by a basket of possessions placed on the grave of a Corinthian girl who had died on reaching marriageable age. This basket had a roof-tile over it and had been placed over the root of an acanthus plant which had then grown up around the basket. Callimachus, attracted by this, used it as the basis for a design for a new type of column capital. An interpretation of this legend is shown in illustration (e).

The myth explains the slender proportions of the column, which are said to derive from those of a young woman, but it may tell us more. Callimachus was famous for his bronzework and the city of Corinth was so well known for its bronzes that these could be referred to merely as 'Corinthian work'. A bronze original could provide an explanation both for the name and the way the leaf decoration seems to be applied like repeated castings to a central core. The connection with death and possessions for the afterlife may be the reason for the acanthus decoration. The acanthus was associated with funeral celebrations in Greek antiquity and gravestones, or stele, such as the one illustrated (c), enlarged for comparison with the column, often had acanthus or anthemion decoration similar to the first known Corinthian capitals.

The use of plant decoration for columns was not new and column (a), reduced for comparison, is one of many from Egypt. The first known Greek example, however, from the Temple of Apollo at Bassai, (b) and (d), of 400 BC was centrally placed in significant isolation in an internal Ionic colonnade. This would normally have been the position of a cult statue, so the column may itself have been the object of veneration, perhaps a reference to one of Apollo's many attributes as the god of sudden death.

The internal position of this Corinthian column among Ionic columns is also informative. The Corinthian entablature did not develop with the column, as with the Doric and Ionic. Rather, the column at first tended to be added to an Ionic entablature, only developing distinct features in Rome. In its early development it was also used exclusively internally, and usually on buildings with Doric exteriors such as the Tholos at Delphi (f) of about 375 BC. It did not make an appearance on the exterior of a major building until 174 BC in the Temple of Zeus Olympius in Athens.

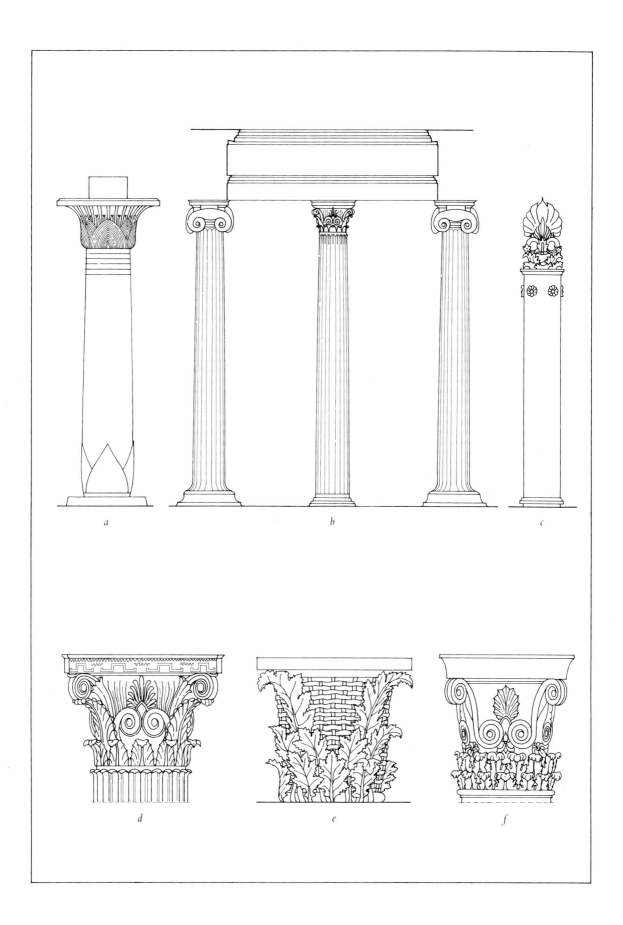

a   b   c

d   e   f

# THE CORINTHIAN ORDER

Corinthian cannot really be regarded as a developed order prior to its use on major buildings in the late second century BC. The principal use of the order in the ancient world was, consequently, under Roman influence, or executed by Roman architects.

The Corinthian order started as a variation of the Ionic; most Corinthian details owe their origin to their Ionic ancestry. The Corinthian column is essentially an Ionic shaft and base lengthened by substituting the low Ionic capital with a tall Corinthian capital. This gives an increased height to Corinthian columns to somewhere between 9.25 and 10.5 diameters. A significant number of ancient columns were exactly 10 diameters and when authors published ideal proportions after the Renaissance they tended to select simple figures such as 9, 9.5 or, more frequently and more accurately, 10. Both the large-scale example (a), a version of Vignola's Corinthian order of 1562, and the column from the Temple of Serapis in Rome (b) of AD 215 are 10 diameters high, while the columns of the Arch of Hadrian in Athens (c) of AD 131 are 9.5 diameters high.

Below the capital the similarities between Corinthian and Ionic are exact. The Corinthian base is the Ionic Attic base with a projecting torus moulding above and below one or two concave scotia mouldings. All early examples of the order have the same twenty-four half-round vertical flutes cut into the shaft, as do later versions of Ionic columns. In several Roman examples the column shaft is left uncut, either for economy or where special coloured shafts of figured marble, granite, porphyry or other special stones are used. After the Renaissance, the use of fluting became simply optional.

The distinctive aspect of the Corinthian order, other than the unique capital discussed on page 94, is the entablature it developed during the Roman period. At about 2.33 diameters it is broadly the same as, but often a little higher than, an Ionic entablature. The architrave, with two or three divisions, is identical in detail to the Ionic, but rather taller, at about 0.66 of a diameter. The Corinthian frieze is also either plain or an uninterrupted panel of sculpted decoration. The details of the cornice, however, differ significantly from the Ionic. Some cornices, such as on the Temple of Serapis (b), retained the distinctly Ionic decoration of dentils, but soon an extended and widely spaced dentil, like a bracket, was introduced, as on the Arch of Hadrian (c). This bracket was later embellished by being carved into the shape of a small scroll, or modillion, supporting reduced projecting mouldings above. The dentils were not, however, abandoned. Either the cornice was modified to include dentils or, as in the interior order of the Pantheon in Rome (d) of AD 120, a plain detail was put in their place. This arrangement became normal, if not universal, Roman practice and in this form has been widely adopted since the Renaissance.

*a*      *b*      *c*      *d*

# THE CORINTHIAN CAPITAL

The Corinthian capital is a formal but relatively realistic representation of an acanthus plant growing around a solid core. Leaves and tendrils of the common wild Mediterranean plant are gathered around a plain cylindrical centre separated from the column shaft by a small, round, astragal moulding. This round core is usually shaped like an inverted bell and capped by a square abacus with four inward-curving sides to create four projecting diagonal horns. The bell is divided horizontally into three parts, which can be equal or vary in height, and these divisions mark the lines of the leaves. The lower two divisions have simple rows of leaves, identical in each row and turned over at the top, which alternate with one another around the bell. In the uppermost division leaves and tendrils sprout out of two stalks on each face and divide up to terminate in a total of sixteen spirals. These join at their tips to create large volutes under each horn of the abacus with smaller volutes between them. Between the smaller volutes a flower rises up to sit in the centre of each inward curve of the abacus.

The accuracy of the representation of the acanthus leaves on the Corinthian capital can vary considerably and the acanthus plant itself has different species with different leaf forms. The large illustration shows a typical capital from the Temple of Vespasian and Titus in Rome of AD 94, but there are many different interpretations of the traditional design.

Illustration (a) is an example from the first known external use of the Corinthian order, the Choragic Monument of Lysicrates in Athens of 334 BC. The lower leaves are plain and the middle range delicate with flowers between them while the tendrils above seem to belong to a different plant capped by a small anthemion. Example (b) is from the Temple of the Sybil at Tivoli near Rome of 80 BC and has a very much reduced range of middle leaves, heavy volutes and a very large flower. The capital from the Temple of Castor and Pollux in Rome (c) of 7 BC is of a more standard type, with distinctive, lively leaf-carving and intertwining smaller volutes. The capital from the Colosseum in Rome (d) of AD 80 is an example of a common simplified form with uncut leaves either for economy, deliberate effect or to contrast with more elaborate capitals. Example (e) is an early-eighteenth-century Baroque design by Diderot and d'Alembert and is an inventive reinterpretation of the traditional form to create a new style. The tendrils are replaced by curled leaves which descend to the top of the middle row of plain leaves. The last example (f) would be of a smaller size than the others and is from the Palazzo della Scrofa in Rome. This Renaissance capital demonstrates a type of reduction of elements that is often used to reduce the scale of detail to a level appropriate to a smaller size of capital.

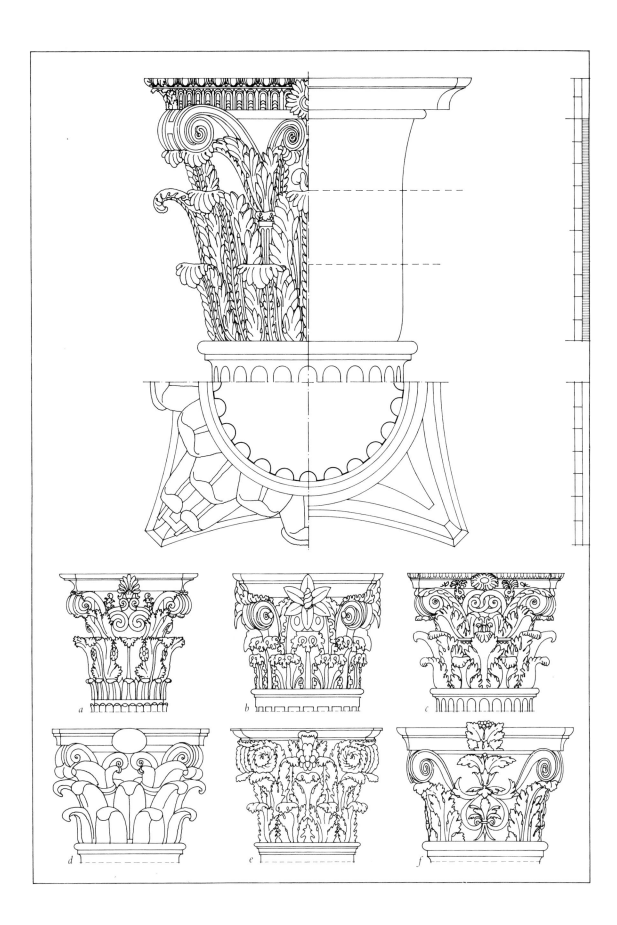

a    b    c

d    e    f

# THE USE OF THE CORINTHIAN ORDER

The Corinthian order had none of the ethnic associations of the Doric and Ionic and was only widely used when such distinctions had lost their significance. Only the column had a meaning in antiquity; the development of a distinct entablature did not evolve until later and the column was often used with the Doric or Ionic order. From the legend of the invention of the capital discussed on page 90, it would appear to have had female and funerary associations. As it was also first used internally, the more decorative character of the column must have been thought appropriate for the greater opulence of the interior. This may also be linked to the female significance of the column as, in antiquity, the passive domestic role of the female was contrasted with the outdoor active role of the male. The association of the order with a young woman has persisted, preserved by the survival of the ancient writings of Vitruvius, and is represented here by a column from the Temple of Zeus Olympius in Athens of 174 BC placed alongside a version of a Hellenistic statue of Venus.

The Corinthian order became a firm favourite of the Romans and earlier temples in earlier orders were at times rebuilt in that style. The strongly decorative and sculptural nature of the order was probably considered to be more attractive, and the evident expense of the decoration gave greater glory to the deity and donor alike.

The widespread use of Corinthian by the Romans ensured its survival throughout the medieval period, early Renaissance and beyond in a virtually uninterrupted sequence until the twentieth century. The elegance of its proportions, the sculptural opportunities of the capital and the prestige attached to the opulence of the carving have maintained its popularity.

In order to understand some of the more particular associations intended by architects since the Renaissance it is often necessary to examine the style of the decoration. The Pazzi chapel (c) by Brunelleschi was built in 1429 in Florence in a geometrically ordered Corinthian design with capitals of a Roman Imperial type; it is one of the first Renaissance buildings strongly to evoke the character of antiquity. The central section of Robert Adam's Register Office in Edinburgh (b) of 1774 is also intended to reflect the architecture of ancient Rome but is overlaid with features that had become established in the Renaissance. Thomas Hamilton's Royal College of Physicians (d) of 1845 in the same city on the other hand, by the use of a Corinthian order from the Tower of the Winds in Athens, seeks to return to an historic purity that pre-dates both Rome and the Renaissance. A house designed by Arthur Mackmurdo in north London (a) in 1883 has simplified capitals and squat columns in a bold and original design which draws its inspiration from the Arts and Crafts Movement and sixteenth-century Mannerism.

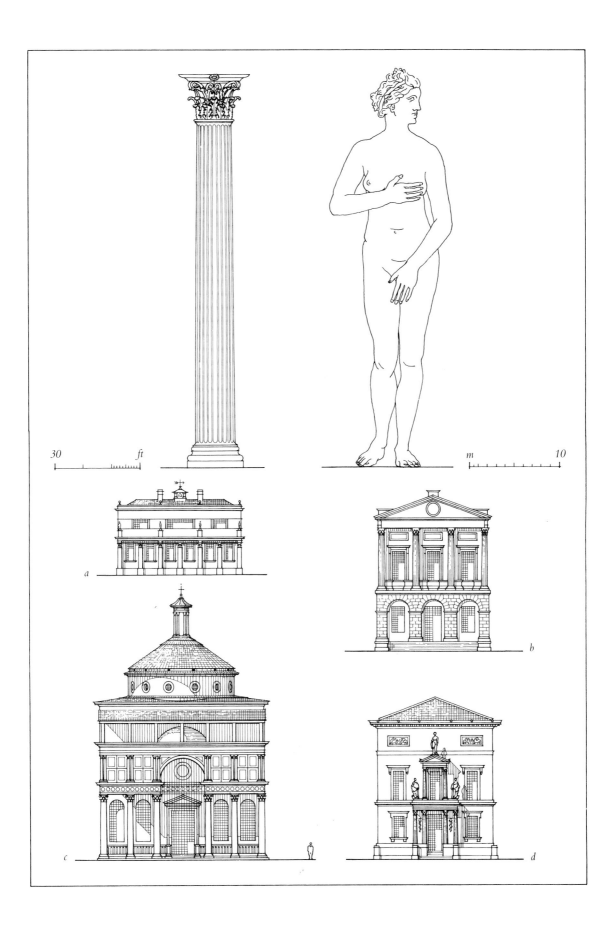

30              *ft*

*m*            10

*a*

*b*

*c*                            *d*

# THE COMPOSITE ORDER

The Composite order is the only wholly Roman order. It is first known in the Forum in Rome on the Arch of Titus of AD 82 although it may have been invented about a century earlier. The order was subsequently used on the Arch of Septimus Severus (c) in about AD 204, and on a number of other triumphal arches, monuments and baths. It seems to be a derivative of the Corinthian order, which was a favourite of the Romans and also used extensively on triumphal arches. In many respects it is identical to the Corinthian order, but it is distinguished by its column capital which was considered in the Renaissance to be a combination of Ionic and Corinthian and hence called Composite.

The capital shares the two lower rows of acanthus leaves of the Corinthian order with the four diagonally placed, decorated volutes of the Roman Ionic order. It may therefore owe its origin more to a development of the Ionic order than the Corinthian. Early Ionic capitals often have a deep decorative anthemion band below the volutes and Roman examples exist with various kinds of decoration in this position combined with diagonal volutes. As the Corinthian entablature is also derived from the Ionic, evolution from this source must remain a possibility.

Once the capital type was established in the first century AD both its distinguishing characteristics and its relationship with the column and entablature were retained. It was therefore sufficiently established as an order to be recognized as such in the Renaissance without any ancient literary references.

The capital is generally 1 diameter high and below the abacus is divided into three parts of approximately equal height. The lower two parts consist of two rows of acanthus leaves, as on Corinthian capitals. On each face two small flowers rise up out of the top row of leaves to penetrate the upper part of the capital. The egg and dart moulding of a typical Ionic capital sits immediately below a two-part Corinthian abacus and the volutes of the capital always penetrate the lower part of this abacus. A flower rises directly out of the egg and dart and covers the centre of both parts of the abacus.

The total column height is generally about 10 diameters, but on the Arch of Septimus Severus (c) the columns are 9.66, while in the Baths of Diocletian (b) of AD 305 they are 10.5. Renaissance authors, when placing the Composite as the last of a sequence of all the orders, related the height to the Corinthian. Palladio (a) made the Composite 10 as the last of an ascending sequence, compared to Corinthian at 9.5. Scamozzi (d), on the other hand, made the Composite order 9.75 diameters high – lower than, and a subservient derivative of, his Corinthian order of 10.

All the other details of the order follow the Corinthian example, both in the variety of their combination of dentils, modillion brackets and other mouldings and in the varied proportion of the elements in the entablature.

*a*     *b*     *c*     *d*

# THE USE OF THE COMPOSITE ORDER

There are no certain literary references to the Composite order from antiquity and the name was not created until the Renaissance. The Roman author Vitruvius mentions the existence of different inventions in the design of Corinthian column capitals in the first century BC but, as such inventions existed within the range of standard Corinthian capitals, we cannot tell if this is a reference to the Composite capital. A century later a reference by Pliny to the orders makes no mention of anything new of this type. There is, however, little doubt from the evidence of buildings and the consistency of design over some three centuries that the use of the order must have had some significance other than as a variant of Corinthian.

The use of the order in association with triumphal arches, such as that of Septimus Severus (c) of AD 203, with some temples to the cult of the imperial family and with other monuments to imperial power, tends to suggest a specific connection with the conquering glory of the Roman state. The celebration of victory and the humiliation of the vanquished were highly formalized events in Roman life and the use of an architectural order not directly copied from a conquered nation may have had some attraction for the creators of the monuments that recorded these victories.

As all the other orders have been represented here by figures and as Renaissance authors created symbolic figures for the Composite order, a column from the Arch of Titus is here placed alongside a Roman figure of Victory poised to crown an emperor with a victor's laurel wreath. The combination of the female Ionic and Corinthian in the Composite order makes the choice of a traditional female figure of winged Victory to represent the order seem particularly appropriate.

The symbolism of victory was inherited by the Christian Church and used to signify the victory of Christ in the Middle Ages. However, Composite was little used for complete buildings after the Renaissance. The lack of literary reference, the attraction of the Corinthian and the view of the order as a derivative of Corinthian seem to have limited its appeal.

Palladio used the Composite order for his incomplete Loggia dei Capitani in Vicenza near Venice (a) in 1565. Here the opulence of the order and its association with victory may be intended as a reference to the Venetian state. The choice of the order for Easton Neston, a house in northern England (b), designed by Hawksmoor before 1695, is probably more arbitrary. The church of S. Marcello in Rome (d), by Carlo Fontana in 1682, is located a short distance from the Arch of Septimus Severus and the use of the Composite order here may be a return to the medieval symbolism of the victory of Christ. Baroque architects made the most frequent use of the order, but they also embellished the Ionic order in a way that closely resembled the Composite and thereby reinforced the ambiguous relationship that already existed between the Ionic, Corinthian and Composite orders.

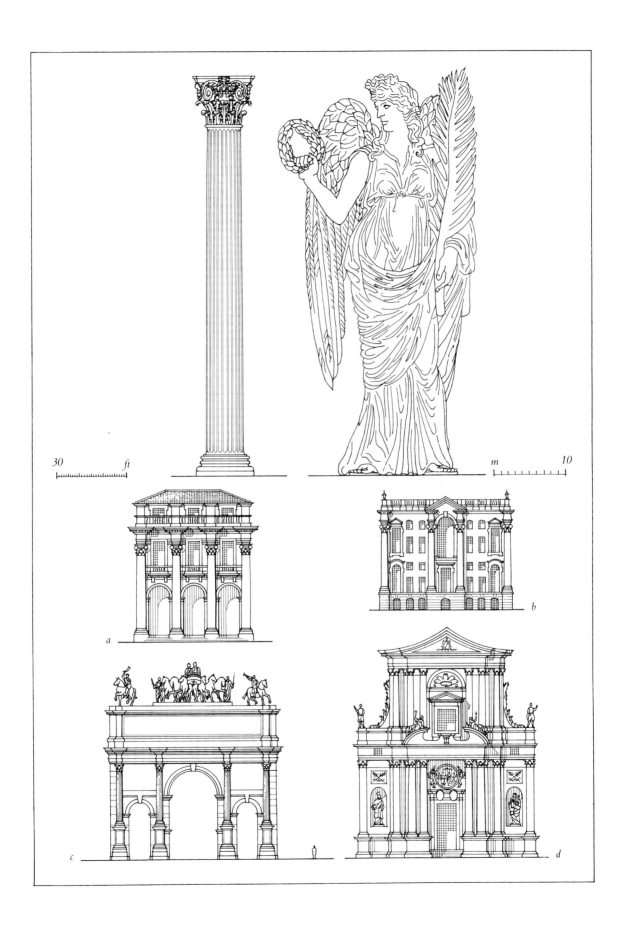

30        *ft*

*m*        10

*a*

*b*

*c*

*d*

# Variations and Inventions: Columns

The column is much more than a means of supporting a building. The vertical tapering shape not only represents different human figures, but refers back to the tree trunks and plants that were the origin of the form and its decoration. Over the centuries the column itself has from time to time been embellished and distorted, either to suggest this natural ancestry or to add more decoration to an order or to refer to some other idea specific to the building, patron or architect.

A free-standing column from the Greek sanctuary at Delphi (f), probably from the third century BC, takes the form of an acanthus stalk. Decorations of leaves recurred in antiquity and can be seen on Roman columns (g). This theme was taken up by the sixteenth-century French architect Philibert de l'Orme (i) and passed on to nineteenth- and twentieth-century followers of the French Renaissance such as McKim, Mead and White in New York (j). The column is most obviously reminiscent of the tree-trunk columns of primitive temples. Literal references to this origin are found in antiquity and the Renaissance. Bramante's cloister of the church of S. Ambrogio in Milan (h) of 1477 is a powerful fifteenth-century example.

When decoration extends over the whole shaft of the column (k) this is only an expression of architectural exuberance. The decoration can be limited to the upper (l) or the lower (m) part of the column, the division normally coming at the top of the lower third of the shaft.

Twisted shafts were often used by the Romans and were revived in the Renaissance. A narrow spiral (e) is quite common and creates the impression that only the fluting has been twisted. Most later columns with a broader, or wreathed spiral owe their origin to imperial Roman examples re-used in St Peter's in Rome (a), once thought to have come from the Temple of Solomon. These complex shapes were enthusiastically copied by Baroque architects in the seventeenth century, most notably by Bernini to support the canopy, or baldacchino, over the altar in the rebuilt St Peter's (b).

The spiral is set out by dividing the shaft horizontally into forty-eight parts and drawing a small cylinder in the centre (d). Eight points on the circumference of the cylinder (c) are joined progressively up the column in forty-eight stages to create a spiral on the surface of the cylinder which is projected on to the surface of the column. The diameter of the column is measured from the surface of the cylinder at each point on the spiral. At the top and bottom the spiral is eased into the base and capital by returning to the true centre in four equal stages, A, B, C and D at (c).

In 1524 in the Laurentian Library in Florence (n) Michelangelo reversed the taper of some columns in a manner reminiscent of Roman furniture. This new shape associated the column with herms, the half-human, half-pillar sculptures of antiquity, and has since become an accepted variant form (o) most frequently used on smaller elements such as windows, fireplaces and furniture.

a     b     c     d     e

8   1   2   A   7   D   B   3   C   6   5   4

48     0

f     g     h     i     j

k     l     m     n     o

# Variations And Inventions:
## The Capital And Base

The sculptural inventiveness of the designer and craftsman are often concentrated on the column capital. The most conventional column capital can reveal the intentions of the architect. There is more variety than the conventions suggest.

The simple form of the Doric capital has often been given additional decoration, such as on the Cancelleria in Rome (a) of 1486 and on the gate arch at Syon House in England (b), by Robert Adam in 1762. The volute, on the other hand, is so specific that extreme variations to the Ionic capital are relatively rare. An unusual arrangement of the volute from a house in the Roman city of Pompeii (c) shows how domestic architecture in antiquity often featured quite original versions of the orders.

The complex sculpture of the Corinthian and Composite orders has led to a large number of inventions and experiments. Early Corinthian varieties such as the order on the Tower of the Winds in Athens (d) of about 40 BC have been copied many times. The Corinthian capitals from the Council House at Miletus on the Turkish coast (e) of 170 BC, show how a reduction in the rows of leaves can accommodate the design to suit smaller-scale buildings. A Composite capital from the Forum in Rome (f) has a marked similarity with decorated Roman Ionic capitals. Later Composite inventions include a fanciful floral capital (g), by William Chambers in the late eighteenth century, and a special maize capital symbolizing the New World for the United States Capitol (h) by Benjamin Latrobe in 1815.

Figures and animals in capitals often refer to the use or ownership of the building. Allusions to victory characterize such Roman examples as (i) and (l), while a capital from the Temple of Concord (j) of AD 10 depicts sacrificial rams. Such figured designs inspired Gothic capitals, and early Renaissance examples such as on the Palazzo Pazzi in Florence (k) unite medieval concepts with classical inspiration.

The flat column, or pilaster, necessitated a modification to the Corinthian or Composite capitals to accommodate the change of shape. In a Roman example (m) the Corinthian volutes are replaced by winged horses, while the reversed volutes on example (p) from the Cancelleria are typical of the early Renaissance. The egg and dart below the abacus on examples (n) from Bologna and (o) from Brescia suggest that these capitals were intended as variants of the Composite order.

Column bases can also be varied. An early example is from the Greek Temple of Apollo at Didyma in Turkey (q) where the decorated bases distinguish the entrance columns; they probably date from the first century BC. Heavy decoration such as that on example (r) was often applied to Roman bases while the addition of leaves on (s), from the Baptistry of Constantine in Rome, is unusual. Occasional inventions such as the base (t), by the sixteenth-century French architect Jean Goujon, from the Louvre in Paris, have continued since the Renaissance.

*a*          *b*          *c*          *d*

*e*          *f*          *g*          *h*

*i*          *j*          *k*          *l*

*m*          *n*          *o*          *p*

*q*          *r*          *s*          *t*

# The Column: Refinements

From the earliest classical buildings onwards, columns have been reduced in diameter towards the capital with a taper unevenly distributed over the height of the column. This tapering, or bulging, effect is known as entasis; it probably echoes the natural reduction in the diameter of the tree trunks first used as columns.

Early Greek columns could also be narrower at the base than at the widest point of the swelling. Various systems were used in antiquity for setting out entasis, and further methods have been developed since the Renaissance, which generally keep the width of the column within the width of the diameter at its lowest point.

The starting point for Renaissance calculations is the difference between the lower diameter of the column measured just above the base and the upper diameter measured just below the capital. Although there is some variety in this difference the upper diameter is usually about 0.85 of the lower diameter in all the orders.

Example (a) tapers from the base. A setting-out point X is found by extending a line from the outside of the upper diameter, at point A, to the level of the lower diameter, through point B. Point B is found by extending half the width of the lower diameter down from the top of the shaft with compasses to meet the centre line of the column. The column shaft is then divided into equal parts and, from point X, lines are extended to cross the points C where these divisions meet the centre line. From point C each line has half the diameter of the column added to it to produce a series of points D which give the curve of the entasis.

Example (b) tapers in the upper two thirds of the shaft. The upper diameter is extended downwards to meet a circle of the same diameter as the lower third of the column at point A. The circumference of the circle from point A to point B, outside the column, is divided into the same number of equal parts as the upper portion of the column. The points on the circumference of the circle are extended vertically to meet the horizontal divisions of the upper part of the column at points C which are connected to give a gradual curve.

The different methods of fluting columns are also illustrated. Doric columns have twenty shallow flutes, meeting at sharp edges, and the other orders usually have twenty-four deeper channels which can have complex curves or the simpler semi-circles shown. Where the sharp edges are vulnerable to damage, the lower part of the column can be left unfluted, as in example (c) from Pompeii, first century AD, or can be partially filled with a curved detail known as cabling, as in example (d), also from Pompeii. Cabling can itself be decorated like a rope or a ribbon and very elaborate examples such as (e) were devised by the French architect Philibert de l'Orme in the sixteenth century.

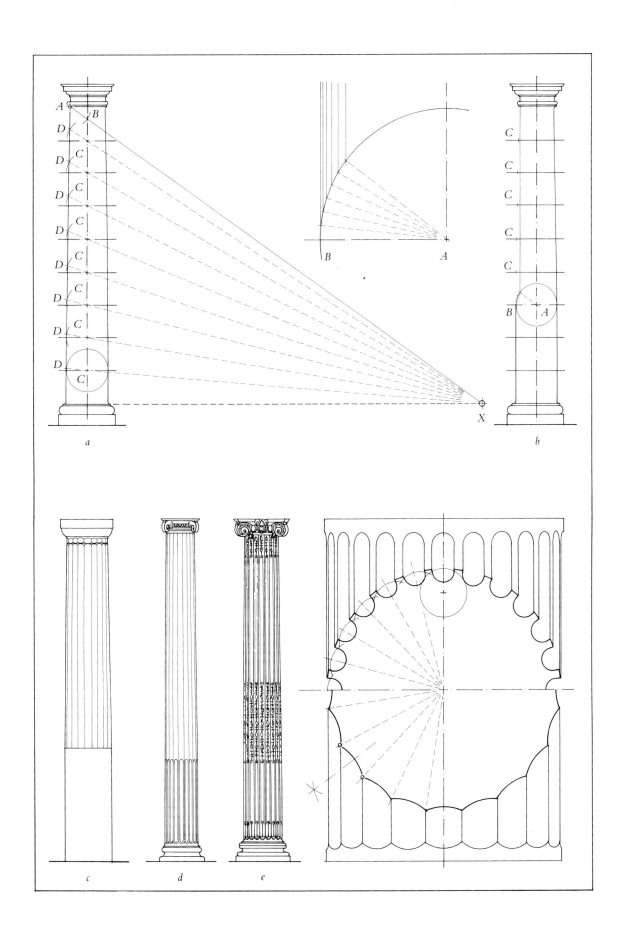

a

b

c

d

e

# THE PILASTER

It is not always practical or desirable to use free-standing columns in a building. Although the orders originated with independent columns, it was not long before imitations of these colonnades were built by applying the same decorative system to projections in walls. These projections are called pilasters when they are shallow and engaged columns when they project more than half a column width.

The early introduction of the pilaster allowed plain walls to be decorated in a way that related to free-standing columns on other parts of the building and gave the opportunity to apply the orders to any kind of structure.

The face of a pilaster can be set at different distances from the wall behind. Example (b) is an engaged column. The connection with the wall is concealed by the inward curve of the shaft, thereby giving the impression of a free-standing column. If this is changed to a square profile as in (c) the effect is lost and the rectangular section of the engaged column gives the impression of greater bulk. If a square engaged column is the full depth of the lower column width the apparent bulk is further increased, since the entasis of the column is lost as it connects to the wall behind. Example (d) is a pilaster half a column deep and is the minimum depth possible for a circular shaft. The curve of the pilaster diminishes the visual effect of the projection. The use of a rectangular form as in (e) can compensate for this. As the depth of the pilaster becomes shallower (f) a rectangular form has to be used. If there is to be any entasis this can be restricted to the two faces that return into the wall.

When a free-standing column sits adjacent to a wall, there is often a corresponding pilaster on the wall as in example (a). The Romans further developed the decorative effect of colonnades against plain walls by setting free-standing columns against the wall and bringing the entablature out in individual sections, called ressauts, over each column.

Pilasters are more often than not rectangular and this has resulted in a series of details specific to pilasters. None of the examples (g) to (k) has any entasis. Example (g) from the fourth-century-BC Temple of Apollo at Didyma is very much more slender than any contemporary free-standing columns and has a capital of a type that is only found on pilasters. The two pilasters (h) and (j) illustrate two versions of a panelled outer column face which can have inset marble or other decorative finishes. This is a popular variation and the panels can, as in example (k), be decorated with figures or other naturalistic or geometric decoration in relief. It is also possible to adapt fluting and capitals to the rectangular form. In the Baths of Diocletian (i) of AD 305 the flutes are reduced in number. Examples (j) and (k) show Renaissance capitals of a simplified Corinthian type modified to accommodate the square profile.

*a*      *b*      *c*      *d*      *e*      *f*

*g*      *h*      *i*      *j*      *k*

# COLUMN SPACING

The spacing of columns, or intercolumniation, is an important consideration in the application of the orders. Not only are there different effects to be gained by varying the spaces between columns, but the introduction of alternating and clustered spacing, particularly after the Renaissance, has given architects an almost unlimited range of options and combinations. Each type of spacing will itself, as with any choice of detail, express the stylistic preferences of the designer.

The Roman author Vitruvius has left us with the earliest surviving categorization of column spacing, based on the fronts of temples. This is measured by the number of column diameters that can be fitted between two columns. He gives five classes: pycnostyle (a) with 1.5 diameters spacing, systyle (c) with 2 diameters, diastyle (d) with 3, araeostyle (e) with 4, and eustyle (b) – his favourite – with 2.25 diameters between the columns, except for the central spacing opposite the entrance, which has 3. Vitruvius further comments that a spacing of 4 diameters, the araeostyle, looks too wide and is only suitable for native Tuscan temples with their timber architraves. Certainly free-standing columns with a spacing any wider than this can look too wide if accompanied by details directly derived from stone buildings.

Vitruvius was primarily interested in describing a system of rules. We know that the variety of column spacing in antiquity was much more diverse than he would have us believe. Variations occurred even in the same building – refinements such as closer spacing at corners are not unusual.

Wider spacing for a central entrance is common and can be quite pronounced. The arrangement in (f) shows a centre spacing of 3 column diameters with 1.5 at the sides. This strengthening of the sides of openings with closer spacing can make a central spacing of 4 look quite acceptable as in (g) and (h). The close spacing of 0.5 diameters on the sides of (h) makes a double pedestal necessary although this could also be satisfactorily used on (f) or (g).

The visual termination of a colonnade with coupled columns (i) can be effective and it can be combined with irregular column spacing between, as in (j) where widths of 4 and 2 diameters between columns alternate. Where greater visual or structural strength is required on ends or corners, columns can be joined together. Example (k) shows two columns linked to form a single heart-shaped column and, although this is quite unusual, it is found both in antiquity and the Renaissance at external and internal corners. It is more usual to form a more positive stop by attaching a column to a heavier rectangular block which can, as in (1) be expressed as a group of linked square and circular columns. All of these variations and more were often combined in Baroque buildings to give the sort of complex and restless impression seen in the hypothetical example (m) which also disguises in its complicated clusters of columns quite large structural supports.

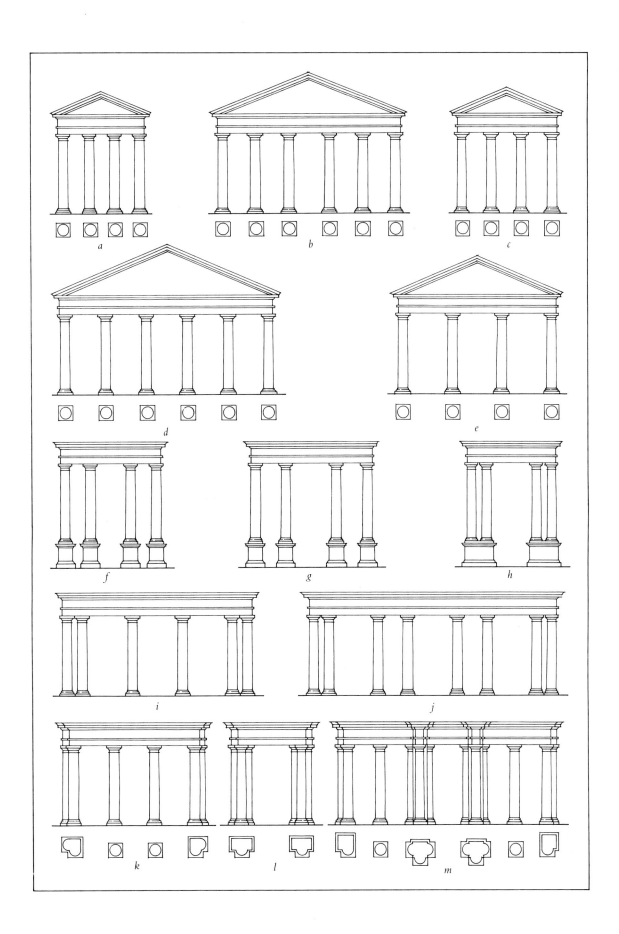

# 4. THEORIES OF PROPORTION

## PROPORTIONAL SYSTEMS

**B**y establishing the mathematical relationship between two or more dimensions, similar shapes and forms can be repeated in different sizes. By this means a room of 1 metre by 2 metres, for example, will be the same proportion in plan as a room of 2 metres by 4 metres or 30 metres by 60 metres. The mathematical relationship in this case is expressed as the ratio 1:2 and all these rooms will be proportioned according to this ratio.

In the past the absence of standard dimensions and the lack of accurate instruments led to the use of proportional methods of surveying, such as the use of 3:4:5 triangles for creating right-angles, and the reliance on proportion rather than dimension for the transfer of information for construction. This can be seen in Serlio's diagram for a door (a) in his *Five Books of Architecture* of 1575. Dimensions were at first derived directly from the physique of the architect and then, until the advent of the metric system, from idealized proportions of the human body. The belief that the human body was created by and even in the image of a god, when combined with the ancient conviction that mathematical proof was divinely ordained, gave proportions a mystical or religious significance.

The ancient idea that beauty is not arbitrary but a vision of the divine, and the more recent conviction that it is subject to scientific analysis, has led to the formation of theories about proportions and ideal systems such as Francesco di Giorgio's church plan (b) from the late fifteenth century.

The classical orders have evolved over the centuries to constitute a sophisticated proportional system. Buildings can be designed according to proportions established by generations of usage without resorting to imitation. The smallest part can be related to the largest through the module of the column width, shown by Philibert de l'Orme (c) in his book *Architecture* of 1567. The conventions can be modified without losing their integrity and the system is not closed to further development. There are families of proportions, or orders, each with their own identity, variations and mythology. An understanding of the orders and their proportions is an entry into an ancestral code appreciated by everyone but never fully understood by anyone.

The orders are only one architectural method of creating harmony in a confusing world. Additional systems of proportions can be applied to the orders. These systems can give an added unity to a design almost regardless of the sometimes fanciful philosophies that lie behind them and seem to give them an enhanced gravity.

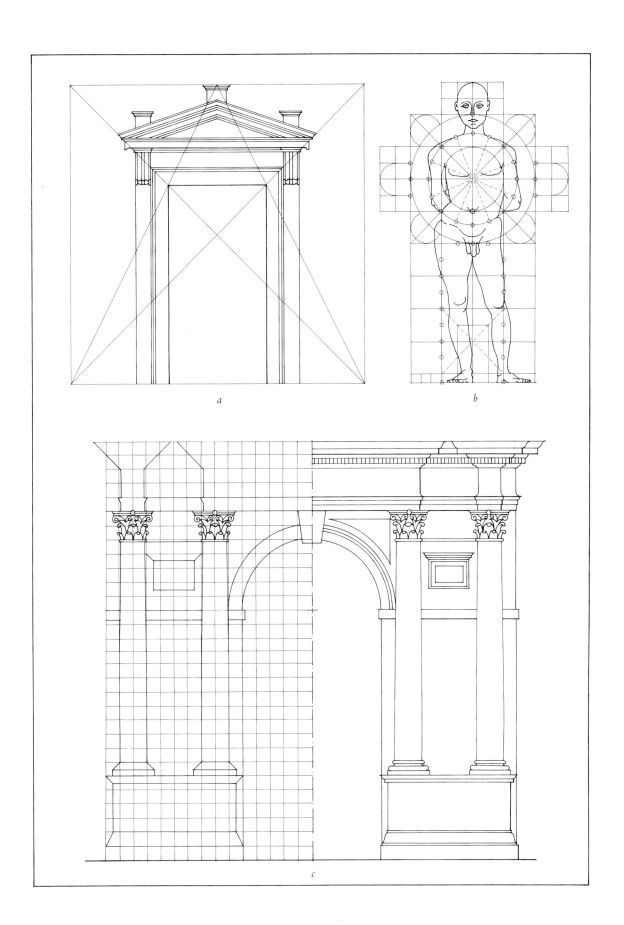

*a*

*b*

*c*

# SIMPLE PROPORTIONS

The circle and sphere (c) and the square and cube (a) are often represented as ideal forms. The equilateral triangle and the pyramid (d) and other figures are sometimes included. These shapes lend themselves to easy construction with the square and compasses and have been given mystical properties. The square and the circle can be related to one another and were both associated with the proportions of the human form by the Roman author Vitruvius. This unification of simple geometry and nature was particularly influential in the Renaissance. It has been illustrated by many authors and artists including Leonardo da Vinci (b).

Belief in the perfection of the circle and the sphere is based on the absolute regularity of the distance of the perimeter from the centre. This perfection has been associated with eternity and divinity. Circular and spherical forms are found in all architectural periods, but their use is limited by their self-contained geometry. Variations are often created with geometric forms related to the circle such as the octagon, hexagon and, more rarely, the pentagon (e).

The square and cube not only have regularity in the equality of their parts but are also easier to manipulate and subdivide than circular figures. Ancient and Renaissance authors described room plans by their relationship to a square. So, a ratio of the sides of a room of 4:5 was a square and a quarter and 3:5 a square and two thirds and so on (f). Plans, façades and volumes could be divided into interlocking series of shapes reducible to a series of small squares or whole numbers (h).

In the sixth century BC Pythagoras discovered that the first four notes of the harmonic series could be related to precise divisions of the length of a taut string when plucked and that these divisions were governed by a series of simple ratios 1:2:3:4. Plato developed these numbers into two series, one which multiplies by two, 1–2–4–8, and the other by three, 1–3–9–27, usually shown together in a figure based on the Greek letter $\Lambda$ (g). These figures were thought to represent the harmony of the universe, a philosophy that unified religion, mathematics and music until the eighteenth century. It was assumed that the mathematics of musical harmony would create visual harmony and Renaissance architects used these principles to develop a coherent proportional system which could generate an intermediate third figure, and therefore dimension, out of two. There were three methods of finding this intermediate or mean figure: arithmetic, geometric and harmonic. The arithmetic mean (A) is found by the equation $M - A = A - N$, or $A = \frac{1}{2}(M + N)$. So the arithmetic mean of 5 and 9 is 7 since $5 - 7 = 7 - 9$. The geometric mean (G) is found by the equation $\frac{M}{G} = \frac{G}{N}$, or $G = \sqrt{(M \times N)}$. So the geometric mean of 4 and 9 is 6 since $6 = \sqrt{(4 \times 9)}$.

The harmonic mean (H) is found by the equation $\frac{1}{M} - \frac{1}{H} = \frac{1}{H} - \frac{1}{N}$ which simplifies to $H = \frac{2MN}{M + N}$. So the harmonic mean of 12 and 6 is 8 since $8 = \frac{2 \times 12 \times 6}{12 + 6}$.

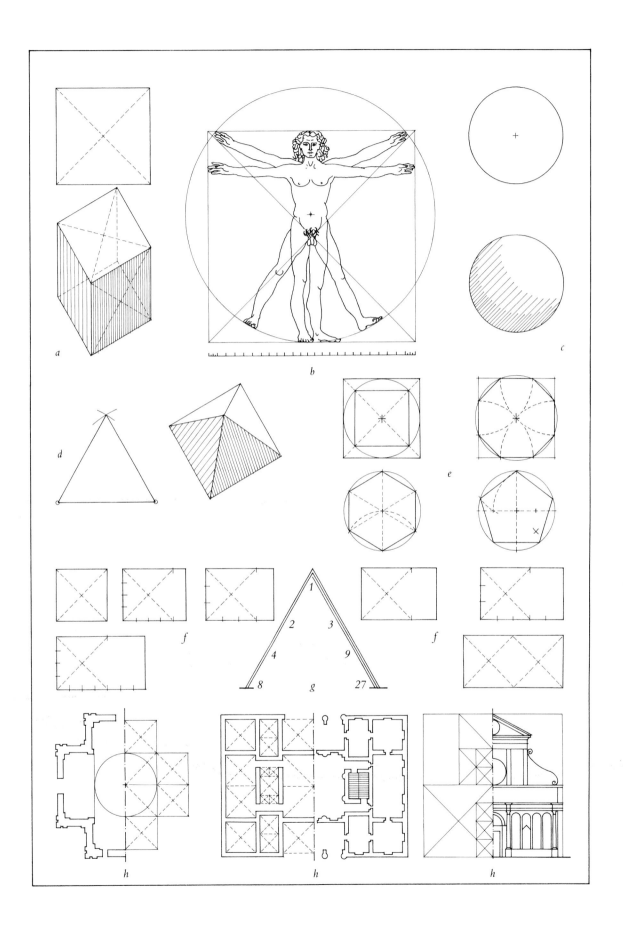

a

b

c

d

e

f

f

g

1

2    3

4    9

8         27

h                    h                    h

# COMPLEX PROPORTIONS

Proportional systems in antiquity and the Renaissance were most frequently based on ratios of whole numbers. Not only was this practical when accuracy in construction was difficult, but even sophisticated theories could be expressed in terms of relatively simple mathematical, geometric and musical principles.

Only one rectangular figure with proportions based on a complex ratio was advocated in the Renaissance, taken from the Roman author Vitruvius. This figure was the root-two rectangle (a) which combined the geometry of the square with the circle. Although the sides of the rectangle have a complex ratio $1:\sqrt{2}$, or approximately 1:1.414, it is very simple to set up geometrically with the diagonal of a square and compasses and has some useful characteristics.

The root-two rectangle can be divided up in the same way as a square to give symmetrical parts of equal proportion and the subdivisions can be varied to include a mixture of root-two rectangles and squares (b). It is also a part of the geometry of the octagon, a common intermediary between the circle and the square, and can be used for setting up and expanding an octagon or a star octagon (c).

Another rectangular figure with a simple geometry and a complex ratio is the golden rectangle (d). A square is divided into two and a diagonal of one of the half-squares becomes a radius with its centre on the central division of the square. This radius is swung outwards to extend to the side of the square, creating a rectangle with a ratio between the sides of approximately 1:1.618. The ratio of the golden section has some unique and remarkable characteristics. Many of these were known by mathematicians in antiquity and the Renaissance, but there is no documentary evidence of any architectural interest before the nineteenth century. At that time experiments sought to link its mathematical versatility with a scientific standard of beauty and circumstantial evidence of its use was claimed from earlier buildings. While no proof of the eternal beauty of this figure or its conscious use in any period but the recent past can be found, its characteristics are of some interest.

The golden rectangle can be divided up to give a square and another golden rectangle, a series of interlocking golden rectangles and squares or diminishing patterns of squares and golden rectangles (e). The permutations are seemingly endless and are based on the equality of the ratios of the parts (d) such that 1:0.618.., BD:CD, is the same as 1.618..:1, BD:AB. The ratio of the golden section is found in the star pentagon and diminishing star pentagons (f). It also has an interesting relationship with a series of numbers set down by the Italian mathematician Leonardo Fibonacci of Pisa in the twelfth century. In the Fibonacci series each successive number is the sum of the two previous numbers, 1–1–2–3–5–8–13 and so on. Growth according to this principle is often found in nature and the ratio between any two adjacent numbers gradually approaches 1:1.618 as the series progresses.

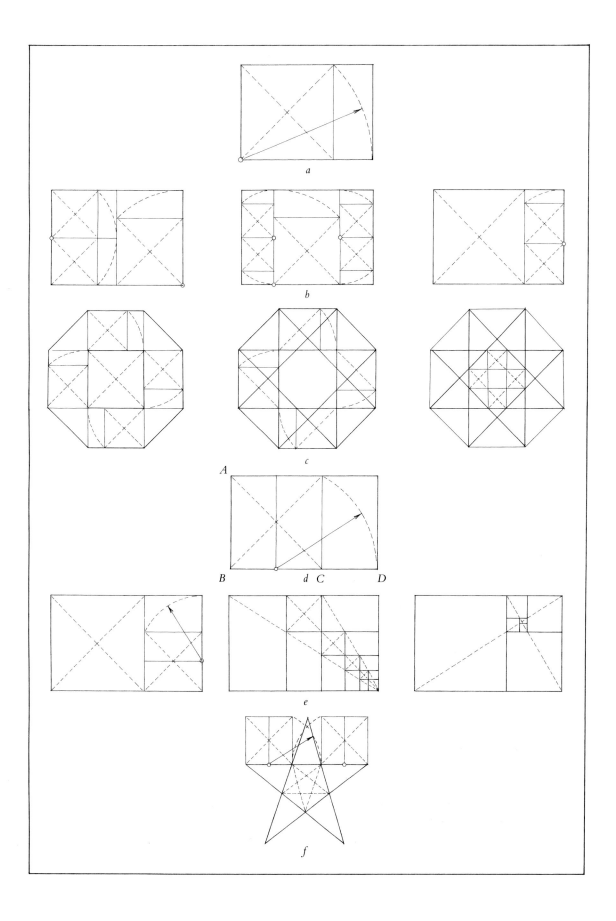

*a*

*b*

*c*

*d*

*e*

*f*

# 5. MOULDINGS

## SIMPLE MOULDINGS

The details of the orders are made up of a series of straight and curved projections and recesses. These are called profiles, or mouldings. Although some are identified with a particular classical order, the same range of mouldings are put together in a specific way to make up the details of each order. Their form, location and relationship to one another have developed over the centuries to create principles which loosely regulate their composition and decoration. A knowledge of the mouldings is essential to a full understanding of classical architecture.

Mouldings can be left as simple shapes or decorated with carving, painting or both. On ancient buildings, mouldings, in common with the rest of the structure, were covered with brightly painted decorations and the origin of many of the early forms of sculpted decoration probably lay in painted patterns.

The fillet (i) is no more than a small square projection which can, as indicated, curve outwards to its face on one or both sides or merely project horizontally on both faces. It is rarely decorated but it sometimes has a simple wave-scroll design, (ii) and (iii). The fillet often sits immediately above the flat vertical face of the corona (iv) which is universal to the cornice of all the orders. In more heavily decorated Roman or later cornices, the corona is occasionally carved with a vertical fluted pattern (v) which can in turn be embellished with stiff leaves (vi).

The astragal (vii) is used more frequently than any other moulding. It is a small semicircular projection and is found on column capitals, between vertical faces on architraves, between larger mouldings on cornices, in the outer face of scrolled brackets and elsewhere in the orders. Astragal mouldings are often decorated. Beading (viii) and various bead and reel mouldings, (ix) and (xiv), were originally specifically associated with the astragal, but in time it was also decorated with cable or rope designs, (xv), (xvi), (xvii), (xix) and (xxi), and other twisted forms such as ribbon moulding, (xviii) and (xx). Many of these decorations continued to be used in Romanesque and Gothic architecture. The variety of possible astragal designs is huge and (xxii) to (xxvii) illustrate only a few of the natural forms and mixtures of natural forms that have been used in the past. Directional natural forms such as (xxiii) and (xxvi) often reverse at the centre of their length to make the pattern symmetrical.

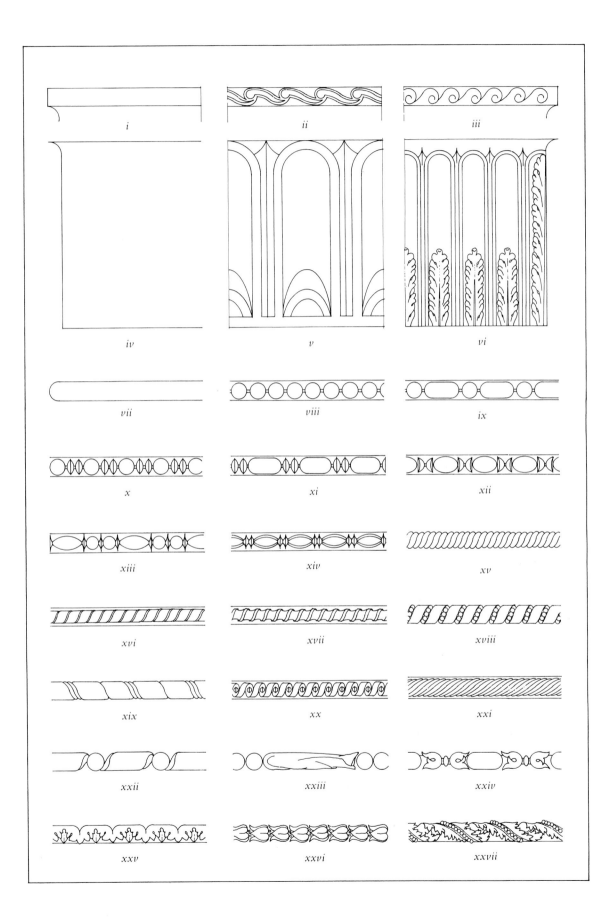

*i*

*ii*

*iii*

*iv*

*v*

*vi*

*vii*

*viii*

*ix*

*x*

*xi*

*xii*

*xiii*

*xiv*

*xv*

*xvi*

*xvii*

*xviii*

*xix*

*xx*

*xxi*

*xxii*

*xxiii*

*xxiv*

*xxv*

*xxvi*

*xxvii*

# FURTHER SIMPLE MOULDINGS

The torus moulding has the same semicircular profile as an astragal, but is consistently larger than an astragal on the same order. Torus mouldings are most commonly found as a part of the base of a column of any order and are often left undecorated. The origin of the torus moulding was, however, as a bulging flat disc at the base of the first Ionic columns in Samos and Ephesus and had a series of concave channels of different widths running around its circumference (a). The frequency, spacing and number of these channels could vary considerably. The form was transferred to the Corinthian order, and in Rome to the Tuscan, Doric and Composite orders, but the channelled decoration (a) was reserved for the base of the Ionic order. Generally it has remained a base moulding and can be used as a continuous band at the base of buildings.

The substitution of a series of concave channels with a series of convex curves like a bundle of rods (b), but without ribbons, is found on early Ionic buildings; an interlacing guilloche pattern, (c) and (d), can be seen on Ionic bases of the fifth century BC. Decoration in the form of bundles of rods resembled the Roman symbol of judicial authority, the fasces, and ribbons were added to reinforce the association (b).

Since the Roman period a number of natural and formal decorations have been applied to the torus moulding. Some of these are illustrated in (e) to (g). Two further examples can be seen on page 273. The torus has received other types of decoration which are illustrated elsewhere, such as the egg and dart, and anthemion.

Many of the devices used to decorate the torus are also used for the cushion, or pulvinated, frieze seen on the Composite order on page 99. The pulvinated frieze, however, is rarely a complete semicircle and its decorative range does not include the horizontal grooves found on the Ionic base (a).

Dentils, (i) to (n), are a row of tooth-like projections that originated in the lower part of the cornice of early Ionic buildings and probably represented beam-ends. From the Ionic order they became a part of the Corinthian order and hence the Composite order. In Rome they were occasionally used on the Doric order and in the Renaissance a specific 'denticular' Doric cornice was evolved.

In their most simple form (i), dentils are no more than a series of vertical rectangular projections. On Roman Ionic buildings an isolated corner dentil was sometimes suspended from an underlying projection (j). This illogical arrangement for a beam-end was often resolved by suspending a purely decorative pine-cone in the corner, (k) and (l). On Corinthian and Composite cornices the underlying projection was at times itself decorated with a curiously specific device (l). On later buildings any association that might have remained with a timber structural origin was lost and dentils were treated as a solely decorative feature, (m) and (n).

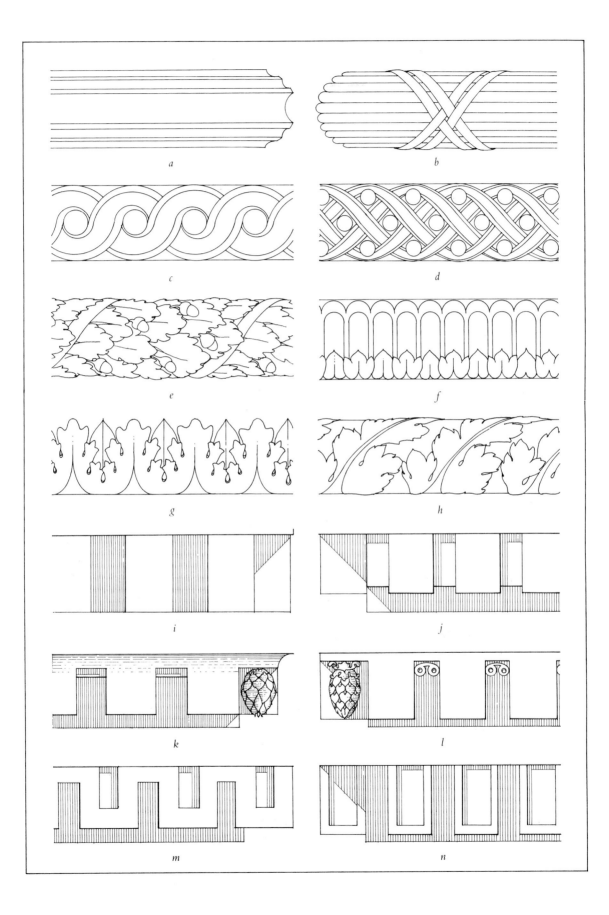

*a*

*b*

*c*

*d*

*e*

*f*

*g*

*h*

*i*

*j*

*k*

*l*

*m*

*n*

# COMPLEX MOULDINGS

A series of complex mouldings has evolved that is specifically identified with classical design. Each of these complex profiles has its own name and geometric structure, but there is a great deal of variety within this framework.

The cyma recta, or ogee, moulding, (a) to (f), is a double curve, concave above and convex below. With the exception of some Doric examples, the cyma recta is the uppermost moulding on the cornices of all the orders. It is also found on pilaster capitals, on the cornices of pedestals and upside-down on pilaster and pedestal bases as well as in other parts of some orders.

The cyma recta seems to be associated with no specific form of decoration. Generally the shallower forms (a), (d) and (e), were favoured by the Greeks and the deeper, stronger forms by the Romans. Examples (d) to (f) have larger concave than convex curves, and when the radius varies it is always in this relationship.

The cyma reversa, or reverse ogee, has the convex curve uppermost and the concave curve below, (g) to (l). The shape evolved to accept tongue and dart decoration and is found in the cornices of all the orders: crowning the architrave of the Ionic, Corinthian and Composite orders, on the abacus of some Ionic capitals and in other parts of some orders. It is usually smaller in scale than the cyma recta moulding above the corona on the same order.

The ovolo moulding, (m) to (o), is specifically associated with egg and dart decoration and in this form is one of the most distinctive and widespread classical ornamental details. It is prominent in cornices, architraves, Ionic and Composite capitals and, in its simpler form (o) or even as a quarter-circle, can be used as the echinus of a Roman Doric or a Tuscan capital.

The Greek Doric echinus, (p) to (r), is shown in the sequence of its evolution from early temples (p), through the classic Athenian form (q), to the late Hellenistic type (r). The name echinus, meaning sea-urchin, refers exclusively to Doric and Ionic column capitals, although a similar profile sometimes appears as a very small scale variant of ovolo in some Greek entablatures and as the uppermost moulding on early Doric cornices.

The cavetto moulding, (s) to (u), is a useful and often undecorated profile which can be a principal moulding on its own or can perform the function of easing the junction between wider and narrower features. The scotia moulding can be used either way up, (v) to (x), but keeps the longer radius below in its most common position separating, either singly or in pairs, the torus mouldings of some Doric and all Ionic, Corinthian and Composite bases.

All these examples have been set out with precision and selected to show how changes in geometry alter the fall of light on the different shapes. With a sure hand and experience, more subtle variations can be drawn without the aid of compasses.

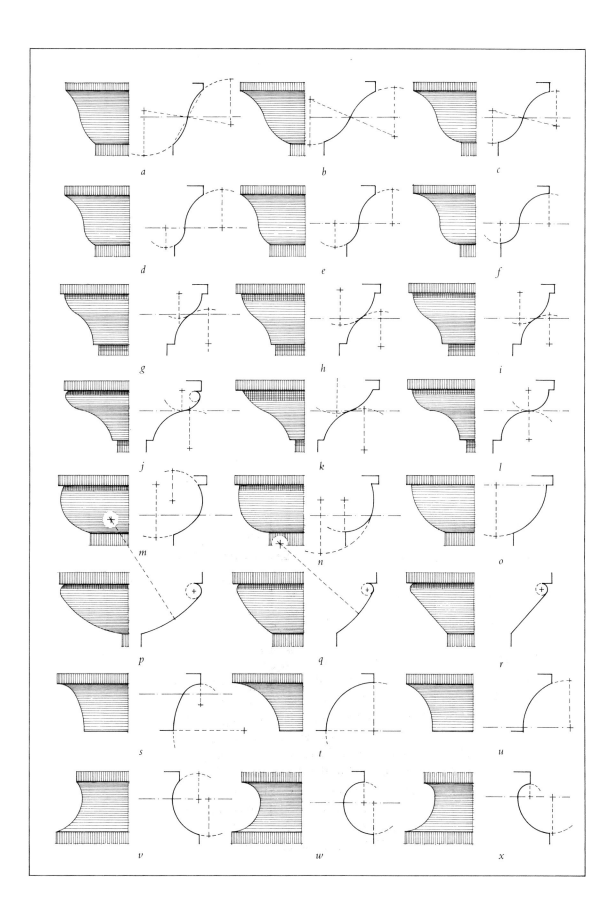

*a*

*b*

*c*

*d*

*e*

*f*

*g*

*h*

*i*

*j*

*k*

*l*

*m*

*n*

*o*

*p*

*q*

*r*

*s*

*t*

*u*

*v*

*w*

*x*

# Egg And Dart And Tongue And Dart

Two mouldings are particularly associated with two forms of decoration. The ovolo moulding is so closely associated with egg and dart pattern that the decoration itself is also called ovolo. Cyma recta moulding is usually decorated with a form of leaf design called tongue and dart or leaf and tongue. It is quite possible that both of these mouldings developed specifically to accommodate these types of decoration, either in painted or carved form. Certainly the consistent association of these two forms of embellishment with their respective mouldings over the centuries has given them a linked identity and a particular association with classical design.

Egg and dart decoration is the most widespread decorative form in classical design. It is most clearly identified, as its name suggests, by its row of hanging egg shapes. Early examples of the decoration on primitive Ionic capitals of the seventh century BC (a), however, do not have such an obvious association with the form of eggs. But by the time it appears on Ionic buildings in the fifth century BC (b), it has developed the characteristics that it will display in the succeeding centuries.

Many variations are to be found, but, as example (c) from Greek colonies in Italy demonstrates, these often display more of the egg shape and so serve to reinforce the association. The Romans adopted the design with unusually little alteration (d), but the dart, which in Greek examples was more like the stem of a leaf, takes on the arrowhead or dart shape of its modern name. In the Renaissance the dart was often further emphasized by a wider spacing between the eggs (e). A similar wider spacing may be incorporated into a simplified form (f) which is suitable for smaller mouldings where the inclusion of all the details is impractical.

Tongue and dart decoration on cyma reversa mouldings (h) appears on fifth-century-BC buildings together with an undercut bird's beak moulding (g) which fell out of use until revived in the late eighteenth century. Investigation of traces of paint on the bird's beak mouldings indicate that it was decorated as a stylized drooping leaf. The pointed-leaf decoration of tongue and dart has the same fundamental design except that the leaf has turned down to the bottom of the moulding and eliminated the undercut. The Romans, while adopting the Greek form (h), at times elaborated the design. In some cases the elaboration derived directly from the original concept of turned-down leaves (i) while, particularly at a large scale, the shape of the original design could be taken as little more than a background for sculptural enrichment (j). The Roman forms were adopted in the Renaissance (k). When used for very small mouldings (l), the individual leaves can be made very much broader in order to accommodate sufficient detail to make the design recognizable.

Both egg and dart and tongue and dart decorations are taken around corners by the application of a special leaf or an undecorated moulding of a similar shape.

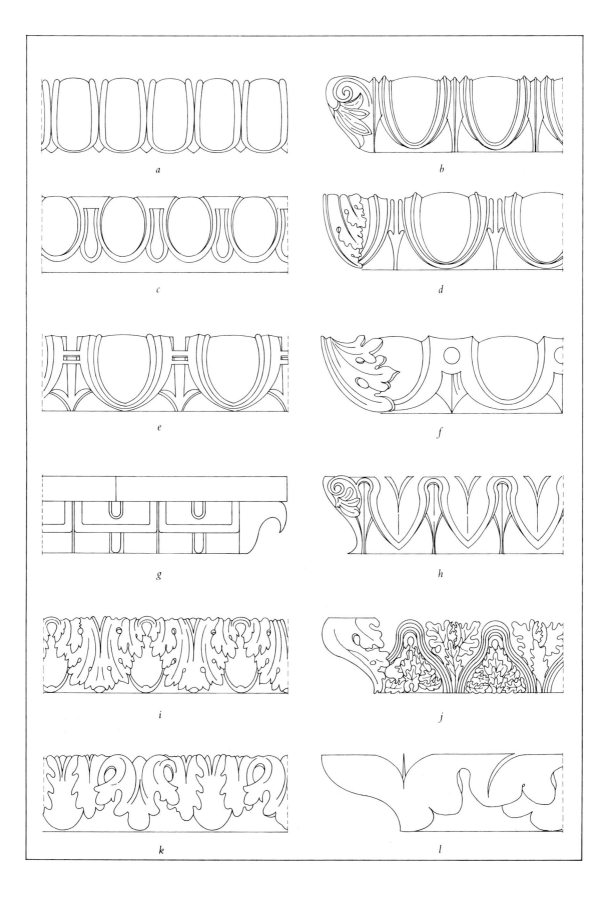

*a*

*b*

*c*

*d*

*e*

*f*

*g*

*h*

*i*

*j*

*k*

*l*

# FURTHER COMPLEX MOULDINGS
## DECORATED

While ovolo and cyma reversa mouldings have a relatively consistent decorative vocabulary the same cannot be said for the other complex mouldings. The addition of decoration to these mouldings seems to have followed no discernible pattern. In common with all details of classical buildings, however, all these profiles were often elaborately enriched with carving, painting or gilding. The only exception is the scotia moulding which is rarely decorated.

Since the Renaissance, the study of the buildings of antiquity has been the study of ruins or much-altered survivals. The only remaining enrichments on these buildings are carvings, which were often originally intended as a foundation and enhancement for painted decoration. The passage of many centuries, however, removed much of the original paint and the idea grew up that the buildings of antiquity were designed without colour. In the early Renaissance, the painting of buildings was common, but the Greek Revival of the late nineteenth century was founded on a desire for sober refinement to counteract the decorative exuberance of the Rococo. It came as a great shock when research revealed that early Greek architecture was a riot of bright colour. Roman architecture, too, relied on painted colour and to this the Romans added gold leaf and the natural colours of bright marbles.

When the evolution of a moulding is not related to a single form of embellishment, the decoration that is applied in carving is likely to be the same as might be found in painting. The tongue and dart on the echinus of an early Greek temple (i) is painted, but tongue and dart and, more often, egg and dart are found carved on echinus mouldings. The range of embellishment is only limited by what is suitable for the shape of the moulding. It is, therefore, not surprising to see variants of the popular classical abstracted leaf designs, such as the anthemion, painted on a Greek echinus (j), carved on a nineteenth-century echinus (k), and carved on two cyma recta mouldings, (e) and (g). Equally, versions of the stiff leaf can be found on another nineteenth-century echinus (l) and on a cyma recta moulding (d) by Palladio in the sixteenth century.

Other examples are shown to illustrate the possible range of embellishment. The rosette pattern on a cavetto (a) is only one of many alternatives for this relatively simple decorative surface. On a cyma recta, the acanthus design (f) and repeating dolphin design (h) from Roman buildings are only two examples from a wide variety of Roman treatments, while the vertical channels from an eighteenth-century French pattern-book (c) are relatively unusual. Finally, the bay-leaf ovolo decoration from a late Roman building (b) demonstrates that even the moulding normally reserved for egg and dart embellishment can receive a varied treatment.

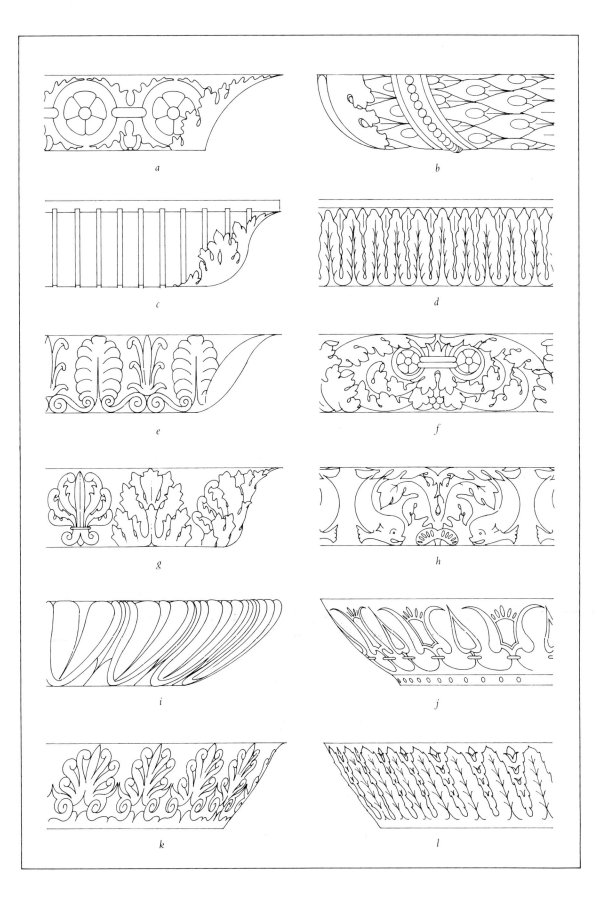

*a*

*b*

*c*

*d*

*e*

*f*

*g*

*h*

*i*

*j*

*k*

*l*

# 6. ADDITION AND SUBTRACTION

---

## The Orders In Order

Classical architecture is not restricted by the use of the orders to buildings of a limited size or form. Since antiquity the orders have been manipulated to accommodate buildings quite unlike the simple temples that are their foundation. Over the centuries conventions have evolved for solving the design problems created by different buildings and these have become part of the classical tradition. There are a huge number of these devices. Some are specific to certain historical periods and rejected by others, but where they have been successful they have been repeated as contributions to the development of the tradition. Many design problems have been solved by these inventions, but the list can never be complete.

In order to achieve a height greater than a single storey the orders can be placed on top of one another. Early examples are in the interiors of Greek temples, such as the Parthenon in Athens (a) of 438 BC, where a smaller row of Doric columns was placed directly on the architrave of larger columns below. The taper of the lower columns is continued through to the upper columns so that the upper columns are significantly smaller.

In later two-storey buildings, such as the Stoa of Attalos in Athens (b) of 150 BC, the more slender Ionic order was used for the upper floor. The principle of placing more slender orders above stouter orders gave a natural reduction in weight which corresponded to structural requirements. It was taken to its fullest extent in the construction of the Colosseum in Rome (d) in AD 80, where Doric, Ionic, Corinthian and Composite are set in an ascending sequence. Although this arrangement was not universal in antiquity or the early Renaissance, the survival of the Colosseum and the categorization of the orders in the Renaissance led to a general adoption of this vertical sequence of the orders.

The Roman author Vitruvius recommends that upper columns should be three quarters of the size of those below. His recommendation seems to apply to two-storey buildings where it can be quite satisfactory but, as illustrated in (c), if continued upwards it can become quite extreme. It is more usual to follow the recommendation of Renaissance authors and make the upper diameter of the lower order equal the lower diameter of the upper order, as shown in (e). This illustration includes pedestals for all the orders although other arrangements can be used.

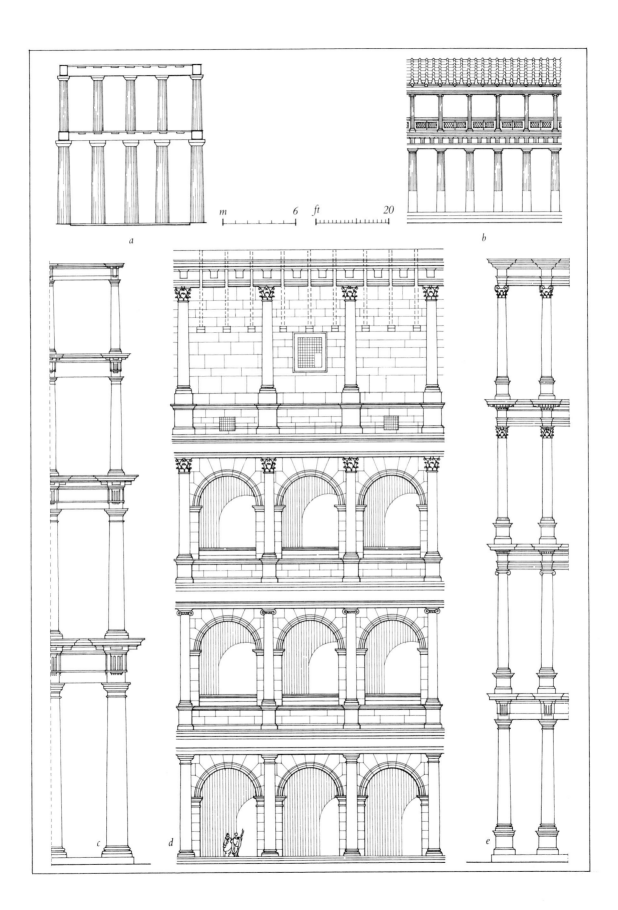

*m*     6    *ft*     20

*a*

*b*

*c*

*d*

*e*

# MANIPULATING THE ORDERS

The visual or functional needs of a building may not be satisfactorily answered by a simple application of the orders in their basic form.

The height of an entablature can be raised by adding a small block (a), or further raised by adding details to this block (b) that correspond to the proportions of a column pedestal of an imaginary upper order. The pedestals can be expressed more literally, as in (c), and provide more interest at the top of the building.

Example (c) has sufficient height to become a separate storey, known as an attic storey. Robert Adam's Luton Park House (d) of 1767 shows an attic storey with windows. Palladio's design for the Palazzo Valmarana (e) of 1565 is similar, but statues on the attic pedestals create an appearance of greater height. Placing a balustrade on top of the attic storey, as on George Dance the elder's Mansion House in London (f) of 1739, gives a still greater impression of height.

The central bay of the Roman triumphal arch in Orange, France (h) has a lower attic block that acts as backdrop to an applied pediment. The pedestal for the statue sits above. In the Ashmolean Museum in Oxford (g) of 1841, by C. R. Cockerell, the principal order sits below a large cornice, proportioned according to the total height of the building, and the attic sits between the two cornices. On the Westminster Insurance Office in London (i) Cockerell turned the attic storey and its pedestals into a squat upper order with its own pediment. These attic orders can have their own short columns and special capitals.

At a low level, height can be gained with pedestals. On the Casa del Diavolo (j) Palladio raised the columns on high pedestals and fitted windows between them. The upper two storeys of the doorway of Philibert de l'Orme's Château d'Anet (k) of 1547 have very heavy pedestal blocks to control the heights of the ascending orders. Palladio's Palazzo da Porto Festa (l) illustrates the common device of turning the whole lower storey into a rusticated pedestal.

The height of the entablature can cause problems with the location of windows. Example (j) has low windows in the frieze but the designer of the Archbishop's Palace in Sens, France (m) of 1535 has taken the radical, but not unique, step of increasing the height of the lower frieze and reducing the height of the upper entablature. A distinctively Baroque detail at Cound Hall, England (n) of 1704 limits the frieze and architrave to a vertical block, called a dosseret, above the column in order to allow windows to pass by the entablature. Architects such as Hawksmoor in his unexecuted design of 1712 for the Radcliffe Camera in Oxford (o) avoided the problem altogether by so simplifying and modifying the order that the remaining details gave little clue as to the conventional position of the classical elements.

a

b

c

d

e

f

g

h

i

j

k

l

m

n

o

# GIANT ORDERS

When floor-to-floor heights are relatively modest, a vertical series of orders can be individually small and collectively make the whole building appear insignificant. To give buildings of two or more storeys the same impact as the large temples of antiquity, a complete classical order with columns the full height of the building was used. This is called a colossal, or giant, order.

Although giant orders did not come into use until the sixteenth century, Roman architecture often combined columns of great size with smaller columns for lesser features. In the interior of the Baths of Caracalla in Rome (a) of AD 216 the wide concrete roof-vault is carried on granite Corinthian columns 11.5 metres high with screens of a smaller Corinthian order between them.

One of the early and influential uses of a giant order was in the group of buildings on the Capitol in Rome (b), designed by Michelangelo in 1546. Two bays of one of the three buildings are illustrated. The façades are unified by pilasters of a giant Corinthian order on pedestals. Inset between the giant orders on the ground floor is a subsidiary Ionic order with full columns one storey high.

The façade of S. Giovanni in Laterano, Rome (c), designed by Alessandro Galilei in 1733, is based on a giant Composite order with columns 20 metres high. Inside the giant order are two one-storey tiers of Corinthian columns. The ground-floor subsidiary order is higher than that on the upper floor and carries an entablature. On the upper floor the columns carry an arch so avoiding any conflict between the entablatures of large and small orders.

Palladio's church of S. Giorgio Maggiore in Venice (d) of 1565 is, in effect, two temple fronts interwoven with one another. A giant Composite order of round pilasters on pedestals supports the larger central pediment and a smaller Corinthian order of square pilasters supports a lower pediment, which is split to provide the lower roofs for the side-aisles. The Corinthian order reappears as quarter-columns framing the central door and the pedestals of the Composite order become the bases for small niches between the Corinthian columns.

With the Freemason's Hall, in London, of 1866, part of which is illustrated (e), C. P. Cockerell avoids a potential conflict between the entablatures of the giant and subsidiary orders by combining them. The giant order is suppressed with rustication and given a squat Corinthian capital the same height as the capital of the Corinthian subsidiary order, which is brought up to the same level on a high rusticated plinth.

On a row of houses in Glasgow (f), built in 1859, Alexander Thompson combined a giant and subsidiary order with the same entablature but, by using exceptionally slender columns for the giant order, made the entablature seem to be an appropriate height for both. He also removed the small upper columns from between the giant order columns, so avoiding any visual conflict at entablature level.

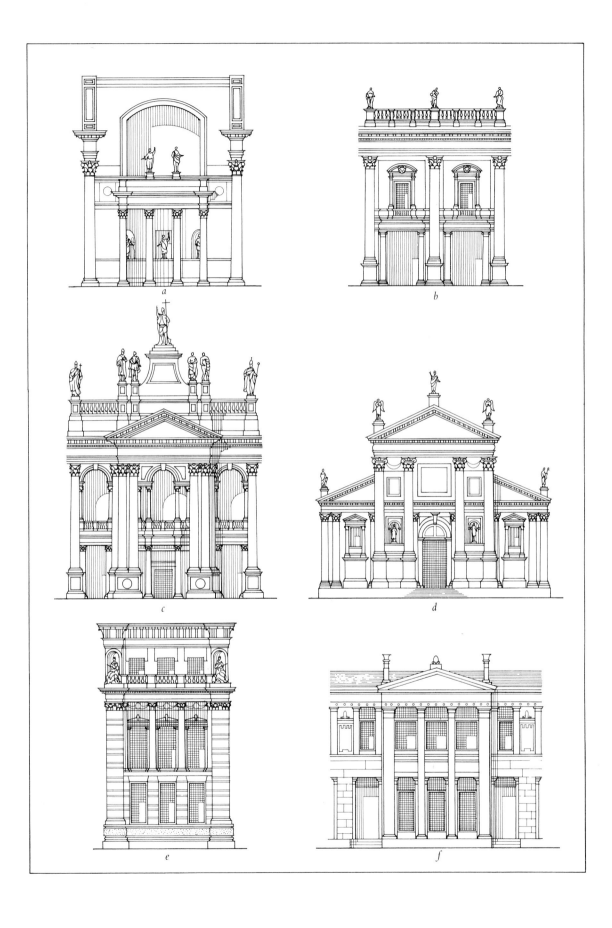

*a*

*b*

*c*

*d*

*e*

*f*

# CHANGING SCALE

---

The orders can be applied in a number of different ways to alter the appearance of a building. To illustrate this, a series of alternative applications of the orders to the same underlying three-storey building (a) are shown together. The examples all have the same proportions, but in practice it would be possible to manipulate the design to produce more refined results.

The simple application of ascending Doric, Ionic and Corinthian orders of diminishing height (b) produces a delicate character due to the small size of the individual orders. The strong horizontal divisions of the entablatures give the building a low appearance. When the first order is raised on a plinth (c) the tall windows above become more important and the whole building tends to look more imposing. This can also be a more practical arrangement as the decoration on the vulnerable ground floor is more robust.

Examples (b) and (c) are typical early and High Renaissance applications of the orders. In both cases the distance between the columns might be better reduced by introducing more columns and spacing them at alternate widths.

The introduction of a two-storey giant order on the rusticated plinth (d) transforms the character of the building. It becomes more impressive and the individual columns are given greater importance. The use of a single order allows the whole building to assume the character of that order. The replacement of the rusticated lower floor with tall column pedestals (e) gives the feeling of greater height, and the pedestals become important design elements at street level.

The increased height of the entablature in examples (d) and (e) can just be contained in the space over the top window on this façade. The projection of the cornice and the detail of the entablature now become significant. Both of these giant order arrangements were used from the sixteenth century onwards and popularized by Palladio. In modest buildings the height of the entablature caused problems and it is not uncommon to find the frieze or the architrave omitted.

When giant order columns extend to three storeys (f) the building looks both taller and more dramatic. The wide columns divide the building so forcefully that the horizontal arrangement of the windows is lost and they are seen as vertical groups. This typical Baroque use of a giant order makes it impossible to accommodate a full entablature so the frieze has been omitted.

The strong entablature of a giant order can be used with an attic storey to reduce the apparent height of a building. By taking the cornice to the sill of the upper windows and leaving the upper floor plain (g) the impression of a two-storey building is created. A more decorative treatment of the attic floor (h) will give it more emphasis, but the heavy entablature will divide the façade into two parts.

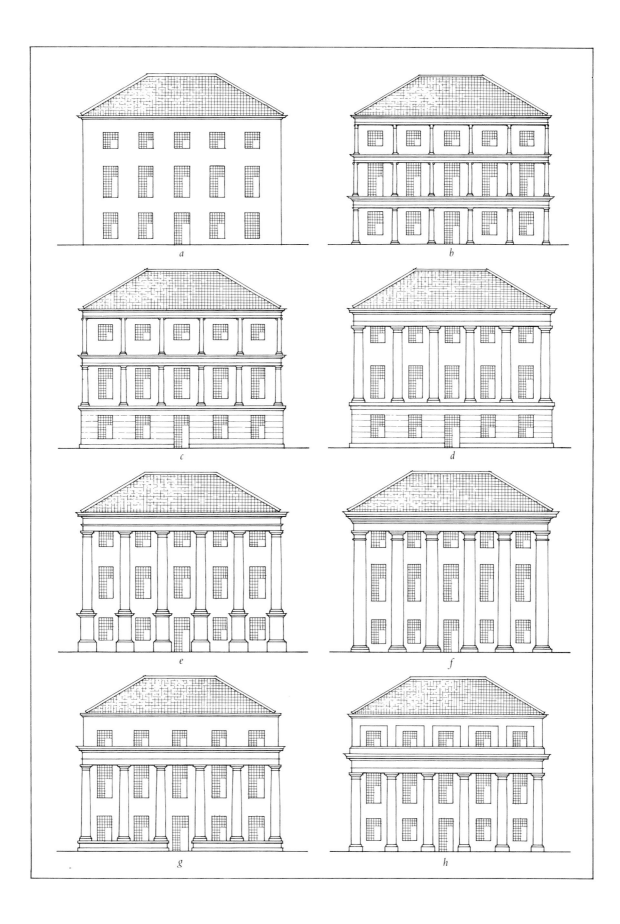

a

b

c

d

e

f

g

h

# 7. HIDDEN ORDERS

## PROGRESSIVE OMISSIONS: THE ORDER

The full range of decoration associated with the orders is not always appropriate. The extent of decoration can be increased or decreased while retaining the character and proportion of the orders; the potential presence of a full decorative scheme can be suggested by introducing selected decorated elements. The ability to manipulate the orders in this way is the product of centuries of familiarity with the classical tradition and is an essential part of classical design.

The Roman Doric order illustrated (a) includes the complete range of details traditionally associated with the order. When this is to be constructed in a small size, at a low cost or to create a bold impression, many of these details can be inappropriate.

Illustration (b) shows the fluting on the column removed and most of the triglyphs omitted. It is possible to use a smooth column shaft on any of the orders, but the progressive omission of the triglyphs on the Doric order has some unique characteristics. The retention of single triglyphs over the columns and the rather peculiar survival of the associated details on the architrave indicate the basis for the horizontal proportioning of the frieze.

The next stage (c) has square columns and no triglyphs or metopes in the frieze. The column retains its entasis and there is a full cornice. The fine detailing on the cornice can also be progressively reduced before the cornice itself is simplified as in (d). This example also shows the omission of the entasis on the columns. The simplified cornice and frieze blur the distinction between Doric and Tuscan.

Reducing the details further, as in examples (e) and (f), produces a very simple assembly of parts while retaining the proportions and a suggestion of the full order. In the simplest expression of the order (f) there is no trace of the column details and the cornice acts as the last reminder of the details that have been lost.

This is only an illustrative progression of reducing an order. It is equally possible to retain some elements in full detail while reducing others. In example (g) only the frieze and architrave have been reduced to a plain face. The cornice and the square column base in (h) have been simplified, but bare versions of triglyphs remain. A full cornice in (i) sits over the most unadorned expression of the proportions of the order. These are just a few combinations, many more are possible.

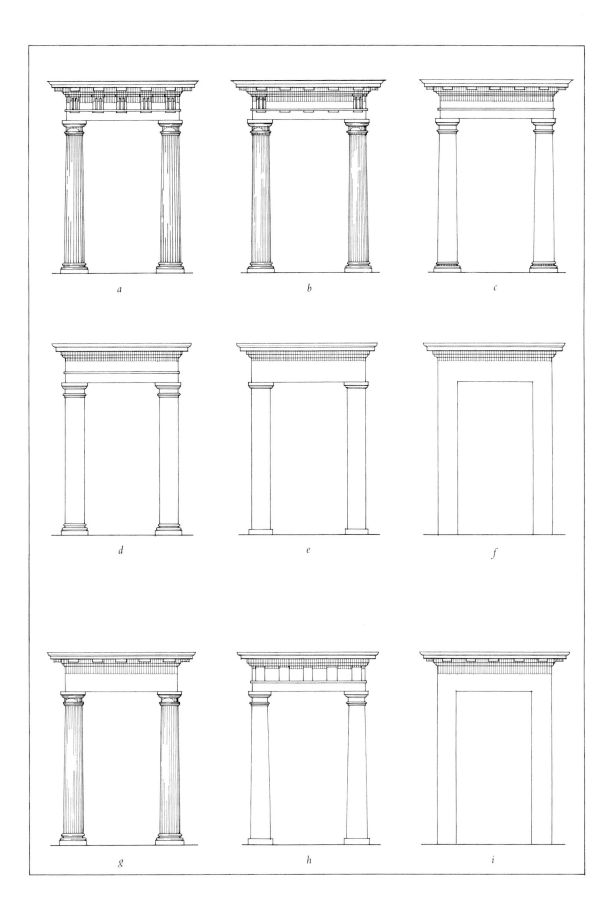

*a*         *b*         *c*

*d*         *e*         *f*

*g*         *h*         *i*

# PROGRESSIVE OMISSIONS: THE BUILDING

The reduction of detail on classical exteriors has created some buildings of such simplicity that their classical origin is not always obvious. Many English houses from the late eighteenth century have little more than the details of the door to reveal the classical principles that underlie their design. The elegance which has made these buildings so admired is, none the less, derived from the classical orders that are the foundation of their proportions. In a classical building the orders are always present even if they are not immediately visible.

A progressive reduction of a classical façade is illustrated here with four slightly modified examples taken from a row of houses in Bedford Square in London, designed by William Scott and Robert Grew in 1776.

The first example (a) has a complete temple front applied to a brick face. A rusticated base in painted stucco contains the front door and supports four Ionic pilasters below an entablature with the architrave omitted. A full pediment hides part of the roof. In the second example (b) the columns have gone and with them the pediment. The design is much more modest but retains the rusticated ground floor of the first example, and the reduced entablature. A balustrade has replaced the pediment and its solid plinths correspond to the positions of the lost columns. In the next stage (c) the rustication has gone, to reveal the brickwork below. The arched door-opening is still rusticated, but in a modified way; otherwise a horizontal band marks the line of the base of the columns which would set the proportions of the order and the size of cornice on the remaining reduced entablature. The final example (d) has less detail than any of the buildings in Bedford Square, but represents a level of further reduction that was common at this time. It has a sheer brick face with only two horizontal bands to mark the position of the column bases and cornice. In the simple door, the same height and width as the adjacent windows, only two quarter-columns give a clue to the classical basis of the design.

These examples are taken from eighteenth-century London, but the principle could apply to many classical buildings from any period and in any place. The possibility of suggesting that a complete classical front lies just beneath the barest façade and the ability to proportion the most rudimentary building in the same way as the most elaborate are uniquely fertile aspects of classical design.

Decoration can be closely matched to construction budgets and existing buildings can be improved by adding missing parts of their hidden orders. Rows of houses can, as in our example in Bedford Square, be combined to form unified compositions that collectively resemble larger buildings: the most elaborate version (a) is placed in the centre, the next level (b) as pavilions at the ends and multiples of less decorated examples (c) between. Above all, the most humble building can share the underlying design of the most exalted.

*a*

*b*

*c*

*d*

# PROGRESSIVE OMISSIONS: THE INTERIOR

The details of the classical interior are part of our everyday lives. Many people live in rooms with cornices, friezes and architraves without realizing the origin of these words, the place of these elements in the classical orders and the way in which the orders set the proportions of such familiar features.

The example illustrated is from the interior of Derby House in London, designed by Robert Adam in 1773, but the principles of the scheme could apply to almost any classical interior.

The walls of the room are set out to accommodate a complete classical order (a), in this case Corinthian. The window-sills are at the level of the top of the pedestal and from this line the columns rise to fix the proportions of the entablature, which sits immediately below the ceiling. This order, based on the height of the room, establishes the size of the cornice and frieze at ceiling level as parts of that entablature. The top of the pedestal becomes the dado rail or chair rail; its profile is generally a flat version of the cornice of a pedestal. The skirting, or baseboard, is the plinth of the pedestal and its profile is similarly composed. As with the pedestal, the wall between is called the dado. The door has its own entablature, in this case equal in size to the principal entablature. The lower moulding of the entablature, the architrave, is carried around the door to meet the baseboard. The windows have a similar detail, but with no frieze or cornice.

This arrangement can differ. The columns often start at floor level and the details and proportions of the cornice, frieze and baseboard change accordingly. A dado is not necessary, but it can still be included when the column bases start on the floor and should be seen as a solid balustrade between columns. The doors and windows frequently have their own independent classical order, sometimes with their own columns and pediment, and the details are correspondingly smaller. In a tall room, the cornice may sit below the ceiling level and be joined to it by a large continuous inward curve, called coving, or a vault may span from one side of the room to another. In a very tall room it is even possible to have two orders, one above the other, or a giant order and subsidiary orders.

These details only appear in full in the most splendid rooms. It is much more usual to find a reduced version. Example (b) retains a number of impressive features. There is a full decorated frieze, a full entablature over the door and a dado. Example (c) is the familiar simple room which retains only the ceiling cornice, the architraves around the door and windows and the skirting. This last example, however simple, is set out according to the same proportions as the first and retains the potential to be improved or decorated to reflect the classical principles shared by both interiors.

*a*

*b*

*c*

# SELECTIVE EXTERIOR DETAILS

The selective addition of full classical details without the complete classical order from which they derive is a particular feature of classical design. The proportional and decorative systems of the orders make it possible to suggest the full ornament of the order by the presence of a few decorative elements. The success of this type of design relies on our everyday familiarity with classical buildings, but can fail when selective details are repeated without an underlying knowledge of their origin and of the orders.

Some examples of the selective use of individual details on an identical building (a) are illustrated here. In these examples the proportions of each building are repeated exactly, in order to make the comparison direct. In reality, minor adjustments would be made to accommodate the particular details of each illustration.

In example (b) an ascending series of orders – Doric, Ionic, Corinthian – is suggested by the retention of all or part of the entablature of each order. The lower Doric entablature is retained in full while on the Ionic order above, only the cornice remains. The eaves have a complete Corinthian entablature. This particular arrangement is dictated by the window positions and it is quite usual to see all the entablatures or just the cornices of each order. This isolated application of the horizontal features of a series of ascending orders in bands is a very widely used design feature in classical architecture of all periods.

The following two examples illustrate other selective applications of the orders when they are arranged in an ascending sequence. In example (c) only the lower floor and the eaves retain any evidence of the decoration of the orders; on the lower floor the Doric order is complete. The Doric order, by its contrast with the upper floors, gives an importance to this floor that would usually be associated with its function. As a contrast, example (d) has a full Corinthian order on the top floor. The balance of the façade is maintained by giving weight to the lower floor with rustication, which in itself can suggest the Doric order. This type of design is normally found where the upper floor commands a fine view or has some other special significance.

The only elements that remain on example (e) are the cornice and frieze of the Corinthian order, proportioned to the full height of the façade. A rich cornice, with or without other elements of the entablature and without any other parts of the order, is found frequently on classical buildings and gives distinction to an otherwise simple façade. It is possible to achieve a similar impression while changing the balance of the design. A more vertical emphasis is given to example (f) by the addition of full-height pilasters. Although the cornice and frieze remain, like the pilasters they are stripped of much of their detail. Full capitals alone give the building the decorative character of the Corinthian order.

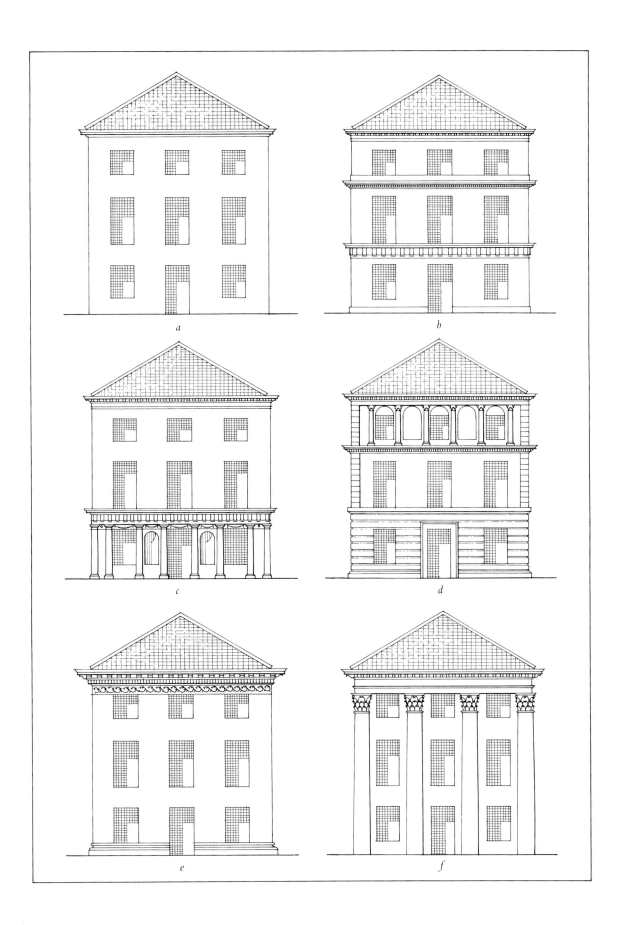

a

b

c

d

e

f

# 8. THE PEDIMENT

## THE TEMPLE ROOF

A pediment is the gable-end of the roof of a Greek temple (a). Greek temples were entered by their gable-end, making the pediment an important architectural feature.

Classical pediments usually have a shallow pitch. The Greek invention of a special type of clay roof-tile in about 700 BC established the pitch of temple roofs. This roof-tile, still in use today, was large, flat and turned up at the sides. The joints between the tiles were covered by smaller half-round tiles. The new roofing system was very efficient and replaced earlier flat mud roofs and steep thatched roofs. The tiles were laid loose and, to stop the outermost tiles falling off, special decorated clay brackets, or antefixa, were secured to the roof beams and hooked up over the end of each row of half-round tiles.

Pediments were often lavishly decorated. The triangular space inside, the tympanum, at times contained sculptural groups and the top of the pediment could have sculpture at the ends and centre called, with their supporting bases where appropriate, acroteria.

The Roman author Vitruvius set out pediments by dividing the maximum horizontal dimension into nine to find the height to the lowest moulding at the top of the pitch (c). In the sixteenth century, Serlio took a distance down from the centre equal to half the maximum horizontal dimension and made this the centre of an arc from the outside of the pediment to its uppermost point (b). These rules are, however, far from universal. Some Roman roofs had a thirty-degree pitch (g) and in buildings of the north European Renaissance, pitches of up to forty-five degrees (f) accommodated local forms of roof covering.

Some details of pediments obey strict rules. The top of the pediment is the same as the cornice of the horizontal entablature on which it rests, but on the entablature the cornice loses its top moulding, usually a cyma, as this was originally the gutter and would be redundant in this position. The corona, below, forms the junction between the pitch and the horizontal.

When the cornice contains projecting features, such as dentils (d), mutules (e) or scrolled brackets, these usually do not tilt over to follow the slope of the pediment but are distorted, so that the sides are vertical while the top and bottom of the features stay at the angle of the pediment. These features are spaced so that they are vertically in line with the equivalent detail below.

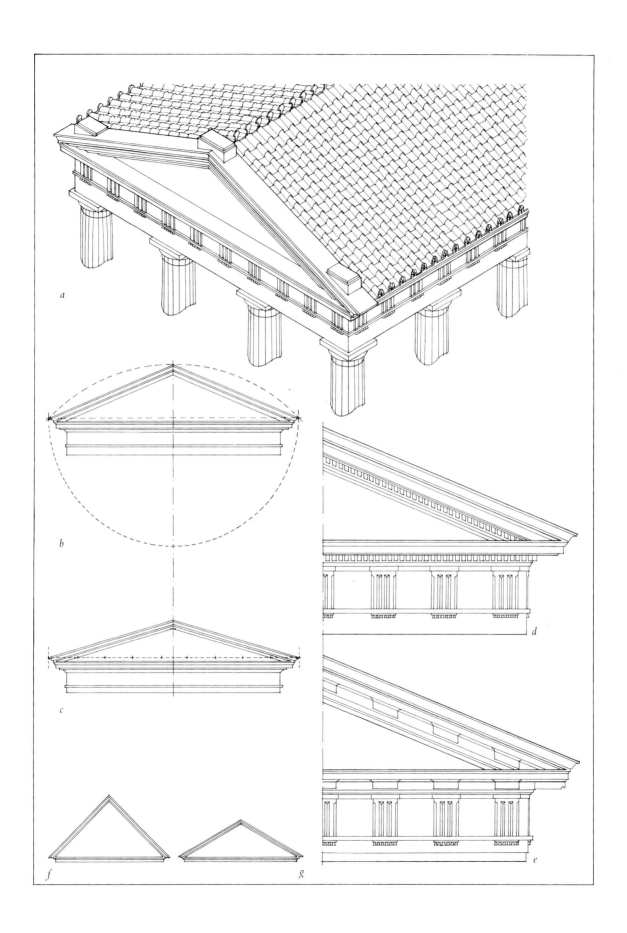

a

b

c

d

e

f

g

# TYPES OF PEDIMENT

The application of the pediment to parts of buildings which do not resemble the gable-end of a temple has, from the Roman period onwards, led to a number of modifications. The importance of the pediment is so well established that its identity survives even when reduced to little more than distorted remnants.

Many of the variations of the pediment involve the removal of different parts. The terminology for these modifications has become confusing. Pediments with part of the top omitted are sometimes called 'open' and sometimes 'broken'; for pediments with part of the bottom omitted, the terminology is similarly confused. There is no universally accepted system of terms.

Part of a pediment can be brought forward on columns or brackets, leaving the central part of the horizonal entablature behind (a). The central portion of the entablature can be omitted altogether, creating an open space beneath the apex of the pediment (b). This arrangement allows an arch or some other vertical feature to rise unhindered past the column capitals.

The pitch of the pediment can be broken and brought forward. The broken entablature and pitch can be brought forward together (d) or the pitch alone can be broken (c). Again, the central portion of the pitch can be omitted, leaving the top of the pediment completely open (e). The gap created in (e) is set by the width of the vertical section of entablature above the column, or dosseret, but it can be reduced. It is also possible to omit both the recessed entablature and the recessed pitch leaving only two vertical remnants of pediment (f). This detail tends to be specifically associated with Mannerist, Baroque and Rococo architecture.

Pediments do not have to be triangular, they can have a curved top. These are generally low segmental curves (g) and of the same height as a triangular pediment. The centre of the arc of the pediment (g) is found by dividing a line from the outermost horizontal point to the equivalent point at the apex into two parts and projecting this centre point at right-angles to meet the centre line. Their equal height allows segmental and triangular pediments to be mixed in an alternating pattern or to give emphasis to one or more features by changing the type. Curved pediments can be varied in the same way as triangular pediments (h).

The pediment can also be a complete semicircle although the uppermost cyma moulding terminates facing downwards. This was sometimes avoided by bringing the bottom of the cyma moulding down in line with the centre of the column or bracket and turning it outward to terminate horizontally (i).

There are many further variations of curved pediments. The pitch can be turned into two scrolls which can meet at the centre or remain apart (j). The pitch can have a double curve (k) or be split into a series of curves, or curves and straight pitches (l). These variations are generally associated with Baroque and Rococo architecture.

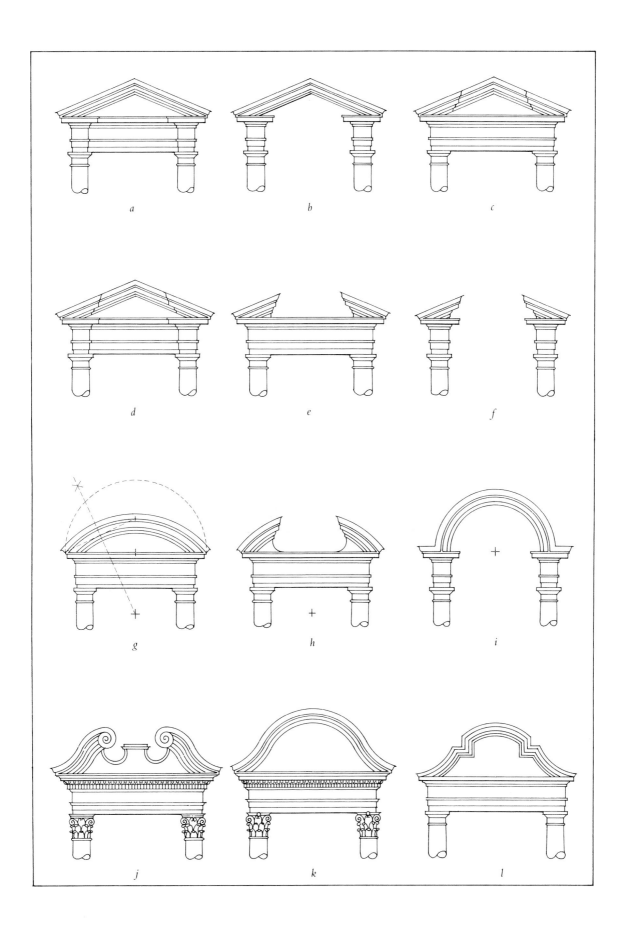

a

b

c

d

e

f

g

h

i

j

k

l

# DIFFERENT USES OF THE PEDIMENT

The significance of the pediment as an element of classical design has encouraged architects of many periods to invent new combinations and variations. This process reached its peak in Baroque and Rococo design, before an atmosphere of neo-classical sobriety encouraged a return to simple forms.

An open top was often created on a pediment in order to contain a specific object. It was an ideal location for a bust (a), a larger statue, an urn or other decorative or symbolic sculpture. When a pediment was placed over a door or filled a space between floors, a window could be fitted into it (b). The window could itself become an important element with its own pediment (c) and a similar feature could be used for an inscription, niche or statue.

A number of Roman buildings have a pediment split into two, each with a single and opposite pitch on either side of a central feature such as a curved pediment. This can be seen on the outer façade of Trajan's Markets (d) of AD 100. Other Roman buildings had pediments inside pediments of a different type, as on the Porta Dei Borsari in Verona (e) of the late first century AD.

Baroque architects invented further variations. Pietro da Cortona, in S. Maria della Pace in Rome (f) of 1660, superimposed one pediment on another by bringing the inner and outer pediments up to the same level. In S. Antonio dei Portoghesi in Rome (g) of 1693, Martino Lunghi allowed the inner pediment to penetrate the open top of the outer pediment, while in SS. Vincenzo ed Anastasio also in Rome (h) of 1664, the same architect superimposed three layers of pediments.

In the following century these distortions developed still further and in the Johanneskirche in Munich, Germany (i) of 1733, Egid Quirin Asam twisted a series of overlapping pediments into a multitude of curves which in turn undulated with the sweep of the façade. Late Baroque designs such as the altar to S. Luigi Gonzaga (j), by Andrea Pozzo in 1700, finally achieve such a complexity that the pediment loses much of its significance in the ambiguity of the composition.

Tha gable-ends of buildings are natural places for pediments. A full pediment located at the end of a pitched roof (k) can have various parts omitted until little more than some cornice mouldings and a short return of the entablature cornice (l) suggest the classical origin of the details. In north European countries the indigenous small flat clay roof-tiles, overlapping in several layers, necessitated steep roofs. In the seventeenth century a great deal of ingenuity was devoted to adapting the traditionally prominent gable façades of these buildings to classical pediments based on the shallow pitch of south European roofs. There is a remarkable variety of these complicated Baroque designs, (m) and (n), which jostle for attention in the crowded commercial street fronts of northern states like the Netherlands, from where they received their English name – Dutch gables.

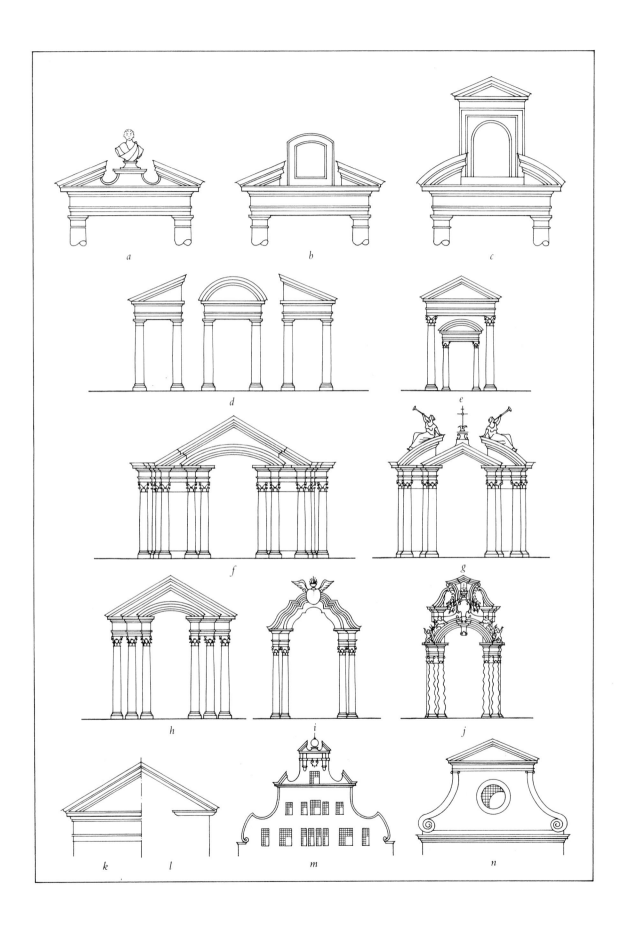

a

b

c

d

e

f

g

h

i

j

k　　　l

m

n

# PEDIMENTS AND DESIGN

The origin of the pediment gave it an importance that it has never lost. From the temples of earliest times to the present day, pediments have been used in classical design to give emphasis both to whole buildings and to parts of buildings.

The Greek temple was dominated by its pediment which, as the gable-end of the roof, occupied the whole end or entrance façade, and its counterpart at the rear. The Parthenon in Athens (a) of 430 BC was heavily decorated with rich sculpture and the tympana at each end were filled with elaborate groups of figures telling mythological stories associated with the life of the goddess Athena.

The combination of columns and pediment was associated with reverence and could retain this association when reduced to two small columns supporting a small pediment. This simple arrangement, the aedicule, can be seen around the statue on Hadrian's Arch in Athens (g) of AD 131, suggesting the religious devotion due to the Emperor. The small pedimented aedicule, forming a niche or frame for a statue, or even empty, has become a recurring theme in classical design.

In Rome and later, in the Renaissance, the pediment was applied to buildings that lacked either the continuous roof or the row of columns that had given it its original form. With his church of S. Sebastiano in Mantua, northern Italy (b), built in 1460 and conjecturally reconstructed here, Alberti was the first to apply the temple front to a church, freeing the pedimented façade from its previous exclusively pagan associations. S. Andrea in Rome (e) was designed by Vignola in about 1550. Vignola follows the example of the second-century Pantheon (page 13) by placing columns and a pediment in front of a domed structure. His little church, however, is oval and the columns are reduced to flat pilasters. The tradition of pedimented entrance façades for churches has continued. In S. Firenze in Florence (f) by Silvani and Ruggieri, completed in 1790, there are three pediments: one segmental, one reversed and one curved, suspended and reduced to a finial.

In the middle of the sixteenth century the Venetian architect Palladio applied the pediment to houses, believing that the Romans would have given an equal dignity to houses as to temples. His designs for country houses, or villas, usually included a large applied porch, or portico, with a pediment, but on the Villa Thiene in Quinto Vincentino near Venice (d) of about 1545, the pediment took over and became the design of the whole house.

The pediment, applied to a gable or false gable and marking small openings and aedicules, is one of the most familiar elements in classical design. It needs neither columns nor whole façades. On Kew Palace near London (c), built by Samuel Fortrey in 1631, pediments are used on several gables in a Dutch fashion and to emphasize windows both individually and in pairs.

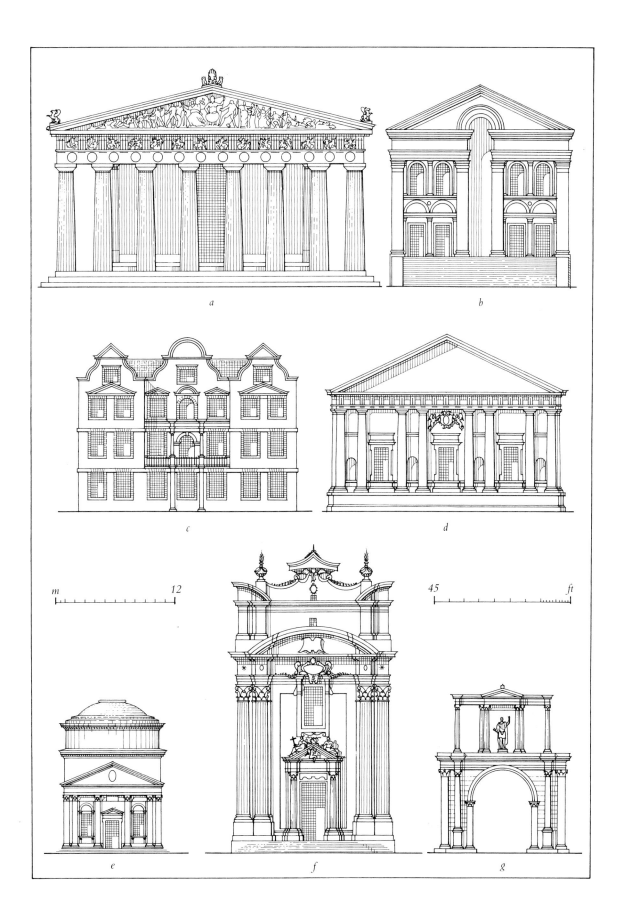

a

b

c

d

m             12

45             ft

e

f

g

# 9. THE ARCH

## THE ARCH IN ANTIQUITY

The invention of the arch was an important technical innovation. By wedging a series of tapering stones together around a semicircle it is possible to span much greater distances using stone or other dense building materials than is possible with flat beams in the same materials. This was known by the Egyptians, who were using full structural arches as early as 1400 BC. The Greeks also used arches, but principally for utilitarian structures. The earliest known decorative example is a market-place gate in the city of Priene in modern Turkey (a) from 156 BC. Neither the Egyptians nor the Greeks used arches for parts of buildings that had any prestige, evidently being averse to the form for stylistic reasons.

It was the Etruscans who first began to develop the arch in European architecture. Like the Romans after them, the Etruscans built permanent roads between cities and brought their water supplies from remote sources. Arched bridging structures were often used for these civil engineering schemes and arches were also used for important visual features such as city gates. A gate in the Roman colony of Falleri in central Italy (b) from the third century BC has all the essential elements of arch design that became an integral part of the classical vocabulary some four centuries later.

The Romans continued to develop the use of the arch, erecting viaducts and aqueducts throughout their growing empire for the movement of people and goods, the supply of water and the levelling and terracing of steep hills. The most impressive survival of these unprecedented feats of engineering skill and daring is the Pont du Gard in southern France (c) from the late first century BC, which not only carried water in an aqueduct 49 metres above the River Gardon to the city of Nîmes, but also a road bridge at a lower level.

The Roman development of the arch as an architectural element is of major significance. One of the principal factors in this evolution was the Roman triumphal arch. These large commemorative structures were built to record a triumph, the coveted public celebration of a victory awarded to a returning general. The form may have originated in temporary wooden gates erected specially for the procession, and structures such as the Arch of Titus (d) of about AD 82 became important symbols of the glory of the Roman state.

a

b

c

SENATVS
POPVLVSQVE ROMANVS
DIVO TITO DIVI VESPIANI·F·
VESPASIANO AVGVSTO

m ⊢————————⊣ 6

ft ⊢—————————⊣ 20

d

# THE CONSTRUCTION OF ARCHES

The Greeks used flat stone beams to span openings in buildings, in imitation of earlier wooden structures. Stone is, however, an unsuitable material for beams as it is brittle and breaks under the stress of downward pressure when unsupported. Hard stone will, on the other hand, offer considerable resistance to being crushed and broken while supported on the opposite side. To make an arch, wedge-shaped pieces of stone or brick are set together over an opening in a radiating pattern so that the weight above each of the pieces pushes them against one another. The resistance of the stone to being crushed prevents the collapse of the arch. The same principle applies to the construction of flat and shallow arches. Round arches are the common classical type, while pointed, Gothic, arches are the most efficient.

A round arch has a single centre (a) which sits on a line (b) from which the arch rises, or springs. From the centre, a constant radius (c) describes the line of the arch from the line of springing upwards. The arch springs off two blocks, or imposts (d), which often project and can be carved with mouldings. The diameter of the arch, the distance between the columns, or piers (e), is the span (f). The arch is made up of a series of tapering blocks, or voussoirs (g), which can be many or few according to the size of stone or span of the arch. The central voussoir, which binds the whole arch together, is called the keystone (h); it is often emphasized through projection and/or decoration. The lower part of the arch is the haunch (i) while the upper part is the crown (j). The entire outer surface or edge of the arch is known as the extrados (k) and the inner surface below the arch as the soffit or intrados (l). The stonework to one side of an arch is the abutment (m) and the area between two adjacent arches is the spandrel (n). The space inside the arch is the tympanum (o).

Arches cannot support themselves until they are complete. They must be constructed on a temporary support known as centering (p). This is usually made of timber and is supported from below. It seems likely that imposts originated as supports for centering. The shape of the arch is formed in the centering and a series of small timber battens (q) is fixed in place in sufficient number to support each voussoir. The voussoirs are laid progressively up from the imposts on each side until they meet and the arch is completed by the keystone. The keystone, therefore, 'locks' the design into place. Large early Roman stone arches were sometimes laid by two gangs, one on each side, and this must have given the keystone particular significance.

The purpose of any structure that spans an opening is to transfer the weight above to the walls on either side and thence down vertically to the ground. The round arch is not the perfect shape for this, the weight tending to push the side of the arch outwards. For this reason arches or rows of arches usually have a substantial section of wall at each end.

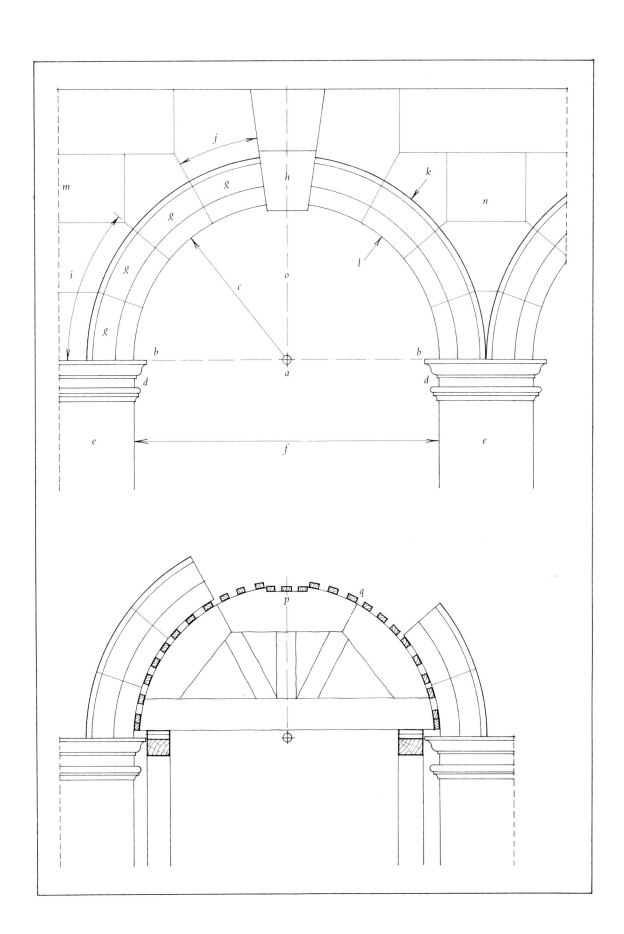

# ARCHES AND THE ORDERS

The combination of the arch and the classical orders led to the introduction of new features that could be associated individually with each order. These are the impost and the archivolt. The impost is the detail just below the point where the arch springs. It resembles either a column capital or a piece of cornice. The archivolt is the profile that follows the line of the arch and is a curved architrave.

As the arch is combined with the orders by sitting between two columns, the proportions of the arch will determine the spacing of the columns. One of the most commonly used proportions has an arch with a height twice its width, (a) and (b). If the columns are to be placed as close to the arch as possible and there is no pedestal, then the column base and the archivolt will establish the width of the arch and this will be about 5 diameters (a). If there is a pedestal, the piers must increase in width to allow for the projection of the cornice of the pedestal, but as the columns will become smaller, the spacing will increase to about 7 diameters (b). If a space of 0.5 diameters is left between the top of the archivolt and the bottom of the architrave, the proportions of the combined arch and order will be fixed.

The relatively late introduction of combined arches and orders by the Romans did not give rise to a clearly established series of conventional forms for imposts and archivolts. In order to maintain the progression of the orders, Renaissance authors keep their Tuscan arch details simple. Examples (c) by Vignola and (d) by Scamozzi are both from the sixteenth century. The Doric is also simple and both Vignola (e) and Palladio (f) show imposts that are versions of Doric capitals.

When the capital for the order becomes more complex it cannot be so readily adapted as an impost. Vignola (g) and Palladio (h) when illustrating Ionic arches continue to use modified Doric capitals, but Palladio adds further decoration to reflect the more decorative character of the order.

The Corinthian order was the most popular in ancient Rome and, perhaps as a consequence, has the most varied arch details. Vignola (i) contrasts the arch with the order by using a Doric capital and archivolt, while Palladio (j) makes the archivolt by adding an egg and dart moulding to a Corinthian architrave and the impost by adding further decoration to a Doric capital. Scamozzi (k) is more conventional, using a late Roman capital and two-part Corinthian architrave with no modifications. The Arch of Constantine (l) offers a complete contrast. Here, the impost is a whole section of cornice above a plain astragal moulding. Similar contrasts are to be found in Composite arches. Vignola (m) only varies his details slightly from his Corinthian arches, while on the Arch of Septimus Severus (n) of AD 203 the impost resembles a section of cornice modified to make an ornate capital and the archivolt is a Composite architrave enriched with an egg and dart moulding.

# Arches and the Orders:
## Variations

———

Although an internal arch width of half the internal height (a ratio of 1:2) is a useful rule of thumb, it is not always possible or desirable to use this precise proportion. The relationship between the piers and the columns, the crown of the arch and the architrave and keystone can also vary.

Guides for the proportions of the Tuscan order are based solely on theory, due to the lack of evidence from antiquity. Vignola in 1562 shows a ratio of 1:2, with no keystone and no form of archivolt when the columns have no pedestal (a). Palladio, on the other hand, writing in 1570, has a ratio of 1:1.65, an archivolt and a keystone (b).

Vignola's Doric arch (c) is also 1:2. It has an archivolt, but again lacks a keystone. The pier has its own base and, only when there is no pedestal, he introduces a moulding on the line of the bottom of the capital to lengthen the columns. This is to be contrasted with one of the earliest examples from antiquity, from the Theatre of Marcellus in Rome (d) of 13 BC, where the ratio is 1:2.4, there is no architrave or projecting keystone and the arch sits well within the frame of the order. Two further Renaissance Doric arches, (e) and (f), have ratios very close to 1:2, but other details vary. The order is much simplified in (e) with the archivolt touching the architrave, while (f) has a keystone and narrow piers.

Vignola's Ionic arch (g) again has a ratio of 1:2 and, although his arch with an order on a pedestal does have a keystone, no keystone is shown for a simple base. The upper storey of the Theatre of Marcellus (h) has a very similar arch proportion, but the lack of an archivolt and the width of the piers create a very different impression. An Ionic arch with a pedestal from the Villa Giulia in Rome (i) of 1550 has the more usual Renaissance configuration, but the arch is lower with a ratio of 1:1.7.

An unusual Renaissance arch (j) sits within an order that combines Tuscan and Corinthian details; the arch is notable for the archivolt unbroken by an impost. The more conventional Corinthian arch from Vignola (k) shares the ratio of 1:2 with his other orders and now has a keystone. This ratio is repeated in Palladio's Corinthian arch with a pedestal (m). The Arch of Augustus in the north Italian town of Susa (l) of 9 BC, in common with many examples from antiquity, is much more individual. The ratio is 1:1.5 and the arch sits so far within the principal order that it has its own small pilasters supporting the archivolt.

Vignola's Composite arch (n) is similar to his Corinthian arch and again has a ratio of 1:2. The Composite Arch of Septimus Severus in Rome (o) of AD 203 is of approximately the same ratio at 1:1.8, but the columns of the order sit on very high pedestals, changing the relationship between the order and the arch.

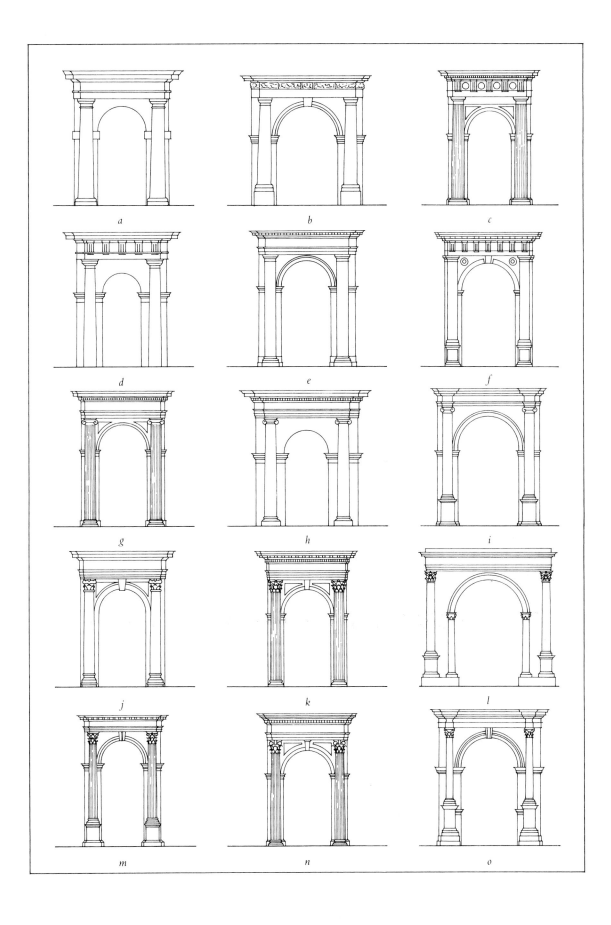

$a$

$b$

$c$

$d$

$e$

$f$

$g$

$h$

$i$

$j$

$k$

$l$

$m$

$n$

$o$

# ARCHES AND THE ORDERS:
## FURTHER VARIATIONS

———————

Classical arches do not always sit within a frame created by the columns and entablature of an order. Although this is how they first became assimilated into the classical vocabulary, the widespread use of the arch in Roman architecture led to an increase in the number of ways of combining the orders with the arch.

Arches were placed above entablatures in the first century AD and the entablature was interrupted to form a high opening. In later years the same principle was applied to continuous rows of arches, or arcades. The arches then sat on isolated vertical pieces of entablature called dosserets, which gave the order the appearance of greater height (a). In the eastern provinces of the Roman Empire another variant form (b) evolved for continuous rows of columns supporting arches. Here, the arch and its archivolt sprang directly from the column capital and the entablature was omitted altogether. This type of arcade spread to all parts of the later Roman Empire and was to influence the development of Romanesque architecture. Both these forms of arch were also popular in the early Renaissance.

In the later Renaissance, arches springing directly from columns were combined very successfully with pediments that had the central part of the entablature left open (c) making the column capital or impost of the arch level with the column capital of the order. This achieved a similar effect to another late Roman detail (d) in which the whole entablature arched over the column. Known as an arcuated lintel, this innovation also reached the late Roman Empire from its eastern provinces. It can be seen either as a central feature in a pediment or alternating with horizontal sections of entablature in an arcade (e). A less pronounced but contemporary treatment (f) involved arching the cornice only from a centre point level with the column capitals.

In the Renaissance a particular kind of arched opening (h) was developed which combined the horizontal entablature and arch. It was invented by Bramante, but both Serlio and Palladio used it frequently to great effect and it has become known as a Venetian, Serlian or Palladian window. It became very popular in the eighteenth-century Palladian revival.

The orders can also be contained within arches. The order can sit independently inside the arch (i) or can line the inner face of the arch, with or without a horizontal entablature, giving added intricacy to the edge of the opening (g). On a larger scale there are many ways of placing the orders inside arches of various sizes. It is, for example, possible to use the orders as a screen across an arched opening. Robert Adam used a simple row of columns supporting a vase to act as the entrance to Balbardie House in Bathgate, Scotland (k) in 1792 and a Palladian window inside a larger arch (j) gives a reduced window size and a crescent of plain wall which can receive a decorative pattern.

*a*

*b*

*c*

*d*

*e*

*f*

*g*

*h*

*i*

*j*

*k*

# TYMPANUM AND SPANDREL

The combination of the semicircular shape of the arch and the rectangular shape of the orders created two intervening surfaces that have developed their own decorative vocabulary. The area inside the arch from the line of its springing to its keystone is called the tympanum. When an arch is created over a rectangular opening and the opening does not rise into the arch, the tympanum thereby created can be decorated or filled with a decorative pattern of openings. The two virtually triangular areas created on either side of an arch inside a rectangular opening are called spandrels, and these are also frequently decorated.

Roman triumphal arches were heavily decorated with statues and inscriptions and sculpture filled the spandrel panels. The central opening of the Arch of Septimus Severus (c) of AD 203, in common with other triumphal arches, had two figures of winged Victory flying with trophies of captured arms and armour towards the keystone. On the same arch there are also side-arches (a) with spandrels containing reclining river gods. This type of spandrel decoration has been repeated many times due to the importance of these monuments in antiquity and their survival virtually intact to the present day. In St George's Hall in Liverpool, England (b), by H. L. Elmes and C. R. Cockerell in 1839, this sculptural theme was modified to suit arches springing above the orders. Allegorical figures fill the T-shape spandrels, their wings spreading towards the keystones.

A simple spandrel decoration (d) has circular details centred on the widest point. These can be decorated or filled with smaller sculptures and can also be placed in the larger spandrels of arcades (e) centred on the column below. More capricious sculptural themes, such as acanthus leaf or other naturalistic designs (f), are frequently used for spandrels, often centred on a dominant geometric form at the widest point.

The decoration of the tympanum can be more varied, due to the broader and less restricted shape of the panel. The semicircular form immediately suggests radiating designs and one of the most common themes is a pattern of radiant fluting which can be abstract (g) or take the form of a shell. Other geometric or natural patterns (i) are often added and are only restricted by convention or the imagination of the designer. Panels of sculpture are frequently placed in arches over entrances or other important positions. The development of tympanum sculptural groups for theological subjects (h) became a particular feature of Romanesque architecture and remained popular for churches in the Renaissance.

Simple circular details are as appropriate to the tympanum as to the spandrel. Circular panels centred on the arch can form a framework for decorative changes of colour, texture or material, or can divide the space for smaller sculptural groups (j). The circles are themselves often windows grouped into simple geometric patterns, (k) and (l), based on their relationship with the semicircle of the arch.

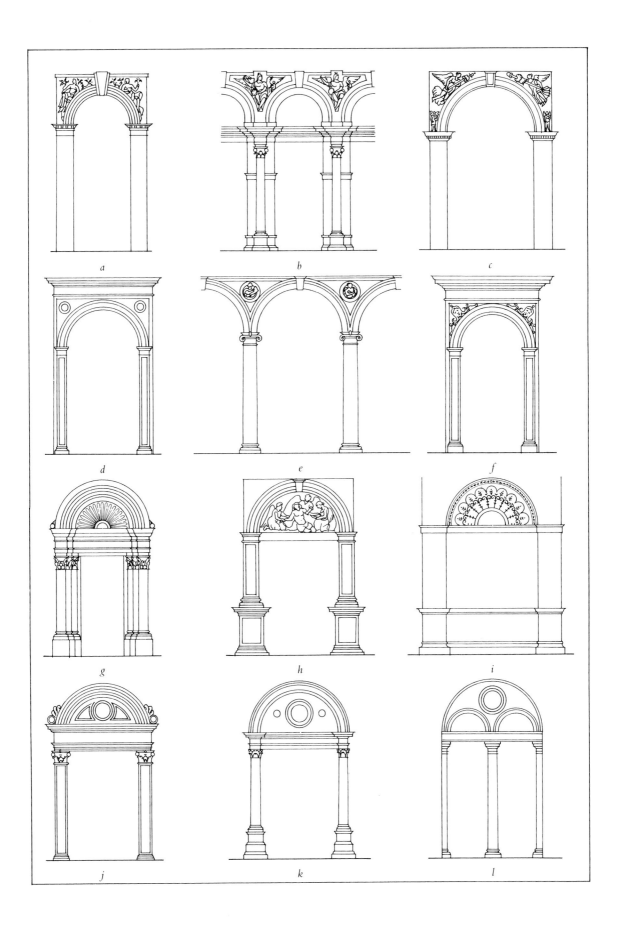

a

b

c

d

e

f

g

h

i

j

k

l

# ARCHES AND VAULTS

When the underside, or soffit, of an arch is lengthened it will cover a space rather than form an opening. This lengthened arch becomes a vault and if it has an unbroken semicircular soffit it will be a barrel vault (a). The barrel vault, or continuous arch, is as old as the arch itself and probably had no separate identity. The Roman invention of concrete, however, resulted in the extension of the old stone arch in three dimensions to create a complete structure which set hard to form one solid mass. This enabled Roman architects to create vast, vaulted structures with relative ease and encouraged the development of the design of vaults. The fluid nature of the wet cement permitted great freedom in the geometry of these structures and the use of permanent thin brick structures to contain the wet material while it hardened did little to limit this freedom. Stone was often added later as a thin decorative surface and, with the temporary structural requirements of the brick skin, an appearance of independent arched structures was maintained.

The barrel vault can have small windows added in its length. If these are also arched (b) a complex, curved shape is created in the vault. If two equal barrel vaults intersect (c), four curved lines will mark their point of intersection, crossing the square space diagonally. These lines are groins, and this type of vault is a groin vault. Concrete groin vaults spanning up to 25 metres were constructed for Roman baths and basilicas.

In the interests of construction, strength or solely for aesthetic purposes, the arches over the points of support in vaults are sometimes expressed by dropping the soffit. This can break up the line of a barrel vault (d) or define the plan of a groin vault (f). The effect of separating the vault structure from real or apparent supporting arches can be taken further and clusters of columns or a mixture of columns and piers (e) provide visually independent supports for each element. This late Roman design was widely adopted in the Middle Ages.

The decoration of the soffit of vaults can also differentiate arched elements in the structure. Simple square recesses, or coffers, in the vault (g) can be continued as rectangles on the arch. A different design, such as guilloche (i), on the arch will give added contrast to the vault, shown here with diamond coffering. On an uninterrupted vault surface, just the omission of part of the design can suggest an arch in the vault (h) which is shown here as less than a full semicircle.

Roman concrete construction ended with the Western Empire. Byzantine architects used great skill in translating the concrete vault and dome structures into brick and stone. In the west, Romanesque and then Gothic architects, aided by the fashion for pointed arches, simplified the stone construction of groin vaults with diagonal arches, or ribs, to create structures of an unprecedented slenderness. The barrel vault and its derivatives were revived in the Renaissance.

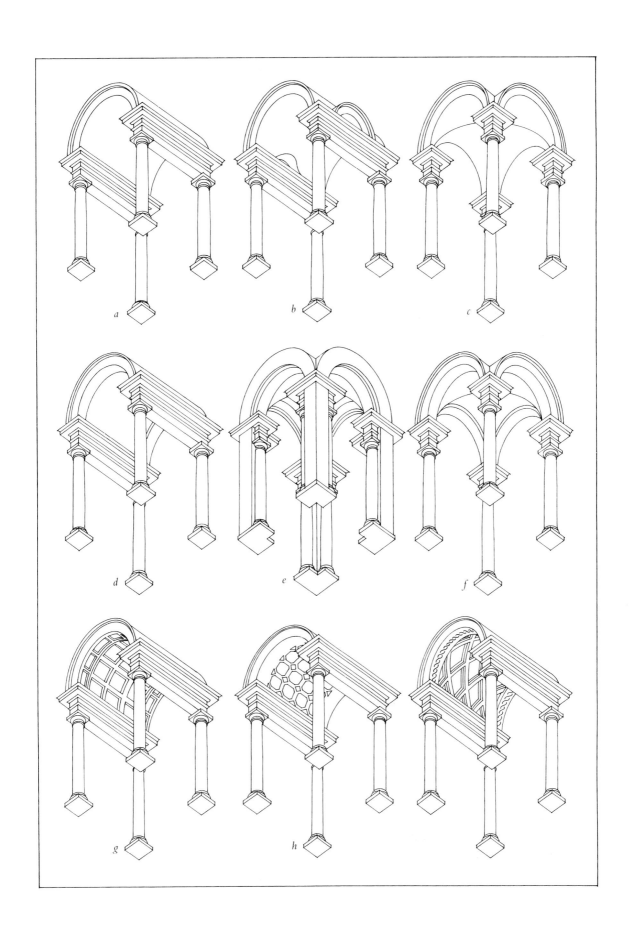

a

b

c

d

e

f

g

h

# ARCHES AND DESIGN 1

Etruscan and early Roman arches were simple masonry structures which occasionally included decorative features related to the construction of the arch, such as keystones or imposts. Long arcades of these arches were constructed on amphitheatres and to support terracing. As Rome expanded her control to the south, and both her wealth and her contact with Greek cities in Italy increased, Roman civilization entered the mainstream of classical culture. It was at this time that the Romans made one of their major contributions to the development of the classical tradition and united the arch with the orders.

It is a significant coincidence that one of the best preserved early examples of this combination is on a theatre – a Greek import – the Theatre of Marcellus in Rome (a) of 13 BC. Although the orders and arches had been used together for a century before, this building displays the simple continuous arcading that characterized the earlier examples. The semicircular façade, which had a high upper storey, relies for its architectural effect on the repetition of the same basic form and the curve of the wall. The varied details of the orders add a contrasting intricacy and some differentiation between the floors.

Almost contemporary with the Theatre of Marcellus, the Porte S. André in the city of Autun in southern France (b) has a similar treatment for the arches and orders on the gallery over the gateway. This row of windows in the form of a gallery was a traditional feature on Roman city gates. The main gates, however, have no applied columns and take the simple form of earlier gates, but the existence of an order is implied by the full entablature that acts as base for the gallery and sits immediately above the voussoirs of the large gates. There is more freedom in the use of arches and the orders on much Roman architecture than many later theorists have argued.

By the late Roman Empire, familiarity with the combination of the arch and the orders had taken the classical arch beyond the application of one system to decorate another to an integrated architectural discipline. The interiors of late Roman churches, such as S. Agnese fuori le Mura (c) of about 350 AD, have simple arcades of columns in an interior springing directly off column capitals and diminishing in scale vertically.

Buildings such as Porte S. André and S. Agnese had a strong influence on medieval architects. The symbolic significance of city gates together with their practical use survived, and late Roman churches enjoyed unrivalled influence. Continuity with the ancient world had, however, been lost and, when architects like Buscheto wished to design classical buildings such as Pisa Cathedral (d) in the mid eleventh century, they relied on selective survivals from Rome. It is, above all, the late Roman use of the arch that gives these early medieval buildings their distinction, even when executed with a vigorous misunderstanding of the classical tradition.

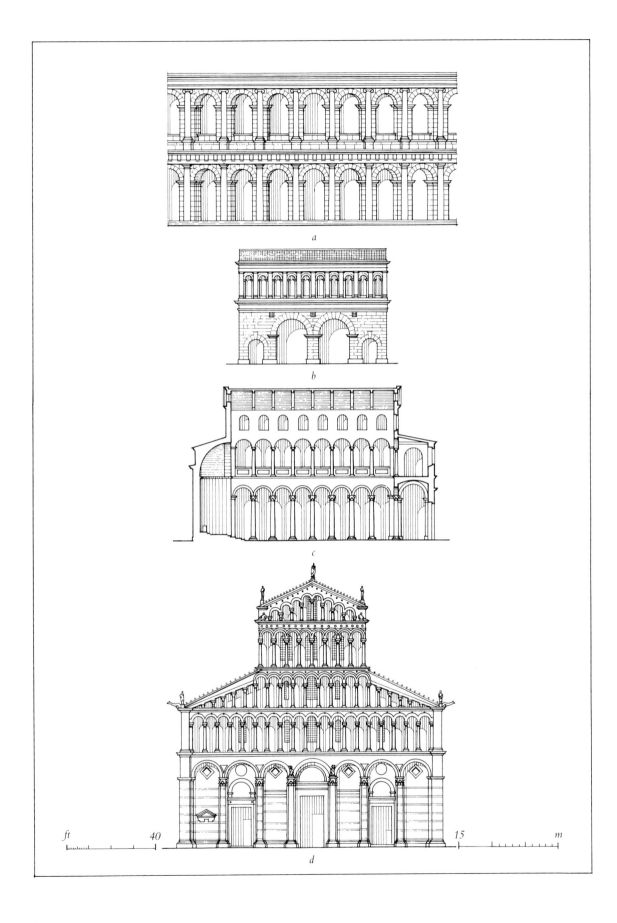

*a*

*b*

*c*

*ft*      40                                           15          *m*

*d*

# ARCHES AND DESIGN 2

Renaissance architects decisively rejected the pointed Gothic arch, incorrectly associating it with the Gothic tribes that destroyed Rome. In the early Renaissance, when the majority of existing buildings were Gothic, the round arch had a unique symbolic association with the classical world. Buildings such as the Palazzo Gondi in Florence (b), designed by Giuliano da Sangallo in 1489, must be seen in this light. The design relies on ordered rows of simple arches set in a graduated rusticated wall. The crowning cornice is the only reference to the orders.

When Palladio won the competition to give a new façade to the medieval basilica in the city of Vicenza in northern Italy (a) in 1545, the arch had become just one of the elements in a universally familiar classical vocabulary. Palladio's design is composed with two arcades of open Venetian windows. Although Palladio had not invented this detail, this is its most explicit use. The arches are a dominant feature in a complex composition which has a Doric order below an Ionic order. Each bay has a subsidiary column of the same order supporting the arch.

Baroque architects again sought out the arch for bold visual effects. The English architect Hawksmoor is notable for striking compositions which use the contrast between solid wall and openings more than fine detail. In his combined tower and portico of Christ Church, Spitalfields in London (d) of 1723, the design is almost entirely made up of arches of different sizes contrasted with a huge Tuscan order.

In the nineteenth century the simultaneous revival of several historic styles gave the classical arch new significance. The revival of Gothic architecture once again drew attention to the shape of arches. An increased interest in the early Renaissance was accompanied by revivals of Byzantine and Romanesque architecture which were called in Germany the round-arch style. Round arches had the advantage of encompassing several favoured revivals and early-nineteenth-century architects like Schinkel designed in more than one of these styles. His theatre design in Hamburg, Germany (c), by the use of arcades of large glazed arches, achieves an ambiguity of style that is characteristic of the nineteenth century.

Classical architecture between the wars in this century was deliberately stripped of much of its decoration to create refined and simplified designs. Familiarity with the classical vocabulary allowed architects to suggest classical form with the barest elements. The classical past was particularly important in the new city of EUR that the Fascist government started to build outside Rome. The parallel with the ancient past was both unavoidable and deliberate and at the centre of the new city was the Palazzo della Civiltà Italica (e) by Guerrini, La Padula and Romano. Nicknamed the square Colosseum, this building uses nothing but six tiers of arches reduced to no more than their shape to evoke the monuments of the nearby capital.

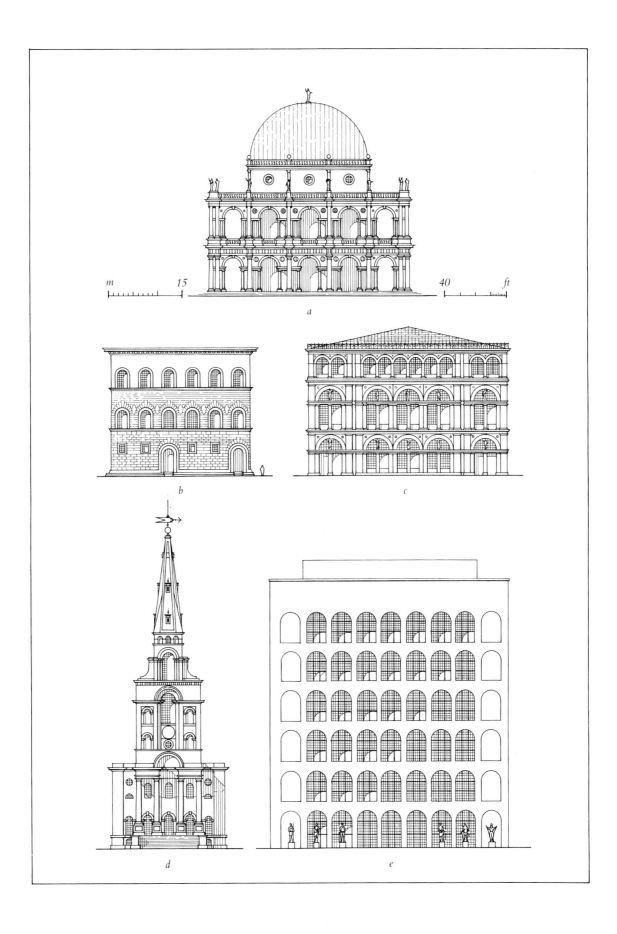

*m* ⊢———⊢ *15*

*40* ———⊣ *ft*

*a*

*b*

*c*

*d*

*e*

# MIXING ARCHES AND SETTING OUT

Arches are not always semicircular. They can have different proportions which permit them to be used in situations where a height other than half the width of the opening is appropriate.

When openings are different widths and are spanned by full semicircular arches (a) the height of the arches must necessarily be different. If the arches need to be the same height, then it is possible to make modifications to the central or side-arches. The narrower arches can be raised (b) so that their centres are above the imposts. The height is then made up by vertical extensions to the arch. These are stilted arches and can be simple semicircles, as on the left, or segmental, as on the right. The height of the large arch can be reduced in two ways: with a three-centred arch (c) or with a segmental arch (d).

The three-centred arch can be drawn in several different ways. It is most useful to know how to set out the arch when the width of the opening and the desired height of the arch are the critical dimensions (e).

First, draw the width at the bottom, or springing, of the arch, AB on the drawing, and the height at the top and centre, point C, and draw a vertical line from C downwards. Draw another line from point C parallel to AB which will meet a vertical line from B at point D, forming a rectangle CDBE. Extend the vertical centre line CE by the same distance again to point F so that CE is equal to EF. Divide EB into two so that EG is equal to GB. Divide DB into two so that DH is equal to HB. Draw a line from point F through point G to point D and draw another line from point H to point C. These lines will meet at point J. Divide the line CJ at point K so that CK is equal to KJ and draw another line at right-angles to CJ through point K which will cross the centre line CEF at point L. Point L is the first centre point of the three-centred arch. LC then becomes the radius of the arc of the larger of the three circles making up the arch. Extend this radius down to a line LM which is parallel to AB and draw a line from point M through point A to meet the arc of the large circle at point N. Connect point N to point L and where this line crosses the line AB, point P, is the second centre point of the three-centred arch. The third centre at Q is an equal distance, but on the other side of point E.

To set out a segmental arch from its height and width, (f), draw a line AB across the width of the opening and divide it at C so that AC is equal to CB. Draw a centre line from C to the height of the arch D. Divide AD at E so that AE is equal to ED and draw another line at right-angles to AD through point E to meet DC extended to point F. Point F is the centre of the segmental arch ADB.

The appearance of different heights of three-centred arches is shown in (g) to (j) and similar differences are shown in (l) to (n) for segmental arches.

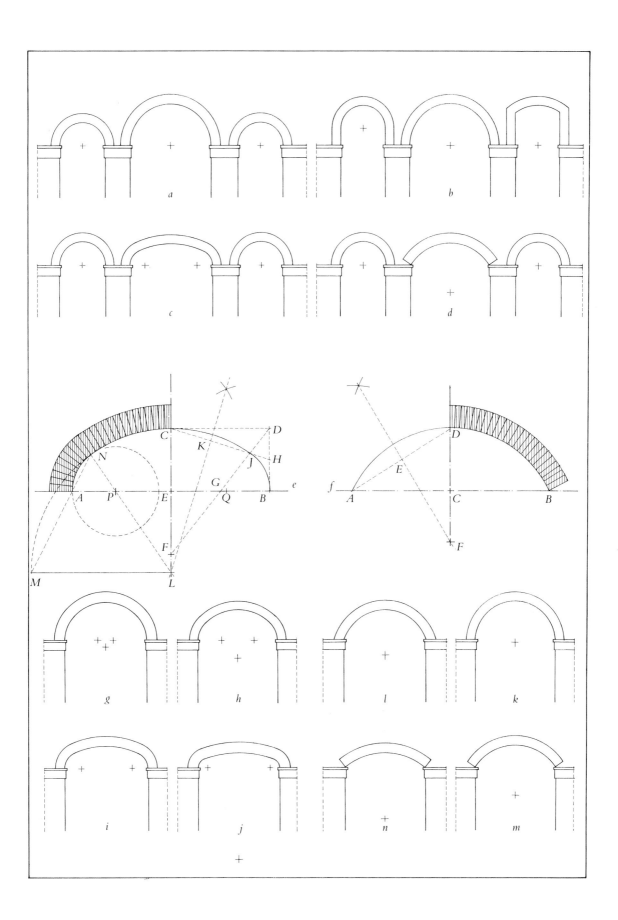

# 10.  THE DOME

## DOMES OF ANTIQUITY

Round buildings with conical or domed roofs and made of mud or branches have been constructed from prehistoric times to the present day. In about 1600 BC the Mycenaeans started to build domed subterranean tholos tombs on the Greek mainland, probably as a traditional or ritual survival of earlier circular buildings. One of the largest of these, the Treasury of Atreus (a), dates from about 1300 BC. The stone beehive shape is created by laying stones flat and stepping them gradually inwards until they meet at the top. This primitive form of dome construction ended with the decline of the Mycenaean civilization.

The Roman discovery in the second century BC of the unique strength of a volcanic sand, pozzolana, for making concrete, revolutionized building construction, allowing architects to abandon the old post and beam form of construction in favour of curved roofs, or vaults, and domes. The dome is one of Rome's great contributions to the development of classical architecture.

Roman architects, as they discovered the structural potential of the new material, also exploited the aesthetic potential of the dome. Great feats of structural engineering were united with traditional classical details to create awe-inspiring vaulted and domed interiors. The greatest of these is the Pantheon in Rome (c), built in the reign of the Emperor Hadrian in AD 120. The inside of the dome is a hemisphere which sits on a circular drum of an equal height so that the diameter of 43.2 metres is the same dimension as the total interior height. Light is admitted only by a single circular opening, or oculus, at the top. The dome is composed of solid Roman cement mixed with light volcanic stone; no metal reinforcement or encircling chain prevents the dome from bursting outwards. For this reason all Roman domes have a saucer-shaped exterior which creates a progressive thickening of the structure, thereby transferring the great weight of the material down to the walls.

Domed structures remained in use until the end of the Roman Empire. A large garden pavilion, known as the Temple of Minerva Medica (b), has survived in Rome from the fourth century. The drum has ten sides, with windows at a high level which merge into the dome. Each side is pierced by an arch which, on all sides except the entrance, opens into a semicircular apse covered by a half-dome. There are brick ribs built into the dome, probably as a part of the construction process.

*a*

*b*

*c*

*m*     10

*ft*     30

# POST-RENAISSANCE DOMES

Byzantine architects continued to develop the tradition of the Roman dome, but changed the construction from cement to brick or stone. When the Renaissance passion for antiquity gripped the cities of Italy in the early fifteenth century, and the construction of domes flourished again, Italian architects turned to the experience of Byzantium rather than to the lost art of cement construction.

Standing at the crossroads of the medieval world and the Renaissance is the dome of Florence Cathedral (b). In 1420 the pioneering Renaissance artist and architect Filippo Brunelleschi solved the seemingly impossible task of erecting a dome over the altar of the cathedral on an existing octagonal structure designed in 1357. The height of the existing walls and a width of more than 42 metres meant that the traditional use of temporary timber supports, or centering, was impractical. Brunelleschi devised an ingenious method of building thin layers of bricks in an interlocking pattern between converging arches, or ribs, which knitted together sufficiently during construction to avoid the use of centering. The Gothic proportions of the dome had been fixed by decree in 1367, but Brunelleschi gave the form a new simplicity of line by using, for the first time, a ring, or chain, of timber and iron to prevent the dome bursting outwards, thereby avoiding the encrustation of stone supports and counterweights used by Gothic architects. The size and ingenuity of the dome became famous and its structural chain, classical details and separation of structural and weatherproofing layers were widely copied.

In 1506 work began on the rebuilding of the holiest shrine in Rome, Constantine's basilica over the tomb of St Peter. Building continued for more than a century and involved many leading Italian architects. Early drawings by Bramante show a huge but simple internal hemisphere with a Roman, inverted-saucer-shaped exterior above a circle of columns. The dome (c) was, however, built to quite different plans prepared by Michelangelo in about 1550. Michelangelo's dome is 42 metres wide, 29 metres high to the underside of the crowning lantern, and its base is 76 metres from the floor. It is constructed of two layers of brick and is bound together with ten iron chains. The complex and dramatic design, with its pointed profile and converging ribs, is a landmark in the development of the classical dome and had a profound influence on the design of innumerable subsequent examples.

The Baroque splendour of St Peter's was too far removed from the concept of antiquity held by neo-classical architects at the end of the eighteenth century. Influenced by archaeology and surviving Roman buildings, architects constructed simple domes with inverted-saucer-shaped exteriors and hemispherical interiors. Un-like the concrete structures of antiquity, neo-classical domes, such as the double dome of the Four Courts of Dublin (a) of 1786, by James Gandon, were built with timber and iron frames to recreate the forms of the ancient world in plaster and wood.

m          25

ft          70

a

b          c

# Types Of Dome

In the history of classical architecture, domed structures have taken many different forms influenced by the shape of the supporting structure, the means of admitting light, the method of construction and the desire for visual effect.

The circular plan of the dome sits comfortably on a circular supporting structure called a drum (a). This arrangement has been used frequently since antiquity. When the shape of the underlying walls is square, however, the relationship between the square and circular plans becomes a significant feature of the design.

The dome can just be placed on the square structure and the geometric difference clearly expressed (b), but this arrangement is not often used as the weight of the dome is only supported by the walls at four points. To overcome this problem the dome can gradually merge into the square. This type of construction is generally associated with arches in each side of a square (c). The triangular space at each corner, between the curves of the arches and the edge of the dome, can be curved down to the springing of the arch and is known as a pendentive. Pendentives were particularly favoured by Byzantine architects. A pendentive structure does not have to merge directly into the circumference of the dome but can support an intermediate drum (d). If the dome is less than a full hemisphere it will eventually merge so completely with the pendentives that the two forms become a single dome, made square by removing four segments from the circular plan of the dome, (e) and (f). In example (f) the distinction between the shallow dome and the pendentives has completely disappeared.

A substitute for pendentives is an arch across the corner of a square. This is known as a squinch (g). It can be a single arch or a series of arches diminishing downwards towards the corner, following the line of a pendentive. In their simplest form, squinch arches form an octagon with the four arches on the sides of the square. This in turn can support an octagonal drum (h) – in this example with arched windows rising into the dome. Squinch arches were another Byzantine device, but domes on octagonal drums are also to be found on early Roman domed structures. The eight sides of the octagon can quite effortlessly merge into a circular dome (i) or extend to the central point of the dome as flat leaves (j). If eight arched openings are placed to rise into the dome (k) the arched forms can be gradually diminished in each segment until they meet in the centre. This distinctive shape gives the name umbrella dome.

These shapes and others have been used in the design of simple domes. There are many varieties and combinations. An umbrella dome can, for example, have twelve sides each with an arched window rising into the dome and (viewed from the inside) concave segments. This can sit on a circular opening in a square, arched structure with pendentives (l).

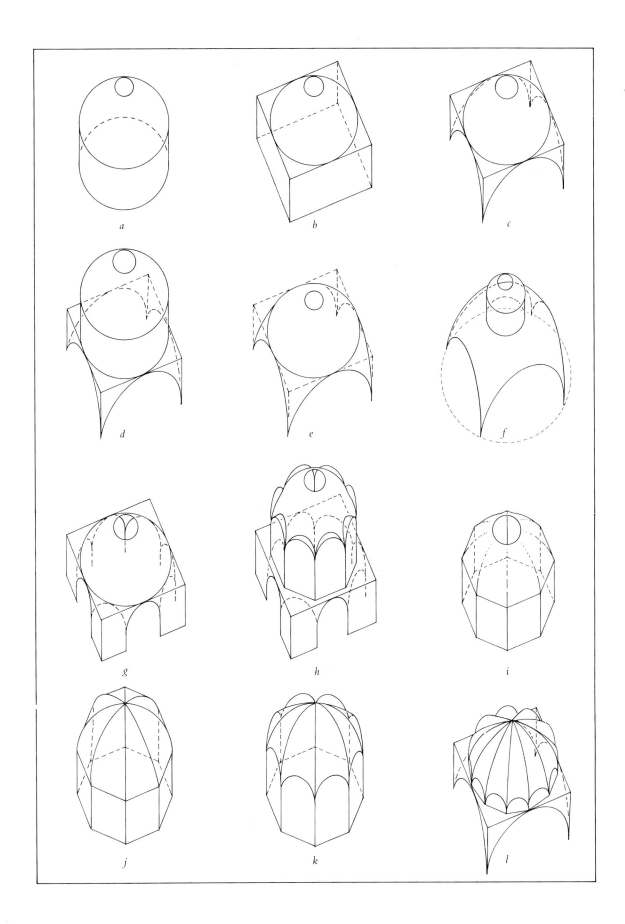

a        b        c

d        e        f

g        h        i

j        k        l

# COMPLEX DOMES

From an early date Roman architects, exploiting the possibilities of concrete construction, designed buildings incorporating several domed volumes. Remains of the Imperial Palace on the Palatine hill in Rome (a) from about AD 90 include an octagonal domed room with a series of recesses on seven of the eight sides. Four of these recesses are semicircular with half-domes and three are rectangular. The rectangular recesses have further recesses within them, two rectangular and one semicircular. The villa of the Emperor Hadrian outside Rome was constructed in the early second century and contains several domes and buildings which experiment with complicated geometric forms. One of these is the Piazza d'Oro (b). This building has an interior of winding colonnades and interconnecting niches thought to have been covered by a large dome surrounded by a cluster of smaller half-domes.

S. Maria della Consolazione, outside the central Italian city of Todi (d), was designed in 1508 and is a symmetrical form focusing on a central domed space. The surrounding half-domes have a simple geometric relationship with the central volume typical of domed buildings of this period.

Baroque architects of the seventeenth century took the design of domes to levels of unprecedented complexity and novelty. In 1634 Francesco Borromini, in the first of a series of revolutionary buildings, designed the tiny S. Carlo alle Quattro Fontane in Rome (e). By taking a cross-shaped plan, lengthening it from the door to the altar and overlaying a pattern based on the geometry of an ellipse, Borromini merged all the conventionally separate elements of the plan into the one space where each part flows into the next in a series of curves. The elliptical structure of the plan is defined by the lower pendentive dome which is penetrated by oval half-domes and supports a further tall oval dome with a small domed lantern at the centre.

The master of these extraordinary structures was the architect and monk Guarino Guarini, who designed throughout Roman Catholic Europe. A number of his buildings are in the Italian city of Turin. In his church of S. Lorenzo (g) of 1668 the dome sits heavily over an octagon formed by eight inward-curving rows of columns and, gathering inwards on four large pendentives, rises on an exposed framework of sixteen interlacing ribs containing eight large oval windows interspersed with smaller openings. His Chapel of the Holy Shroud (f) of 1666 is even more extraordinary. To accommodate three entrances, three large arches rise to support a dome where six arches support from their apex a series of shallow arches containing two small windows each and forming a pattern which ripples upwards to a central lantern. In the church of the Immacolata Concezione (c) of 1673 two relatively simple circular domes, each with four pairs of flat ribs and three windows, are brought together on their fourth sides to merge with a central flattened octagonal dome, creating a restless interior that is neither whole nor divided.

*a*

*b*

*c*

*d*

*e*

*f*

*g*

m    20

ft    40

# FALSE DOMES

Brunelleschi's dome in Florence (see page 174) had an inner structure of brick and a separate outer structure to keep out the weather. This was quite unlike the domes of antiquity and Byzantium, where the structure was solid to the exterior, but was in the tradition of Gothic construction. Although many domed structures were solid, the construction of double domes continued during the Renaissance. The exterior and interior surfaces of these double domes were only separated by a narrow space. In the seventeenth century, however, the visual possibilities of different interiors and exteriors were realized, first in Venice and then, more dramatically, in the northern nations.

The Dome des Invalides (a) was designed by Jules Hardouin Mansart in 1680 to act as a landmark in its own square and in the city of Paris. This public prominence gave the architect special design requirements for the exterior. The dome and its lantern have no visual relationship to the appearance of the interior. The external dome is constructed of timber and lead and sits above a further two domes which can be seen from within the church. The inner dome has a large central opening, or oculus, giving a view of the solid middle dome, which is decorated with paintings and lit by windows invisible from the interior and located in the external upper drum.

St Paul's Cathedral (b) was designed in 1675 by Christopher Wren as a centre-piece to his Baroque replanning of the City of London, following the Great Fire of 1666. Again, this external dome has no visual relationship to the interior dome, but a brick cone was constructed to support the heavy stone lantern. This cone is pierced by a series of concealed circular openings which allow windows in the external upper drum indirectly to light the conical volume, the upper part of which is visible through an oculus in the smooth, painted, plaster-and-brick inner dome. The outer dome is built of timber and lead.

When the architect Jacques Germain Soufflot designed the church of Ste Geneviève (c) – later to become the Panthéon – in 1755, Baroque design was starting to decline in the face of increased interest in ancient and Gothic architecture. His design, none the less, included the Baroque invention of the triple dome. All three domes were of solid construction and the usual heavy supporting piers of Baroque domes were replaced with rows of slender columns, which proved inadequate for the weight of the structure. The inner dome had the simple design of the interior of ancient domes.

Even the revolutionary French neo-classical architect Claude Ledoux had recourse to the triple dome in his design for a library in the principality of Hesse-Kassel in Germany (d) in the late eighteenth century. However, Ledoux offers for the first time a view through the oculus, not of a false sky or painted design, but of an additional, inaccessible, neo-classical interior.

*a*

*b*

*c*

*m*      15

*d*

50      *ft*

# HALF-DOMES, TRIBUNES, APSES AND NICHES

The half-dome was first developed by Roman architects to provide a focal point in a room or external space and, at a small scale, as a feature within the bulk of thick Roman concrete walls and piers. A large half-dome can be called a semi-dome, tribune, apse or exedra, according to its position and function; smaller ones are generally referred to as niches.

Large Roman baths often contain several semi-domes facing internally into the central hall and externally on to gardens or pools. Two monumental exedrae face outwards into the cold pool, or frigidarium, on either side of an arch of equal size in the Baths of Caracalla in Rome (b) of AD 216. Each one of these exedrae contains an arched opening in the centre flanked by two smaller half-domed niches, which probably contained statues. These acted both as visual features and areas separated from the main space for assembly or seating.

The seat of the magistrate, governor, emperor or any person of importance was distinguished by a recess at the focal point of a basilica. This recess was often of a semicircular form and, in recognition of its judicial function, is called a tribune. The significance of the space became as symbolic as practical, and statues of emperors were placed in tribunes to represent imperial authority. The tribune of the basilica in the city of Leptis Magna in north Africa (a), built in the early third century AD, has a display of columns that reinforces the authority of the centre with two giant columns.

The associations of the tribune were passed on, together with the design of the basilica, to church architecture, where it became the apse. Apses were major features in the design of late Roman, Romanesque and Gothic churches, symbolizing the presence of God. At first, a single apse was placed like the seat of the judge at the end of the nave and emphasized by mosaics or paintings in the half-dome and the location of the main entrance at the opposite end. As the cult of the Virgin and the Saints developed, subsidiary apses or chapels gathered around the central apse.

Smaller versions of tribunes were included in domestic buildings. These served a similar function to exedrae by defining a space subordinate to the principal space. These became popular in the late eighteenth century and could form a recess for a serving-table in a dining-room (d), an entrance lobby for two off-centre doors (c) or a recess for shelving in a library separated by a screen of columns (e).

Niches are invariably smaller features containing statues, providing a focus at the end of a passageway or vista, or adding interest to a plain wall. The word niche derives from the Italian for shell, and decorations of shells in the half-dome, (f) and (i), are common. There are many other forms of decoration, either derived from their larger counterparts (h) or of a small scale (g) to suit the size of the niche.

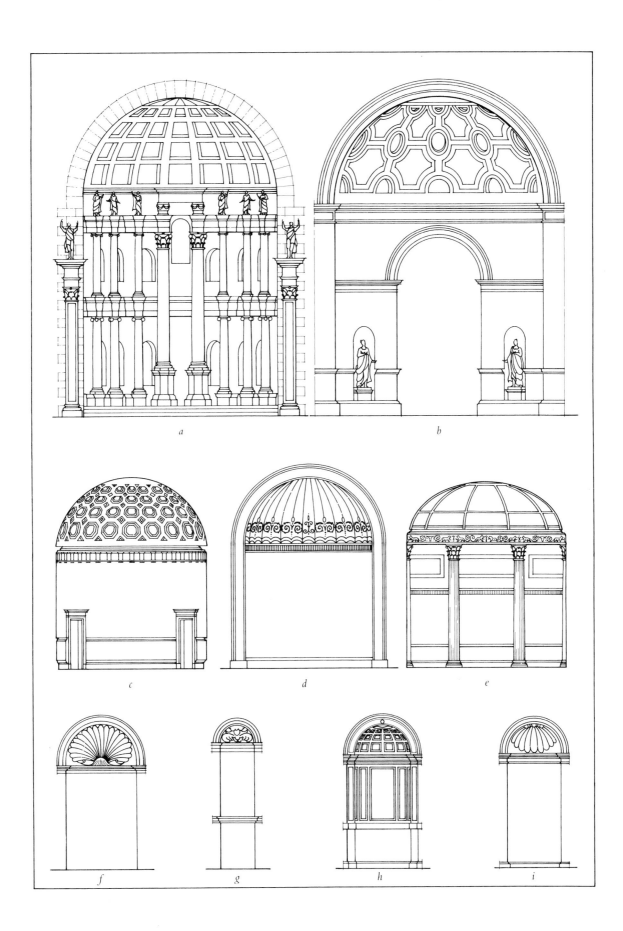

$a$  $b$

$c$  $d$  $e$

$f$  $g$  $h$  $i$

# INSIDE THE DOME

The decoration of the underside, the soffit, of the dome has its own tradition. Painted decoration, mosaic and shallow plaster in relief have adorned innumerable domed surfaces. The nature and variety of these make them impossible to categorize satisfactorily and only decoration in the form of deep relief is shown here.

Roman decorative patterns have, due to the Roman origin of the dome and half-dome, set a standard over the following centuries. The simple coffering of the second-century dome of the Pantheon in Rome (a) has survived virtually intact and has probably been more influential than any other form of ornament. Horizontal and vertical ribs running up and around the dome intersect to create almost square indentations, or coffers, in the surface of the soffit. On the Pantheon there are four additional inward steps set inside each coffer and the faces of the steps are angled towards the centre point of the dome. A decorative rosette may also have sat in the middle of each coffer. As the vertical lines converge towards the top of the dome, so the distance between the horizontal lines diminishes to create coffers of similar proportions and decreasing size. This effect increases the natural drama of a domed interior and is the principle behind most coffering systems.

Other Roman coffering is generally a more complex version of this Pantheon type. The coffers can become an interlocking pattern of hexagons and rectangles, which can be seen in the Basilica of Maxentius in Rome (b) of the early fourth century. Many other geometric variations can be created. The eighteenth-century dome of Ste Geneviève in Paris (d) reduces a similar pattern to circles and squares. The design of the apses of the Temple of Venus and Rome, in Rome (c) from the early fourth century has lines diagonally across the surface of the dome in opposite directions, creating a spiral pattern often used in Renaissance buildings.

Ribs arching over the surface (existing, but concealed, in Roman domes and coffers) were introduced in the Renaissance – probably due to the influence of Gothic and Byzantine architecture. On early examples the ribs are simple and define the flat segments of faceted domes, (e) and (k), but became more exaggerated where Baroque architects sought to enhance the vertical impression of their domes (g). Ribs can also be added to Roman coffering patterns, (h) and (j), to give them a more vertical character, and the omission of alternate horizontal and vertical divisions in a simple, squared, coffered design (i) also gives a subtle vertical emphasis.

In spite of its Roman origin the dome was too well established to be dismissed in Greek Revival designs in the nineteenth century. Philip Hardwick created a ribbed rosette design for his dome over the booking-hall in Euston Station in London (f) while John Soane mixed a central rosette with coffering and fluting to sit over primitive Greek columns in his Mausoleum at Dulwich Picture Gallery outside London (l).

a  b  c

d  e  f

g  h  i

j  k  l

# 11. RUSTICATION

## ORIGINS

Rustication is stonework that is left rough and unfinished except where it fits together at the joints. The even joints form vertical and horizontal grooves in the uneven face of the stonework. A similar effect can be achieved with brick and stucco. The word implies construction that is crude and unsophisticated, but rustication has become one of the most widespread and subtle forms of decoration in classical architecture.

Stone walls where the face of the blocks show the marks of coarse chisel work or bulge outwards between the joints are quite common in antiquity and can be found in utilitarian structures such as Greek city walls (b). There are also some Roman buildings where the joints in masonry are set in shallow channels for deliberate visual effect.

The first evidence of rough stone rustication being used extensively as an aesthetic device is on buildings constructed in the reign of the Emperor Claudius in the middle of the first century AD. A series of remarkable designs, such as the Temple of the Deified Claudius in Rome (a), date from this period and have the same exaggerated mixture of smooth finished and very rough unfinished stone. It is known that Claudius was a keen antiquarian and it is quite possible that this unprecedented architectural phenomenon arose out of a desire to evoke an imaginary antique primitiveness. Whatever the intention behind this work, it was not repeated in this form in antiquity.

In medieval Italian towns another unconnected tradition developed. Urban fortresses or palaces, such as the fourteenth-century Palazzo Comunale in the central Italian town of Montepulciano (d), were built of deliberately massive and rough blocks of stone to express their strength and impregnability, and consequently the nobility of the occupier. Renaissance architects, while striving to emulate antiquity, had to design for the same climate of urban violence and with the same traditional expressions of strength and status as their medieval precursors. Perhaps influenced by the remnants of Claudius' buildings, a more orderly system of rusticated decoration was created, distinct types became recognizable and the imitation of stone eroded by weather (c) became as pronounced as that of unfinished stone.

In spite of its brief flowering in antiquity, the systematic use of rustication is a Renaissance extension of a medieval tradition. Buildings such as the Palazzo Cervini, also in Montepulciano (e), designed by Antonio da Sangallo in 1520, add classical harmony to the established forms of their Gothic forebears.

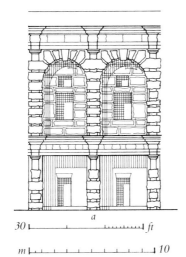

*a*

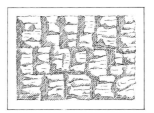

*b*

30 ⊢———————⊣ *ft*

*m* ⊢————————⊣ 10

*c*

*d*

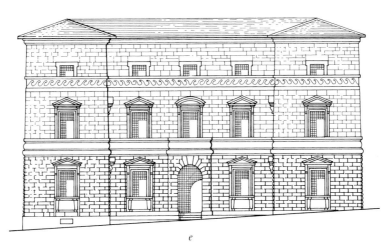

*e*

# Types Of Rustication

The word rustication has in the past been limited to rough stone blocks but has come to mean any form of stonework, brickwork or stucco where the joints are recessed or the face of each stone is separately expressed. Where only the horizontal joints of stonework are recessed, or occasional courses of bricks are set back, rustication is sometimes referred to as banding.

A large number of different types of rustication have evolved. It can be limited to recessing the joints between the stones (a). This smooth rustication is often reproduced in plaster or stucco, or even wood. Variations in the joints, (m) to (r), can significantly alter its appearance. The separation between the stones can be exaggerated by rounding the corners of the projecting faces (b), although this detail is unusual. Bulging, cushioned rustication (c) is much more common and frequently has even joints as illustrated. The face of the stonework can have many different types of finish. Reticulated rustication (d) is covered with a net-like pattern, while vermiculated stones (e) have a series of contorted forms which resemble worm-casts and can be cut to varying degrees of depth and complexity. These two types of rustication are often mistaken for each other. A rock-faced finish (f) has always been popular and is the most straightforward representation of uncut stone. The coarseness of rock-faced work can be diminished by chiselling to give a gentle, pecked finish (g) or a harsher, punched face (h). Most extraordinary of all is the frosted, or congelated, finish (i), used on Baroque buildings and cut to imitate the petrified drops of limestone found in caves. Mannerist architects developed a prismatic, or diamond-pointed, stone (j) which produces a very powerful pattern on a building. It can be emphasized by recessing the joints (k) or embellished by repeating the design (l).

Different types of recessed joint can be used. Simple straight (m) and chamfered (n) joints are found associated with all types of rustication while the half-round joint (o) is less common. Joints with two steps, (p) to (r), can strengthen the effect of smooth-faced rustication but are particularly useful for keeping the joints of rough-faced rustication distinct from the coarse surface.

Rustication is often mixed. Courses can be of different heights (s) and the sizes of the blocks can be varied to produce an irregular pattern (t). Joints can be varied, for example by alternating straight and chamfered joints (u). Rusticated blocks can be mixed with smooth, dressed stone to create textured bands, surrounds or edges (v) and different textures of rustication can be mixed (w). The horizontal courses of rustication are usually level, but a few buildings have random coursing (x).

The illustrated examples are by no means a comprehensive collection of types. There has been a great deal of individual interpretation of rustication, both by architects and stonemasons. Mixing types and details can produce many different textures and effects on the surfaces of walls.

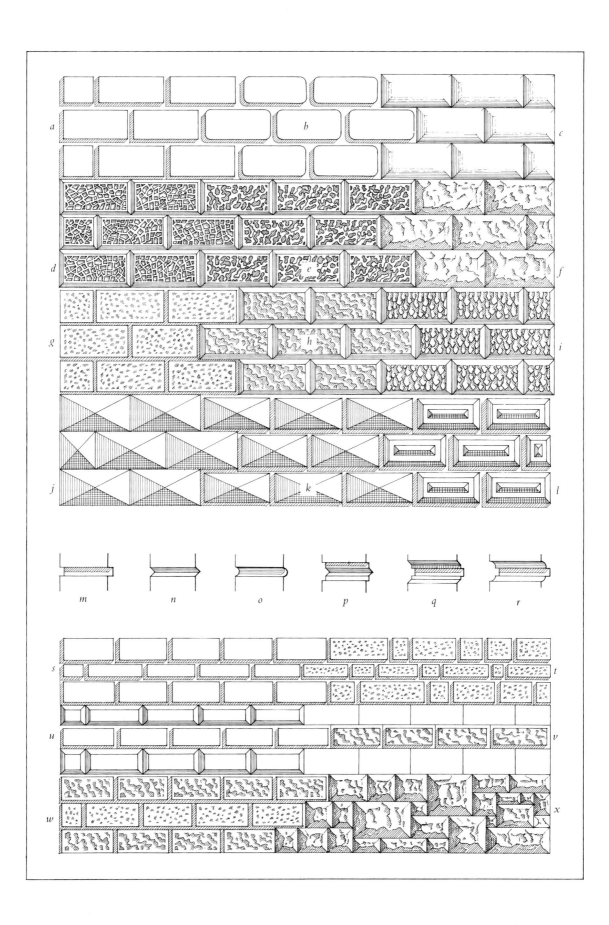

# RUSTICATED ORDERS

Although some of the earliest rustication is Corinthian, when Renaissance theorists fixed the orders in a sequence, according to the slenderness of columns, they established Tuscan and Doric as the orders most often used for lower storeys of buildings. The same theorists enlarged upon the Roman author Vitruvius' mythological human characteristics for the orders, suggesting that robust details such as rustication would be most appropriate for the masculine orders, Tuscan and Doric. The Renaissance development of rustication was, consequently, contemporary with developments in the understanding of the orders that led both to the idea that Tuscan and Doric were most suitable for rustication and to the location of these orders in the often rusticated lower storeys of buildings. Tuscan and Doric rustication is, therefore, much more common than rustication in the other orders.

All the orders can, however, be rusticated, but there is no consistent difference in the details. Features seen on one order can be applied to another and these can take many different forms.

Regular circular blocks on the column shaft (a) give an orderly appearance and leave the finer details such as the capitals and entablature intact. These bands can be set out to reveal more of the true column shaft. Vignola's doorway on the Villa Giulia in Rome (c) of 1550 has the underlying column shaft exposed in line with the imposts of the inset rusticated arch. The spaces between the rusticated blocks can be increased progressively to expose more column, (k), (f), (d) and (i). An archway at Somerset House in London (d), designed by William Chambers in 1776, has no rustication on the columns above the impost of the arch.

Rusticated blocks can be regularly or unevenly spaced, (g) and (l), and can vary from the coarse stones of Serlio's extraordinary design (e) of 1551, to the late-eighteenth-century use of neat, square blocks with vertical joints (b). One of the first uses of heavy rustication, in the Corinthian Porta Maggiore (j) of the early first century AD, has stones like a series of uncut blocks for Corinthian capitals. In another detail by Serlio, the columns are strapped into the wall (f) as if captured by the stones, while illustration (h) shows how square blocks can bind two columns together.

Arches set into the order at times push through into the entablature. The upper voussoirs of the Doric arch at Somerset House (d) are very carefully coordinated with the triglyphs in the frieze, while Serlio avoids this by using simplified Doric details (f). Although the cornice often escapes the intrusion of rustication, at times it can occupy the whole entablature (i).

Rusticated voussoirs from flat arches can be contained within the horizontal zone of the column capital, as on the garden elevation of the Palazzo Pitti in Florence (k), by Bartolomeo Ammanati in 1560. They can also be cut into the entablature (e) or the entablature can, by the addition of voussoirs, become the flat arch itself.

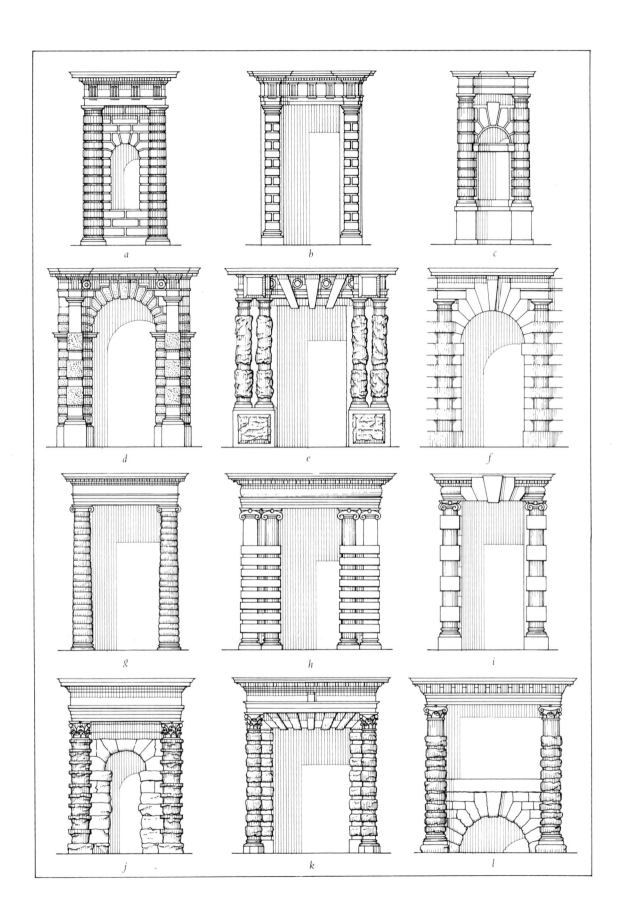

a
b
c
d
e
f
g
h
i
j
k
l

# RUSTICATED WALLS AND OPENINGS

Before the creation of a series of rusticated orders in the sixteenth century, a number of methods of forming openings in rusticated walls had become established. As rustication is essentially an enhancement of the stone normally used for the construction of walls, the details of simple openings are an enhancement of the traditional method of constructing stonework.

A series of voussoirs forming a flat arch can be brought up to the level of an appropriate joint in a rusticated wall (d). A more interesting arrangement is the integration of the voussoirs with several courses of stone to form blocks that turn the voussoirs outwards into the wall (a). The pattern of the rustication on the wall can cut into the voussoirs of the flat arch progressively from the outside by lowering one (c) or more (b) of them to create a series of upward steps that resemble the arrangement of voussoirs for round arches. Example (b) from the Palazzo Costa in Rome is unusual as it has two keystones, instead of one.

Similar variations in round arches are dictated by the way the voussoirs meet the horizontal lines of the wall rustication. With more than three courses of rustication in the height of the arch the voussoirs will step progressively upwards as they meet each horizontal course to form the rough outline of a pointed arch in the stone, (n) and (o). This pattern can be marked with a joint at each intersection (n) or, particularly with banding, can run in unbroken lines into the horizontal courses (o). These two arrangements can be combined to form L-shaped stones (m). The height of the stepped, radiating voussoirs can be limited by stopping them in a horizontal line at a joint above the arch (p).

The rustication of both flat and round arches can be isolated from the wall by forming separate rusticated surrounds, (e) and (i). The surrounds can also be reduced to stone frames that contain no indication of the structural means of forming the opening, (h) and (l).

In the sixteenth century, designs for rectangular openings and surrounds derived from antiquity were rusticated. Blocks were placed around the architrave and penetrated part of the entablature as voussoirs (f) or, as on the window in Vignola's Villa Giulia in Rome (g) of 1550, a rusticated flat arch and classical surround were fused together. Different varieties of this union of rustication with classical detail have evolved and in George Dance's Newgate Prison in London (j) of 1770 the rustication has virtually consumed the surround, which is contained within an arch. This combination of rectangular and arched rusticated openings was established in Italian Renaissance palaces. Palladio's arch from the Palazzo Thiene in Vicenza in northern Italy (k) of about 1550 combines the two forms effortlessly within the pattern of the rustication, while Dance attempts to match the curve of the arch in the voussoirs and so gradually loses their relationship with the horizontal wall.

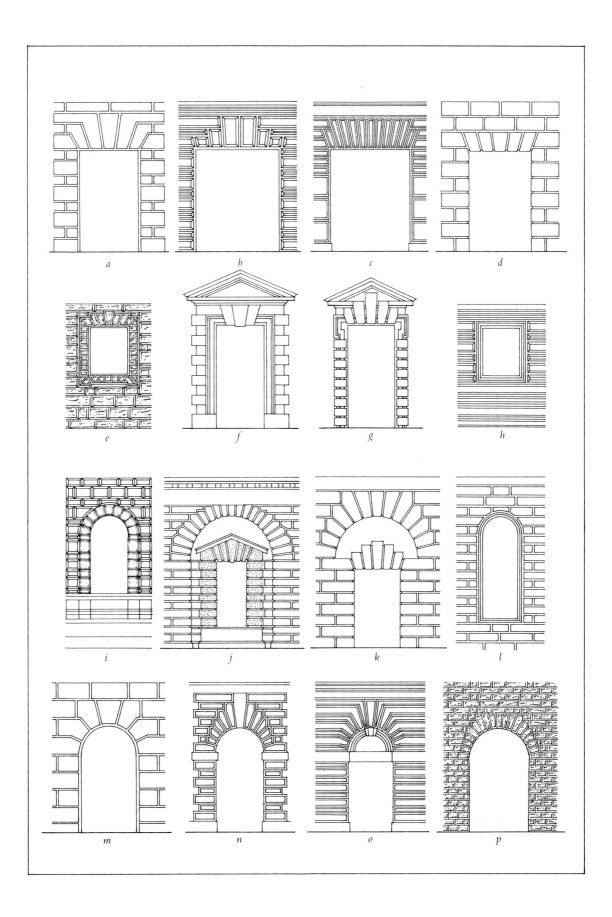

a

b

c

d

e

f

g

h

i

j

k

l

m

n

o

p

# RUSTICATED BUILDINGS

Rustication has traditionally been used on the lower floors of buildings and examples have been illustrated on pages 29, 33, 37, 39, 43, 45, 59, 81, 89, 97, 101, 131, 135, 139 and 143. The origin of Renaissance rustication in the design of palaces firmly established this tradition. These palaces usually had only their stables and service rooms on the ground floor and the fine detail began on the upper floor, or piano nobile. The coarse surface of rustication expressed not only the humble function of this level but also the defensive character of buildings that needed robust and forbidding lower floors. Rustication can also form a rock-like base for the orders or provide the first level of a design that becomes progressively finer as it rises. This follows Greek and, in particular, Roman practice where some buildings were constructed on bases of stone with a rough finish or channelled joints.

Rustication can be a dominant element in the design of buildings. A total surface decoration of rustication for urban palaces was one of the earliest features of Renaissance architecture in Florence. The spread of the Renaissance to other parts of Italy led to the introduction of this surface on similar buildings. In the north Italian town of Ferrara the Palazzo dei Diamanti (a) of 1482, by Biagio Rossetti, is so called because of the encrustation of sharp, diamond-pointed rustication. It is one of a series of north Italian designs with this very distinctive form of rustication.

The Zecca, or Mint, in Venice (d), designed in 1537 by the Florentine exile Jacopo Sansovino, was originally only two storeys. It is one of a series of adjacent but different buildings by the same architect in and near the Piazza S. Marco. As it was to house the bullion reserves of the city it had to be robust and Sansovino chose to express this with rustication which included the first use of columns with the circular rusticated blocks that would become so popular in the following centuries.

The English Baroque architect Nicholas Hawksmoor frequently used banded rustication to add a feeling of weight and solidity to his buildings. His unexecuted design for the Provost's house at King's College, Cambridge (b) of 1712 is an essay in the dramatic application of banded rustication. Column capitals and bases make only brief appearances from within their girdle of rustication, and decoration is limited to lions' masks and two scrolled half-pediments.

Rustication can also be used selectively. The Director's house is the focal point at the saltworks near Besançon in eastern France (c) and was designed by the revolutionary architect Claude Ledoux in 1775. The large portico rusticated with prominent square blocks dominates the building and is one of a series of original rusticated compositions in this manufacturing complex. The rusticated features on the gaol in the English town of King's Lynn (e), by William Tuck in 1784, are restrained by comparison and show the effective use of rusticated corners, or quoins, and other small areas to give some distinction to an otherwise unadorned façade.

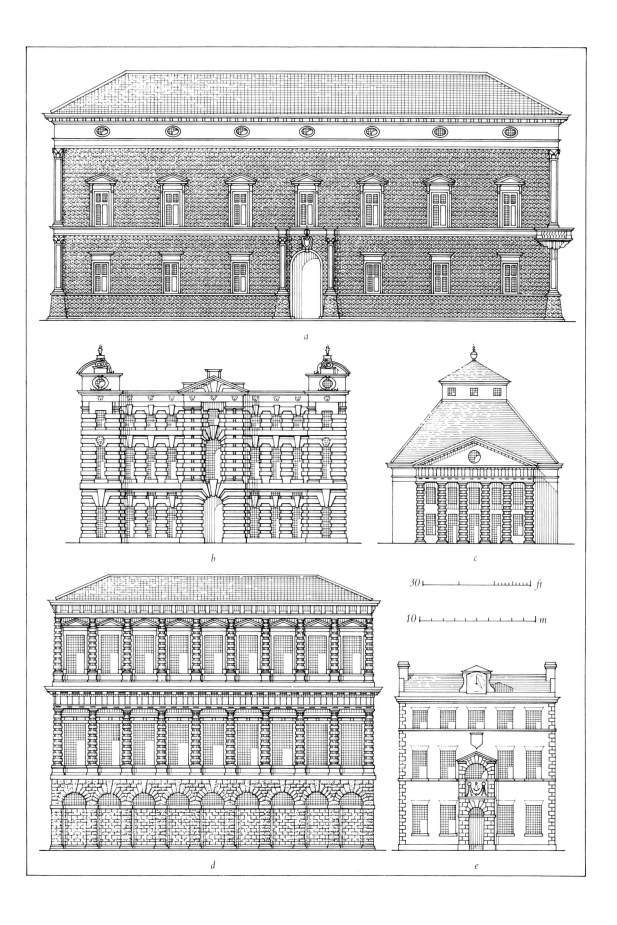

a

b

c

30 |————————|......... ft

10 |—————————| m

d

e

# 12. DOORS AND PORCHES

## BUILDINGS AND ENTRANCES

One of the most important elements in the design of a building is the entrance. It marks the division between the exterior and the interior, the public and the private, the exposed and the sheltered – everything, in short, that the enclosure of a building represents. In architecture of almost all types and periods particular attention has been paid to the door, and the crossing of the threshold can have symbolic and even religious significance.

The location of the entrance centrally on the façade has for centuries been universally accepted and understood. In response to this convention the design of the doorway can assume supreme importance or receive no emphasis except its central position.

The Villa Chiericati near Vicenza in northern Italy (a) was designed by Palladio in 1554 with a portico so large in relation to the size of the villa behind that the portico, which acts as a massive entrance porch, is the only significant element in the design. The Palazzo Caprini, or House of Raphael, in Rome (b), designed by Bramante in about 1512 and since destroyed, includes no detail specific to the entrance except its central location and the lack of shopkeepers' benches.

The decoration of the entrance for additional significance can take many different forms in relation to the design of the building. Robert Lyminge's entrance front to Hatfield House near London (c) of 1609 is richly decorated and the entrance is marked by an increase of decorative detail and height. Two centuries later there were many buildings like the house at Richmond outside London (d) where the detail is so sparse that the classical door-surround is virtually the only decoration.

It is not always possible to locate the entrance centrally on the façade. A narrow width or particular functional requirements can necessitate a door to one side. This is quite common on small houses. In an early-nineteenth-century house in London (g) the door and its adjacent window have been given the same decoration to balance the design. Edwin Lutyens used a similar device in 1922 for his bank building, also in London (e), but matched the door with a blind niche and used a large window for a central emphasis. The Chapel of the Resurrection, a mortuary, by Sigurd Lewerentz in Stockholm (f) in 1925, is much more radical, with a fractionally detached entrance portico sited firmly at one end.

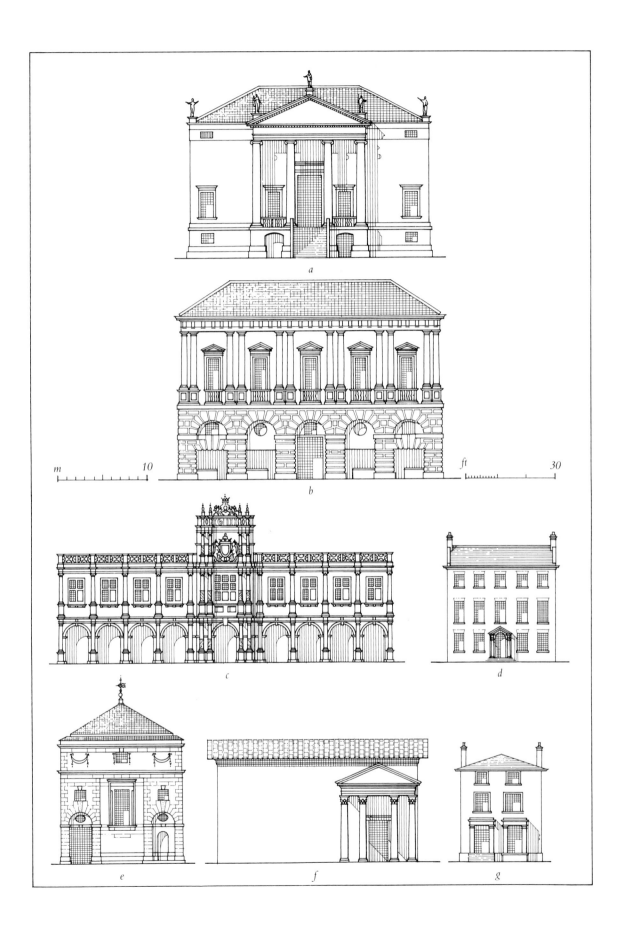

10 $ft$ 30

a

b

c

d

e

f

g

# DOORS OF ANTIQUITY

The principles of design for classical doors were established in antiquity. The history of the construction of early doorways is recorded in the detail of the doors they framed, and, in the case of temple doors, their design expresses the symbolic significance of entering into the sanctuary of the god.

The beam, or lintel, of a door must have sufficient strength to take the weight of wall above and transfer it to the sides of the opening. As wood has the right kind of elastic strength to perform this task efficiently, it is likely that the earliest lintels were timber. Only early stone lintels have survived and they retain the rectangular form and proportions that are more suited to the natural form of wood. The need to limit the length of the narrow beam and, of course, the shape of the human figure have established vertical proportions for most classical doors. Where doors were wider, as in the shop fronts of Trajan's Markets in Rome (b) of AD 100, an arch to relieve the weight on the slender lintel was required during construction.

The door of the Parthenon in Athens (c) of 438 BC has only the posts and beam expressed, with the ends of the lintel projecting into the wall. The edges of these features are emphasized with a simple moulding. In common with many doors in antiquity, the door diminishes in width and this traditional feature may be the survival of a narrowing of openings to reduce the width of the lintel. An Etruscan doorway from central Italy (a) of a similar date has the same design with the details stylistically exaggerated.

One of the doors of the Erecntheion in Athens (d) of 421 BC is more heavily embellished. The stone frame is decorated in the same way as the architrave of the Ionic order of the building. Above and around the architrave is another decorated band, which corresponds to the frieze of the order, and above this is a modified cornice supported on two brackets, or consoles. The wooden doors themselves have not survived but are reconstructed from the evidence of sculpture and paintings. The decorative principles of doorways such as this, derived from the details of the order of the building, have become established conventions. The architrave of the order and the door share a common origin in the wooden beam and are an inseparable part of most classical doors. The frieze, particularly as a vertical feature, is often omitted and the cornice, with or without brackets or the frieze, is also optional.

The huge doorway of the Pantheon in Rome (e), with its original bronze doors, is a remarkable survival from the second century AD. The architrave, frieze and cornice of the large opening are to the conventional pattern but without a reduction in width at the top. Inside this opening are a pair of Doric pilasters, a little higher than the doors, that support their own architrave, or inner lintel. Above this inner architrave there is a large window, or fanlight, in its own frame.

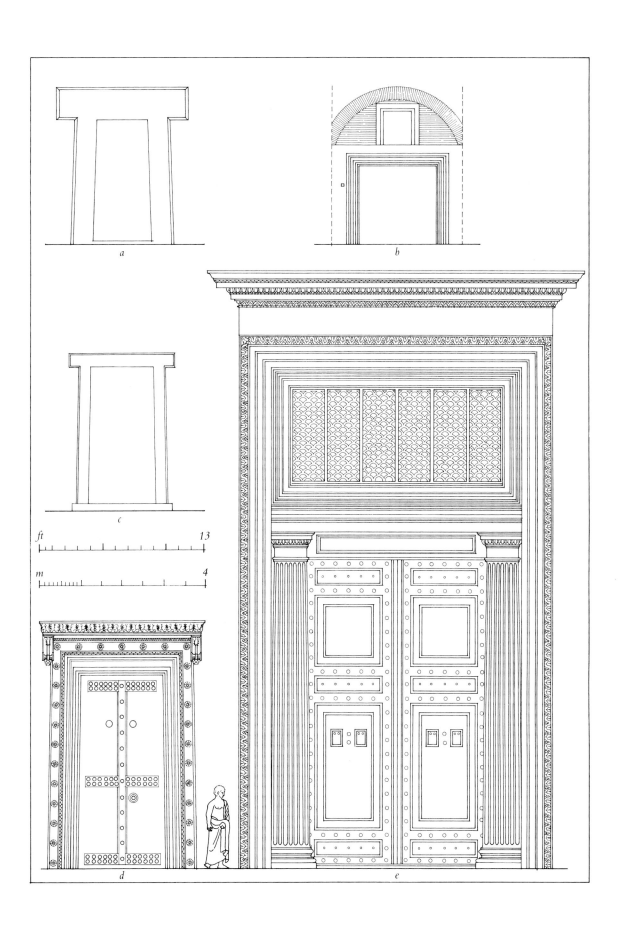

*a*

*b*

*c*

ft                13

m                4

*d*                              *e*

# PORCHES OF ANTIQUITY

The classical temple originated in the simple primitive dwellings of the Greeks and the design survives in the small temples of the Greek and Roman world which have a single room, or naos, faced with a porch, or pronaos, supported on columns in front of the entrance. The Treasury of the Athenians in the sacred Greek city of Delphi (a) from about 500 BC retains this layout.

In warm climates open porches are an important part of living accommodation. In the development of Greek and Roman houses the porch became extended to form complete colonnades around courtyards, known as peristyles, which were hidden behind enclosing walls. The public significance of the porch in dwellings was lost, except in some Greek houses in Asia where a raised section of the colonnade created a porch for the principal reception room.

Porches remained an essential part of the Greek temple. The interiors of Greek temples were not entered by worshippers but housed the image of the god and his treasure. Worship and sacrifice took place at the altar outside. The closest the ordinary worshipper could come to the sacred image was the porch. When the Erechtheion (see page 9) was constructed to house several religious sites under one roof, three porches were erected to represent the multiple dedications of the building.

The temple form was also used for the gate, or propylon, which gave access to sacred enclosures; the roadway in the centre passed through a porch at each end. Public fountains were protected from the weather by small porches and public halls were often constructed with an open colonnade on their entrance façade.

When Hellenistic architects adapted these simple buildings in the Greek temple form to more complex uses, the porch, its columns and its pediment had an established significance and could be taken as an isolated feature and added to the entrances of different buildings to give them additional status. Porches that looked like miniature temple fronts were added to doorways such as the two entrances to the Tower of the Winds in Athens (c) of about 40 BC, the only surviving clock tower from antiquity, containing a water-clock and supporting sundials and a weather-vane.

Roman architects used the temple porch in the same way as the Greeks. The Pantheon in Rome (see page 13) sat inside a courtyard and its circular shape, now dramatically revealed, was disguised by the courtyard walls and the conventional temple porch that dominates the entrance façade. The use of small porches and door-surrounds to give additional importance to doors was a widespread Roman practice. A complete doorway is realistically illustrated in a wall painting in the Italian city of Pompeii (b) of the first century BC, which shows a richly decorated door-surround and doors with grilles. Even a humble second-century-AD warehouse in Ostia, the port of Rome (d), has its own Composite door-surround, executed in brick with a stone plaque in the frieze.

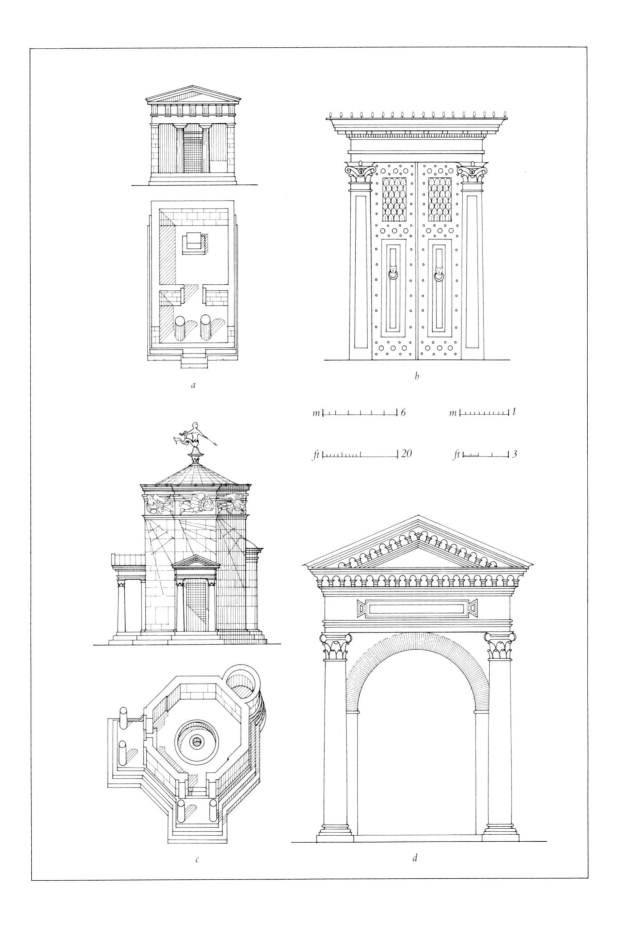

a

b

c

d

m ├┼┼┼┼┼┤ 6     m ├┼┼┼┼┼┼┤ 1

ft ├┼┼┼┼┼┼┼┤ 20     ft ├┼┼┼┤ 3

# Doors And The Orders

T he order of the door-surround may relate directly to the order that governs the proportions of a building or of an individual floor. It may also be a contrast. The proportions of a door-surround will relate to its order although it may lack columns or other features. Variations in the application of the orders to doors are, however, most readily understood when both columns and entablature are included.

In example (a) the door is independent of the Doric details that surround it. The margin between the door and the surround is uneven, but the door-head aligns with the bottom of the capital. A similar relationship is to be seen in the Ionic example (d) but the architrave details of the door differ from those of the order. The top of the door architrave aligns with the bottom of the capital and when a similar relationship is applied to a Corinthian door (g) the space between the two architraves becomes large enough to be decorated with swags. This is avoided in the Composite example (l) where the door-head aligns with the bottom of the capital and the space above is partly filled with the large door architrave.

Where the surrounding order comes into contact with the architrave of the door, a visual conflict can be created between the architrave of the entablature and the door architrave. Where they are identical, as in the Doric example (b), a tablet helps to separate them. In the Corinthian example (h) not only is the door architrave different but the frieze and architrave on the entablature are limited to vertical extensions of the columns leaving a decorated space between. In the other Corinthian example (j) the door architrave is also varied, but only the lower section of the curved Baroque architrave is omitted on the entablature and the remaining narrow space is decorated. In the Ionic example (e) the problem is solved by bringing a fluted architrave only up the sides of the door. On the Composite door (k) the separation is maintained with an arch and keystone.

It is also possible to bring the door-head up to the underside of the entablature so that the door architrave will be in line with the entablature architrave. This creates a problem in the relationship between the columns and the vertical architraves of the door. The Doric door (c), like (b), shows the common technique of halving the columns with the vertical architraves, and further emphasizes the separation with ears on the door architrave and special frieze details above.

In the later Renaissance a more radical method of avoiding any conflict between the architraves was evolved. A column capital sits immediately below its frieze and the architrave, halved with the column, lies alongside the capital. This can be seen on the Ionic example (f) and the Corinthian door (i). Although it altered the normal proportional relationship between the columns of the order and the entablature, this design so successfully dealt with the relationship between the architraves of the door and the order that since its development it has been widely used.

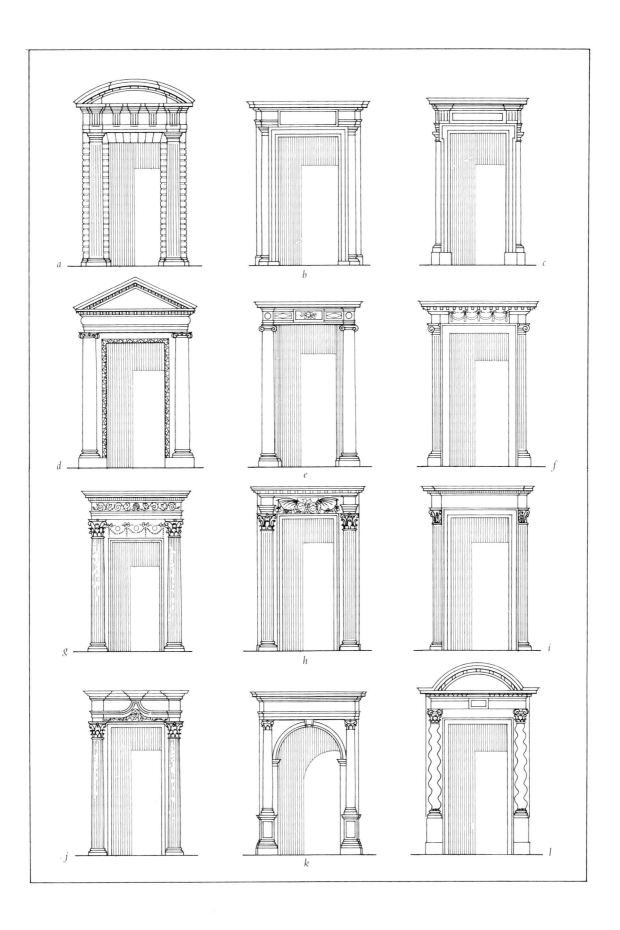

# DOORS AND BRACKETS

The use of brackets on door-surrounds has been a consistent classical tradition since they were introduced in early Greek temples. Brackets first supported the projecting cornice over the door and this has remained their position on most subsequent door-surrounds.

The original Greek position of the bracket outside the mouldings around the door is reproduced in the door-surround of St George's Hall in Liverpool, England (b), by H. L. Elmes and C. R. Cockerell in 1839. This design is taken directly from the door of the Erechtheion in Athens, although the door is an imaginative interpretation. The bracket is more often placed on a special narrow pilaster alongside the door architrave. A Renaissance door from Rome (a) and an eighteenth-century English door (c) show this detail. The position of the bracket, however, differs on the two examples. On the Renaissance door (a) the bracket is above the opening and supports the upper part of the cornice only, thereby reducing the projection of the cornice to the sides. On the English door (c) the brackets project well below the opening and support the full cornice with a correspondingly greater projection to the side.

Brackets can be placed directly on to full pilasters the same height as the door. A tall bracket will then replace the lower sections of the entablature and raise the cornice to a height that will allow a window to fill the space between the brackets. This can be seen on doors of the early eighteenth (f) and early nineteenth (d) centuries. An unusual design (e), by the sixteenth-century Italian architect Serlio, also raises the cornice to a high level on brackets, but places the high cornice above a complete door-surround with its own smaller cornice.

The bracket can be set at the same height as the door-head and support a section of the frieze as well as the cornice (k). Where the space at the side of the door is restricted, it can even sit above and inside the architrave (j) in order to limit the projection of the cornice. Michelangelo, in a design for the Laurentian Library in Florence (l) of 1524, even took a simplified bracket within the door architrave in order to give the impression of support for a rudimentary cornice placed along the top of the architrave.

In Baroque architecture the ears on the architrave developed an ambiguous relationship with the bracket. Ears on an architrave can have a straightforward and independent relationship with the bracket (g). Extra decorative brackets set flat against the wall, as on the door of the university of La Sapienza in Rome (h), by Giacomo della Porta in 1576, had, by the middle of the next century, been reduced to a simple profile on doors, such as those designed for the Casino del Bufalo in Rome (i) by Francesco Borromini. This profile, although by origin a bracket, was transferred to the upper part of the architraves of doors and windows by Borromini and his followers to create a design that was a very literal representation of ears.

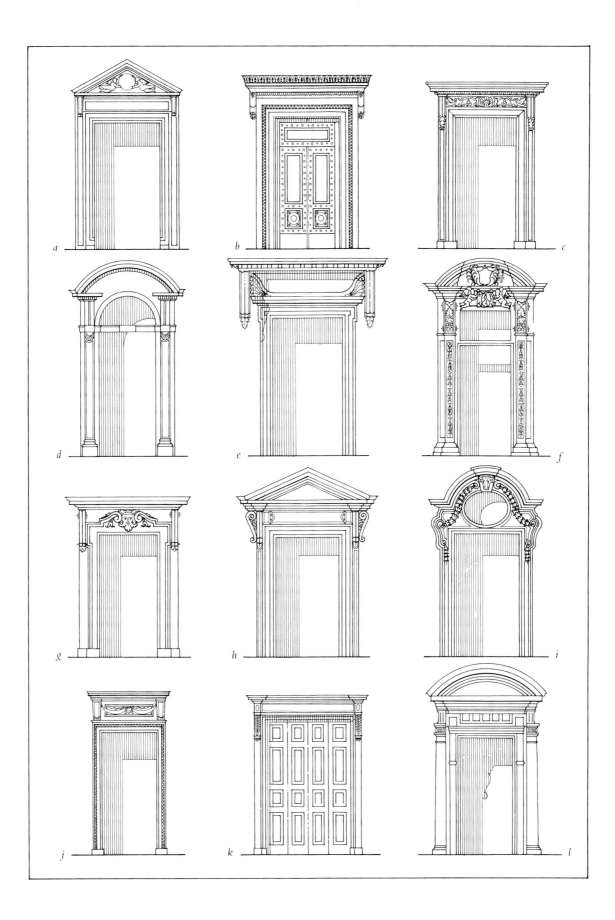

a

b

c

d

e

f

g

h

i

j

k

l

# DOOR-SURROUNDS 1

The standard form of full classical door-surround without columns is illustrated with a Renaissance example from Rome (a). From the head of the door there is a full entablature and pediment. The architrave turns down to frame the door-opening and at the bottom turns inwards to form a base. The pediment can be omitted to leave a simple entablature and the architrave can come down to a block, or end at the floor, without a return. This type of door-surround can have the decoration and proportions of any of the orders with varied degrees of detail and has been used repeatedly in all classical periods.

Other Renaissance door-surrounds are illustrated in examples (b) and (c). Example (b), from Genoa in northern Italy, shows an outer and inner architrave which frame a sculpted panel over the door. The outer architrave and the cornice above are narrow and the frieze has been omitted from the entablature. The inner architrave is wider and the upper corners of the opening contain small brackets. In example (c), from Bologna in northern Italy, the frieze is also omitted and the architrave contains a plain inner frame. An arched cornice, finished with scrolled ornaments, sits independently above the horizontal cornice.

The simple door-surround can be varied too. The top of the architrave can be extended, a bulging, or pulvinated, frieze can be added and the pediment can be broken (d). When the projection of the cornice is difficult to accommodate, the width of the cornice can be reduced by narrowing the frieze in the form of a scroll (e). A Baroque door-surround from Sudbrook Park in Surrey in England (f), by James Gibbs in 1728, shows the width of the pediment decreased by the reduction of the frieze and cornice to a curved panel.

A simple Renaissance door-surround (g) shows how the standard form can accommodate an arch and, in this case, rustication. An undecorated arch can sit within a plain architrave, but Bernini has given his side-door of S. Andrea al Quirinale in Rome (h) of 1658 greater interest with a stepped arch and crowning scrolls. Rustication can itself form the door-surround and the example (i), by Edwin Lutyens in 1901, from Homewood in England, has a rusticated beam suspended inside a plain arch.

There are many departures from the standard classical type. The bold Greek Revival door from St Andrew's Chapel in Plymouth, England (j), by John Foulston in 1823, is revolutionary in spite of its derivation from Greek sources. Equally dramatic is Hawksmoor's side-door from St George-in-the-East in London (k) of 1714, where a savagely simplified standard door-surround is punctured with a rusticated keystone and contains an oval window and severely simplified inner door-surround. Schinkel's weighty design, from the Bauschule in Berlin (l) of 1831, combines a decorative frame reminiscent of the Renaissance with an ancient Greek cornice.

206

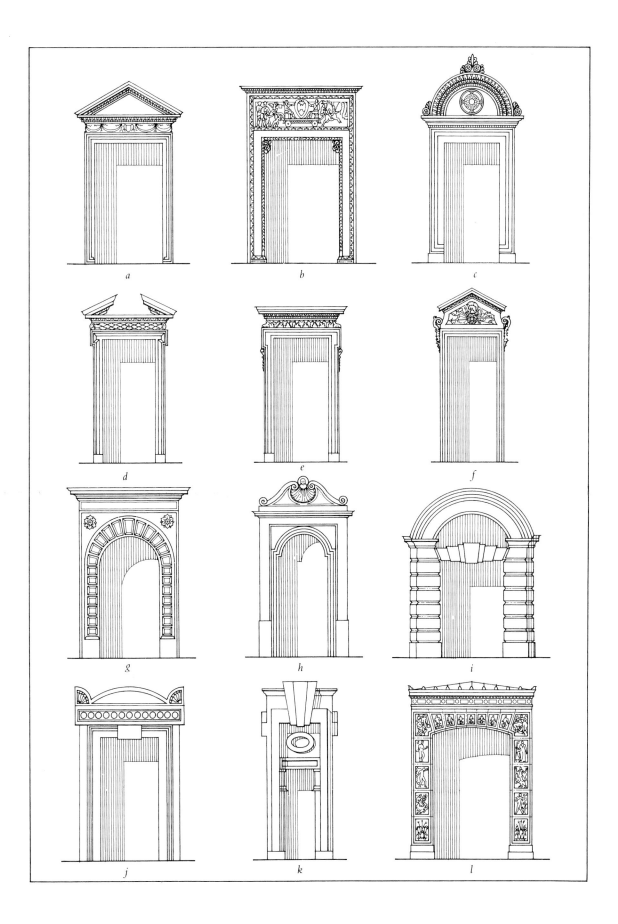

a

b

c

d

e

f

g

h

i

j

k

l

# DOOR-SURROUNDS 2

Door-surrounds are often fitted into arched openings with a semicircular window over the door. This was a common feature in the late eighteenth and early nineteenth centuries and the inventive designs of the semicircular windows gave rise to the name fanlights.

An early example is a bold design by Palladio from the Villa Pojana near Venice (b) of 1548. An inner arch sits above the simplest representation of a cornice and a row of small circular windows rotates around it, giving a distinctive pattern of light to the interior. The details of the order can be more complete (a) contrasting the simple shape of the arch with the details inside. Two more windows can be added on either side of the door and the proportions of the order are sometimes modified to reduce the width and height of the columns and entablature and give more space for glass (d). A similar but less elaborate effect is created by limiting the details around the door to the architrave, and in example (c) a decorative plaster fan has been added to the outer arch, restricting the fanlight to the inner arch over the door.

The orders on Baroque and Rococo door-surrounds can be modified to achieve a rich decorative effect. The architrave in the entablature is often lifted in the centre and a small carved feature added above the door (e). Pediments are frequently varied by omitting sections from above and below, (e), (f) and (h), and by using scrolls or multiple curves to modify the profile. A late-seventeenth-century English door (f) has used the pediment to create a complex decorative scheme in a very small space. The entablature is reduced to dosserets above the columns, the pediment is split with opposing curves and the space inside the pediment contains a double-curved arch, spilling over with carved decoration. A door-surround from Munich in Germany (h) has most of the decoration above the cornice concentrated around an oval window, while the architrave on the late-eighteenth-century door of São João del Rei in Brazil (i) explodes through the entablature to support an ornate frame for a statue of the Virgin. Hawksmoor's monumental Baroque door-surround at Blenheim Palace in England (g) of 1705 is sober by comparison, contrasting the large Doric order with the simple scrolls above the plain arched opening.

Nineteenth-century door-surrounds could also include modifications to the orders, but these were often introduced to create a greater feeling of solidity. The Doric door (k) from a pattern-book of designs is typical and includes a pediment reduced to its upper mouldings, derived from Italian rural buildings. The German architect Schinkel's design for a music academy in Berlin included a door (j) inside an outer order of mixed Doric and Corinthian details with an inner door-surround of a Greek type. A door by Louis Sullivan on the Guaranty Building in Buffalo, New York State (l) of 1894 combines a Renaissance design with novel geometric decoration executed in terracotta.

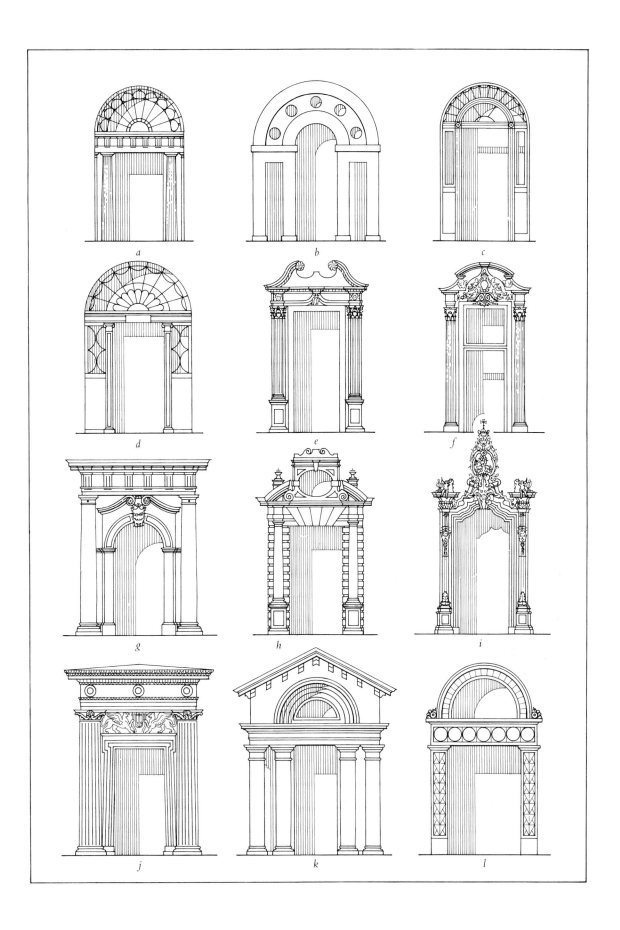

a

b

c

d

e

f

g

h

i

j

k

l

# DOUBLE-HEIGHT DOOR-SURROUNDS

The design of the window above the door and the detail of the eaves or pediment are often varied to give some rhythm to the façade and to give additional emphasis to the entrance or centre. In some designs the section of the building above the door is included in the design of a distinct and separate door-surround. The height of such a design could be any number of storeys, to the full height of the building, but in practice they are rarely greater than three and more often two storeys high.

Three-storey door-surrounds were a common feature in northern European buildings of the sixteenth century and displayed the newly discovered classical orders. The porch of Beaupre Castle in Wales (a) of 1590 has an ascending series of orders diminishing in size, but manipulated with varying or multiple pedestals to create two upper levels of equal height. A gateway to St Catherine's College, Oxford (c) of 1674 is more restrained, containing two upper-storey windows within one large Corinthian order. The gateway below becomes part of a Doric base for the principal columns above. This design is notable for the reversal of the normal vertical reduction in the size of the orders. The German Baroque design of the gateway to St Florian in Kloster (b), by Jakob Prandtauer in 1712, is an extravagant display of figured sculpture and multiple curves diminishing over three storeys.

The elements in the design of the entrance to the Villa Giulia in Rome (e), by Vignola in 1550, could be extended over the whole building, but a difference of detail and decoration makes it an independent element in the façade. An increase in decoration was often used on Baroque buildings to link the door-surround with the window above. On Mompesson House in Salisbury, England (g) of 1701 the door and window are only just brought together by a slight projection in the wall above the door and by the enhanced detail on the window. On Argyll House in London (i), by Giacomo Leoni in 1723, a balustrade and urns overlap with the window above, creating a more unified composition. A door for the Palazzo Fidia in Milan (f), by Aldo Andreani in 1924, has three quite different details just touching one another in a vertical sequence which is distinguished from the rest of the stucco façade by the use of stone and by the individuality of the features.

Double-height entrances do not have to be formed from additive assemblies of orders or features but can be individual designs. Edwin Lutyens's door for the Country Life building in London (d) of 1904 raises the height of a single pedimented order to contain the window above the door in the high tympanum. The remarkable guards' barracks in Würzburg, Germany (h), by Peter Spreeth in 1811, has a door-surround with a colonnaded gallery over a heavily rusticated arch, giving it a visual independence which both isolates the element and allows it to dominate the façade.

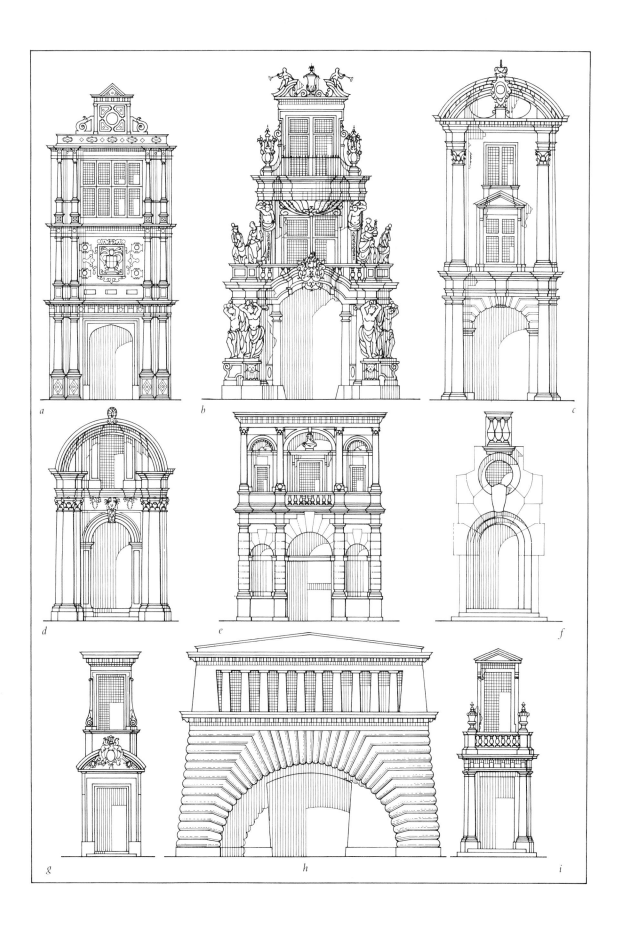

a

b

c

d

e

f

g

h

i

# PORCHES AND PORTICOS

The practical advantages of porches have ensured their continuous use. Located in front of the door, the design of the porch becomes the design of the entrance and shares all the significance of the door-surround. Many of the door-surround details shown on previous pages can, by the addition of free-standing columns or brackets, become porches.

Porches, or porticos, large enough to dominate the façade and generally more than a single storey in height, derive from the transfer in antiquity of the temple front to buildings of a different form. Although low continuous colonnades had been used for the front of churches since their first construction in the fourth century, the addition of giant order columns with a pediment could only be introduced in the Renaissance when the direct association with pagan temples had ceased to be significant. Continuous colonnades are called porticos and the word seems to have been transferred in the English language to isolated porches.

The use of the temple front portico for houses is almost entirely due to the influence of the sixteenth-century Italian architect Palladio, and the popularity of his *Four Books of Architecture*. Palladio held the erroneous idea that the Romans gave as much importance to their houses as to their temples and would, consequently, have used temple front porticos for their houses. Although based on an incorrect assumption, the application of a high portico to houses has become widespread. Temple front porticos, often with but occasionally without pediments, can have one giant order, as on William Wakefield's Duncombe Park in Yorkshire (a) of 1700, or can have ascending orders and a balcony, as on Palladio's own Villa Cornaro near Venice (b) of 1553. Balconies can also be included halfway up giant order columns and this detail, also introduced to house fronts by Palladio, is popular in the United States.

Smaller porches sitting on columns can take many forms. The simple projection of an entablature or pediment on two or more columns (g) is universal and subject to all the variations available in the orders. There are usually two pilasters where the entablature meets the wall and these can be repeated at the sides (c) to enlarge the composition. The porch can be partially enclosed by side-walls and the columns can sit between the walls (d) in the form of a small Greek temple porch. Alternatively, the porch can have a half-circular (e), half-elliptical or segmental plan.

A porch can be made without free-standing columns by projecting a part or all of the entablature on brackets. The brackets can take any of the positions illustrated on page 205. To limit the weight of the projecting canopy it is often restricted to a projecting cornice with the brackets in the frieze (f). Canopies are flat or pedimented or can take other forms such as the English early-eighteenth-century decorative semicircular hood (h).

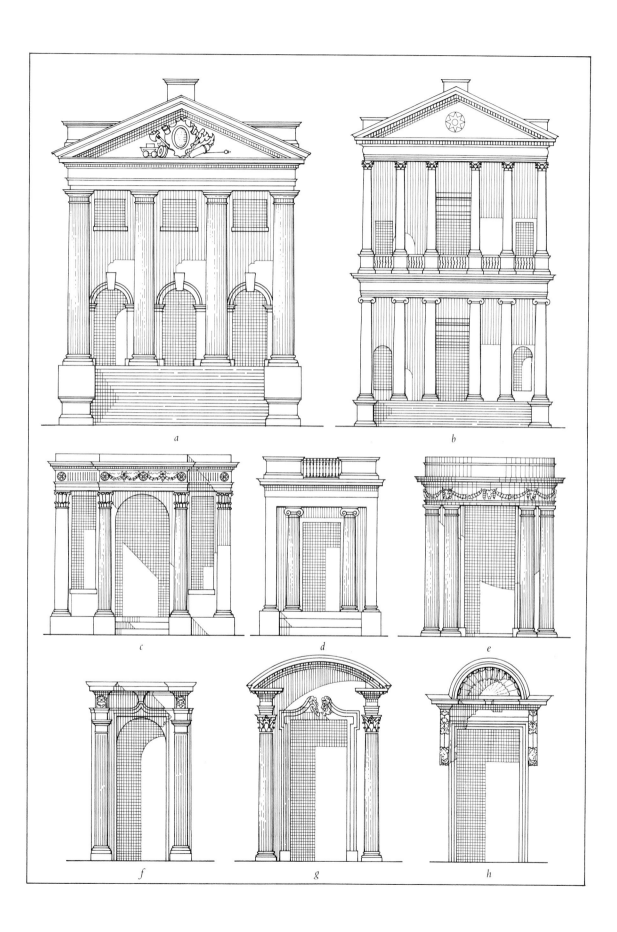

a

b

c

d

e

f

g

h

# A Doric Door-surround

A simple door-surround can be designed by the application of the orders. This Doric surround is based on two versions of the order published by Vignola in 1563, but modified here to suit the small size of a door. This is a door-surround without columns. It can be altered to create the five versions illustrated or, by reference to details of the orders, the pediment and examples of other doors, can be modified in a number of other ways.

A door-surround of this design could be used either internally or externally and could be constructed of stone, plaster, timber or any other suitable material. If it is used externally and constructed of perishable materials the projection of the cornice will have to be protected with a waterproof material and, if it is flat, the top will have to be laid to fall outwards. The waterproof material, usually a sheet metal of some form, must be dressed carefully over the top edge of the cornice to provide protection against windblown rain without overhanging the top cyma moulding.

Vignola's Doric orders include a version with mutules in the cornice (a) and a version with dentils (b). Both versions can have triglyphs, but these are omitted in the dentil cornice to illustrate an alternative which will not be tied proportionally to the spacing of the triglyphs and mutules. If the usual spacing of the triglyphs and mutules is used, the ratio of height to width of the door will have to be 2.6:1 with the number of triglyphs shown, or 1.7:1 if another is added.

It is assumed that the height of the door has already been determined, as this is commonly a standard or dictated by other factors. This height is taken as the height of the column of the order to obtain a module. The architrave will then be one half of that module and will surround the door-opening. If a block is to be added to the base of the architrave this could also be a half-module to equal the height of a column base and to determine the height of the skirting, or baseboard.

If triglyphs are included and located as shown, then the architrave should have ears in order to allow space for the pegs, or guttae, which project into the architrave. The guttae should be half-round, but with small doors this can create a difficult detail. It is possible to notch a flat section of material to achieve a similar effect. The inclusion of triglyphs and, in particular, mutules with their closely spaced pegs will give very fine detail to a door-surround. It is possible to omit the pegs on the mutules, but the pegs below the triglyphs are usually one of the last details to go.

By reference to the details of the other orders, Ionic, Corinthian and Composite door-surrounds can be made. Pilasters can be added and page 203 on door-surrounds and the orders shows some of the ways this can be done.

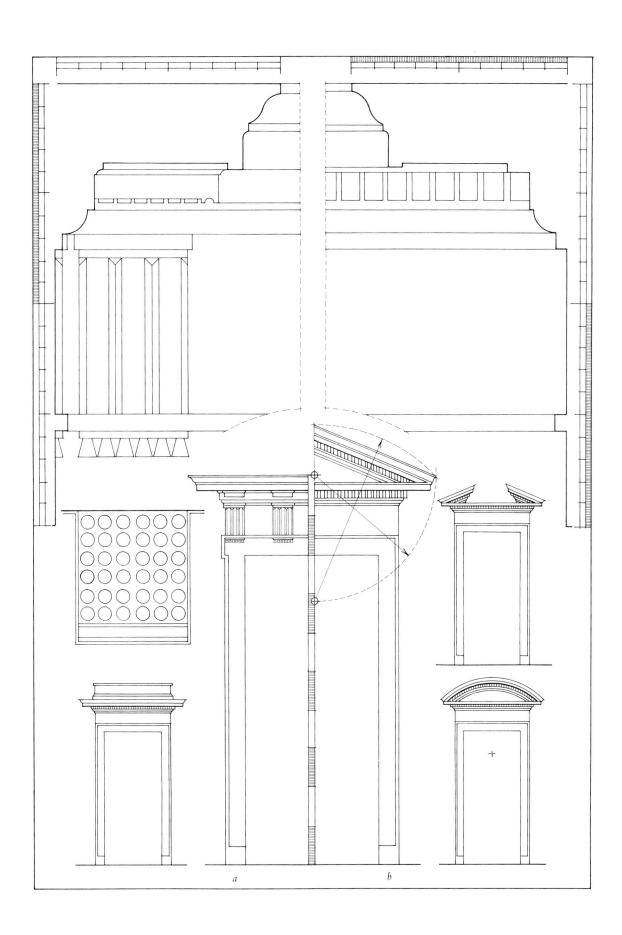

*a*             *b*

# A Doric Porch

The design of a simple porch with two free-standing columns is one of the most straightforward applications of the orders. The principles for setting out this design can be expanded or modified to create many simple variants. The large view of the porch shows a version with a pediment (f) and with a small attic block (e). The small views above show a pediment over an attic block (a), a segmental pediment (c), a simple entablature with a top sloping gently to the front (d) and an example with paired columns half a column width apart and a high attic block (b). The large views also show a full circular column, fluted (g) and unfluted (i), and a square column (h). The pilasters against the wall are shown square but could be half-round. These are only a few of the alternatives possible.

These porches could be made out of stone or timber or any suitable material, or be finished with a coat of fine plaster over a rough brick or concrete core. When there is a pediment or a flat roof the water can be left to fall on to the ground around the porch or, particularly if the porch is large, a gutter can be included. The uppermost cyma moulding is by its origin a gutter and could be used for this purpose. When an attic block is added this will form a parapet and rain-water will collect in the roof behind. To avoid unsightly pipes these can be taken vertically down through a column in areas that do not suffer severe frosts.

A Doric order from the early-fourth-century Baths of Diocletian in Rome is used as the basis of this design, although it has been simplified to suit a small porch. This order is notable for its lack of mutules and the projection of the cornice is, consequently, reduced to a depth more in keeping with the other orders. A version with triglyphs (e) is shown together with a version where they have been omitted (f). If triglyphs are included then the width of the porch will have to be calculated to give them a satisfactory spacing. The column has no base, but a low step below the columns is shown to lift them off the paving.

The porch has columns spaced four modules apart at the front. This is sometimes considered to be a maximum and a greater spacing should not be used without careful consideration. If a significantly wider porch is required, it is better to include additional columns. The spacing of two modules from the columns back to the pilasters on the wall could be increased to four. Columns or pilasters against the wall provide a satisfactory practical and visual method of stopping the entablature against the building.

The remaining details are derived directly from the order and the method of construction would be according to local building practice. Different Doric and Ionic, Corinthian and Composite porches can be designed according to similar principles and by reference to the details of the order.

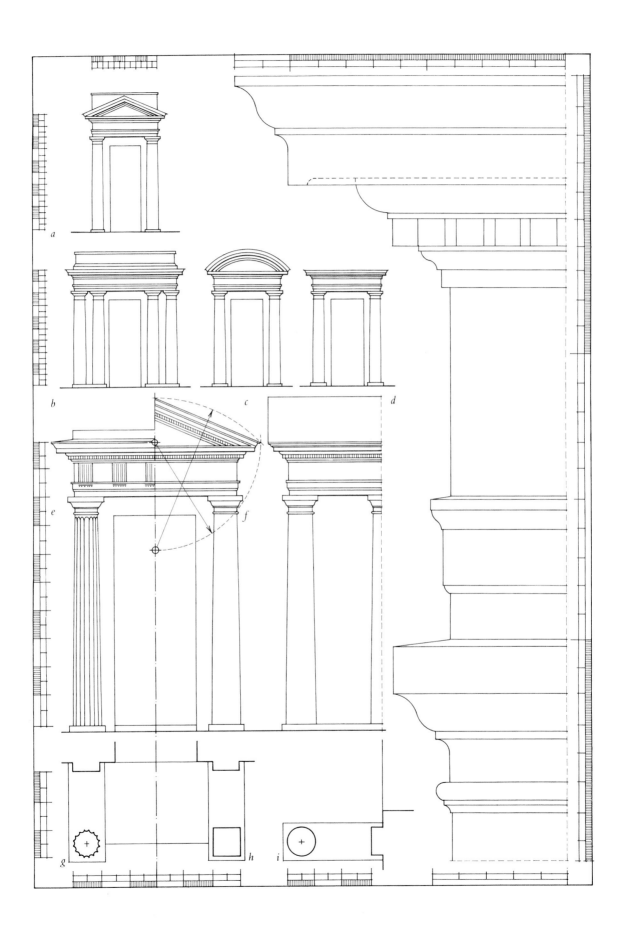

a

b

c

d

e

f

g

h

i

# 13. WINDOWS

## WINDOWS AND DESIGN

In the detail and location of windows, the internal function and the internal and external appearance of the building must be combined. The arrangement of the windows is often a direct expression of the layout of the building and the uses of the rooms.

The Palazzo Pitti in Florence in Italy (a), by an unknown architect in 1458, has an arrangement of arched openings in rustication. No emphasis is given to the door and the upper-floor windows provide the fine detail on the façade. These large windows identify the living accommodation while the small openings below light the service rooms.

The Palazzo Covoni-Daneo, also in Florence (b), designed by Gherardo Silvani in 1620, has plain walls and above them an insignificant cornice. The design depends for its effect on elaborate window-surrounds, different on each floor. Hardwick Hall in Derbyshire, England (c), designed by Robert Smythson in 1590, is remarkable for its ostentatious display of expensive glass in huge stone-framed windows. There is little other detail on the exterior except the crests on the towers and the balustrade on the lower roof.

These buildings all share the identification of principal floors by the size or decoration of windows. The most important floor is often that above the ground floor, known by its Italian name piano nobile. The buildings illustrated also share the horizontal bands of decoration that join the windows on each floor. This detail can be reversed. On the wings of Petworth House in Sussex, England (d), by an unknown architect in the late seventeenth century, the windows have been linked above and below to give a strong vertical accent.

Windows can be placed on a façade without any direct connection between one another. The decorated window-surrounds on one of Poland's first classical buildings, the castle at Piotrków (e) of 1511, probably by Benedikt Ried, have no connecting mouldings or bands. This arrangement is more often found on the severe designs of neo-classical architects. John Soane's design for Blundeston House in Suffolk, England (f) of 1786 is an abstract composition of little more than unadorned window-openings. A similar concept lies behind Frank Lloyd Wright's Charnley House in Chicago in the United States (g), built in 1891, except that the stone lower floor joins the two outer windows above and rises in the centre to contain the front door and two large windows and give a base to the Doric covered balcony.

a

b

c

d

m |⊢⊢⊢⊢⊢⊢⊢⊢⊢⊢⊢⊢⊢⊢⊢| 20    60 |⊢⊢⊢⊢⊢⊢⊢⊢⊢⊢⊢⊢⊢⊢| ft

e

f

g

# WINDOWS OF ANTIQUITY

The principles of classical window design were established in antiquity, and a sufficient number survived to inform the Renaissance. Early Greek and later Roman rectangular windows took the same form as doors and the disposition and variety of details follow the same pattern.

A window from the Erechtheion in Athens (a) from the late fifth century BC is the same shape and design as a contemporary door. The opening is wider at the bottom than the top and the window-sill is a block of stone similar to the threshold of a door. The window is surrounded by a band of flat stone with a moulded strip at its outer edge, corresponding to the top part of the architrave of the Ionic order of the building. At the head of the opening the position of the beam is indicated by a projection of the stone band, or architrave, to form ears.

The internal window-surround from the first-century-BC Temple of the Sibyl at Tivoli outside Rome (c) has a more elaborate architrave which matches at a smaller scale both the full architrave of the Corinthian order of the building and the adjacent door. The ears at the head of the window are matched at the sill. The opening is slightly wider at the bottom, and at the top there is a cornice but no frieze.

Windows lighting an interior gallery in the Pantheon in Rome (b) of the second century AD sit on a continuous moulding which encircles the interior at a high level. These windows are rectangular and include a frieze as well as a cornice. They are of particular interest as sufficient evidence survived of their original divisions and grilles to restore them. The stone hoops are of the same design as the window grille above the door (see page 199) and were a common type. These grilles, or transennae, in timber, stone and metal were used to fill openings for security while admitting light. Shutters were also fitted to seal windows. A Roman relief carving shows transennae between columns in a circular temple (d) and a small iron window grille (g) has been discovered in England.

In the first century AD the use of window glass became widespread. Much of the evidence for this has been lost, but it is known that glass was fixed together with lead and plaster as well as sitting in timber or stone frames. Large fifth-century windows with stone grilles were discovered and restored over the nave in the church of S. Sabina in Rome (h). These grilles contained translucent alabaster which was sometimes used as a substitute for glass. These elaborate designs are a glazed version of early open grilles and are the ancestors of the great Romanesque and Gothic windows.

Larger panes of glass were also made and the framework of a glazed wall from the first century AD has survived in the House of the Mosaic Atrium in Herculaneum, southern Italy (e). Similar large sheets of glass or alabaster were used in windows such as the late Roman example (f).

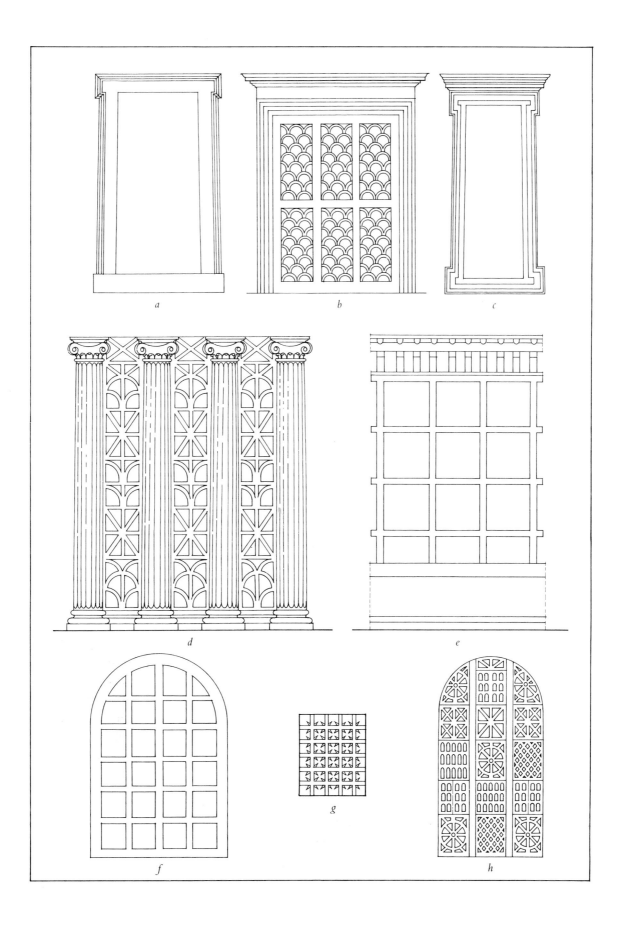

*a*        *b*        *c*

*d*        *e*

*f*        *g*        *h*

# THE VOCABULARY OF THE WINDOW

Window types have developed parallel to the design of doors since antiquity. Examples (i) to (xiv) show many of the combinations of column, pediment, baluster, architrave and bracket that can be used with all rectangular and some round-headed windows. Most of these are also found on doors and are illustrated on other pages. The principal details exclusive to window-openings are the features that are added beneath to link them to the ground or to a lower horizontal band on a façade. Plain panels (vi) or small panels of balusters, (i) and (xiv), can give a base from which a window can rise. Brackets of various forms can also be placed below sills to support heavy decorative details. Full brackets, (ii) and (xiii), and small brackets, (iii) and (xii), will be appropriate to different sizes of window-surround. A Baroque and Mannerist detail (ix) flattens the bracket to a panel of projecting wall below the window, which can be decorated or left as a simple rectangle known as an apron.

The arrangement of glazing within the opening has taken numerous forms, constrained only by the limitations of glass manufacture restricting the size of pane available. Small panes of glass have been contained in grilles of various patterns in, or in imitation of, antiquity, (xv) and (xxix). Lead has frequently been used to bind together small pieces of glass in many different designs, (xx), (xxi), (xxiii), (xxiv), (xxxvi), (xl) and (xli). Stone (xxi) or timber (xx) bars, or mullions, often divided up large areas of leaded windows and, when glass came in larger sizes in the eighteenth century, wooden mullions or bars supported whole panes. Timber bars were originally broad (xix) but later became very narrow, and patterns changed to accommodate larger panes in the nineteenth century (xvii). The invention of plate glass in the nineteenth century made bars or mullions redundant, although the traditional use of small panes of glass continued as a choice not governed by necessity (xxxvi). Large sheets of glass were also used on buildings where bold designs did not need the delicate scale of small panes (xxxvii).

Circular or round-headed windows can be divided in a number of ways. The divisions can follow the line of the circle or ellipse, (xxii), (xxiii), (xxiv) and (xxviii), and can radiate out from the centre. Divisions can form rectangles independent of the circle, (xxxi) and (xxxiii). A particular form, more often used for large semicircular windows, is the Diocletian, or thermal, window, (xxix) and (xxx), divided vertically into three uneven parts. Small semicircular windows, or fanlights, placed over doors have been divided with a great variety of decorative designs, (xxv) to (xxvii).

Classical windows tend to be taller than their width. Width is usually achieved by placing two, or more often three, windows alongside one another. The Palladian window illustrated on page 161 has been very popular for this purpose. On other triple windows a larger centre opening is normal, (xxxvii), (xxxviii), (xxxix), while divisions of two and four, (xxxiv), (xxxv), (xxxvi), (xl), (xli), are equal.

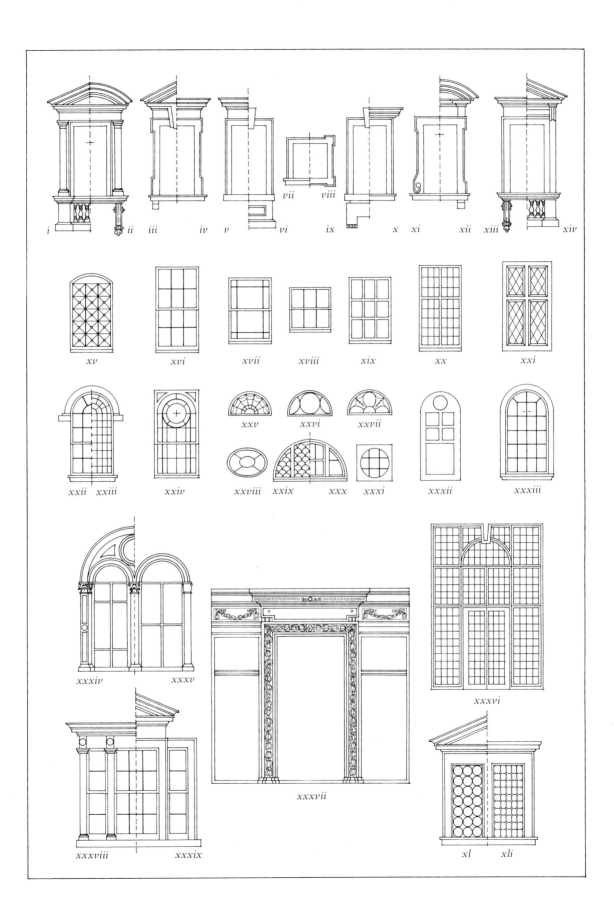

*i ii iii iv v vi vii viii ix x xi xii xiii xiv*

*xv xvi xvii xviii xix xx xxi*

*xxii xxiii xxiv xxv xxvi xxvii xxviii xxix xxx xxxi xxxii xxxiii*

*xxxiv xxxv xxxvi*

*xxxvii*

*xxxviii xxxix xl xli*

# BOW, BAY AND ORIEL WINDOWS

Large domestic buildings in the later Middle Ages often had an oriel window, a window that projected from the façade of an upper floor. Late medieval houses, particularly in England, could also have a large projecting window on the ground floor, known as a bay window, which usually lit the principal room or hall. Although the oriel window was probably defensive in origin, both of these window types came to have a luxurious character with seating space and large areas of glass.

English Renaissance architecture retained this feature of earlier medieval buildings, which was further emphasized in the late sixteenth and early seventeenth centuries due to the status attached to the lavish use of glass. The three-storey entrance tower of Bramshill House, Hampshire (a) of 1605 has a large semicircular oriel window suspended as a principal feature over the door. Wootton Lodge in Staffordshire (b), probably by Robert Smythson in about 1607, although subsequently altered still displays a complete collection of full-height projecting windows. The entrance is through a square bay with splayed three-sided bays to each side and two semicircular bay windows, or bow windows, on the side-walls. These bays may have projected above the parapet to create turrets. The projecting windows not only increased the use of glass, giving a luxurious character to the rooms, but added strong vertical features to the façade reminiscent of medieval towers.

In the early eighteenth century these windows became unfashionable, but by the middle of the century they were extensively revived in Britain and since then have been used on many large and small houses.

Early revivals, such as the single-storey bays in Saffron Walden (g) and the two-storey bays in Colchester (h), both in Essex, tend to be simple extensions of the façade made up either of multiple windows attached to the building as in (g) or, as in (h), of part of the front wall of the house. Later in the eighteenth century curved forms became more popular. On large houses whole walls of rooms and sections of façades were curved and on smaller houses simple bow windows provided architectural interest. A house in Marlow, Buckinghamshire (c) has no features except simple bow windows, one of which sits on columns to provide a porch. A bow window in Weymouth, Dorset (d) has a complete ascending series of pilasters and at street level the lower window is recessed behind free-standing columns. A similar window with pilasters is reduced to a single-storey oriel on a doctor's house in London (e) counteracting the loss of symmetry created by the door.

The convenience of these windows ensured their survival among the large number of small houses constructed in England in the nineteenth century (i). They remained popular and enjoyed particular favour with the renewed interest in English seventeenth-century architecture, seen in the oriel windows of a bank building in a London suburb (f) of 1886, by the Arts and Crafts architect Ernest Newton.

*a*

*b*

15     *ft*

5     *m*

*c*        *d*        *e*        *f*

*g*        *h*        *i*

# 14. BRACKETS

## SCROLLED BRACKETS

The scrolled bracket, also known as the modillion or console (a), is a decorative feature unique to classical architecture. The form is very specific, but its origin and meaning are unknown.

An early example supports the upper cornice of the door of the north porch of the Erechtheion in Athens (c) of 421 BC, shown in full on page 199. The scrolls, or volutes, are complex and have the same multiple ribs as the Ionic capitals of the building. The lower scroll opens out as a back to the bracket while the face of the upper scroll has its own small volutes, out of which grows an inverted anthemion. These details are individual to this bracket and its copies, but in other respects it establishes the principal features of future scrolled brackets (a). It has two scrolls turning in opposite directions, the outer face is divided into two parts, a bud sprouts from the upper scroll and an acanthus leaf from the outward turn in the lower scroll.

In Rome, scrolled brackets were applied to other architectural details. The Roman Corinthian order included a series of scrolled brackets set horizontally in the upper part of the cornice. The bracket details differ from the Greek design. The bracket from the Temple of Apollo in Rome (b) of 36 BC has two scrolls, both of which have flowers in the centre, and what is now the underside has a large acanthus leaf sprouting from the centre of the face of the larger scroll.

The scrolled bracket was also adapted to act as keystone for arches on the Arch of Titus in Rome (d) of about AD 82 and other triumphal arches. The level of decoration has increased in keeping with the importance of the detail. Rows of beaded and fluted mouldings have been added to the scrolls and the outer face is filled with a scale decoration. An acanthus leaf supports a symbolic figure, and the awkward gap behind is filled with a twisting series of buds, leaves and flowers.

The bracket has subsequently been used as a support in many different circumstances and the profile can be modified to suit particular configurations, such as the support of shallow cornices over doors (e). Baroque designers added further variations to the form, breaking the line between the volutes, (f) and (g), and at times carving away all but the essential details, reducing the bracket to a decorative skeleton (f).

*a*

*b*

*c*          *d*          *d*

*e*          *f*          *g*

# OTHER BRACKETS

A series of alternatives to the scrolled bracket has evolved from the orders. The mutule in Greek Doric buildings (a) was a stone representation of the end of the rafters from the pitched roof as they projected over the wall to support the overhanging corona and cyma. In this respect the mutule is a bracket, but on Greek buildings it retained its sloping form. Roman architects often reduced this to a horizontal pattern cut into the underside of the projection of the corona. In the cornice of the earliest monumental Corinthian temple, the Temple of Zeus Olympius in Athens (b) of 174 BC, designed by a Roman architect, there are plain brackets seemingly supporting the corona. These brackets, on later examples substituted for scrolled brackets, seem to be a mixture of Ionic dentils and Doric mutules and perhaps represent projecting beams from a structural tradition now lost. Renaissance architects such as Vignola further modified the Doric mutule (c) so that it no longer resembled rafters and became a horizontal beam-end, like that of the Temple of Zeus Olympius, while retaining the characteristic Doric guttae.

The projection of the corona in stone loses all the structural advantages it had in timber and creates instead a structural problem. It is significant that the introduction of deep brackets capable of supporting the corona did not occur until the later Hellenistic, or Roman, period when the timber origins of the orders had become historic. The cornice of the upper Composite level of the Colosseum in Rome (d) of AD 80 held masts to carry awnings and the corona was given the extra support of cyma reversa brackets. The survival of the Colosseum made this useful detail common. Vignola turned it into a scroll and set it below a standard Corinthian bracket (e) and Serlio combined the cyma reversa profile with a Doric triglyph and joined it to a mutule in a Doric cornice (f).

All these brackets have been used on their own without their cornices. Further modifications have also been made. A French Renaissance bracket (g) shows a scroll put on to a triglyph and a similar combination lies behind the nineteenth-century German architect Schinkel's triglyph bracket (h). On the upper-floor windows of the Palazzo Farnese in Rome (i) of 1546 Michelangelo introduced projecting mutule brackets that dropped down into the frieze. An early-eighteenth-century bracket from France (j) finally loses virtually all association with the traditions of the orders.

The termination of an arch against a wall created the need for a bracket of a type that was unnecessary below barrel vaults. A special column capital bracket, or corbel, had been used for this purpose in medieval buildings, such as the twelfth-century cathedral at Noyon in France (k). This form was adapted in the Renaissance and at first the designs, such as the terracotta corbel capital from Pavia in northern Italy (l) of 1467, were free interpretations of classical capitals, but they were soon adapted (m) to correspond more closely to the Roman orders.

a       b       c

d       e       f

g       h       i       j

k       l       m

# SCROLLED BRACKETS: VARIATIONS

The scrolled bracket has become such a characteristic classical form that it has been adapted to suit a large number of different practical applications and decorative themes.

The original shape of the scroll is not always suitable for supporting large or heavy projections. This has given rise to the use of pairs of scrolled brackets combined in one design. In the early Renaissance these were often grouped around a square or rectangular block (a) to give a greater projection and create a complex design. Example (c) shows an English Baroque porch bracket, which also combines two scrolled brackets, though the individual brackets have in this case been modified to adapt to the required shape. A cherub's head is lodged below the large volute of the lower bracket and an extended acanthus leaf links it to the more conventional upper scrolled bracket. Example (b) shows a Renaissance bracket on which the standard design has been reduced to a barely curved decorative face on a deep triangular bracket supporting a heavy masonry projection. The shape of the bracket is a traditional medieval design, but the decoration has given it a classical character.

Scrolled brackets have often been used as keystones since their first adaptation for this purpose in Roman triumphal arches. These first scrolled keystones were contorted to carry figures and to fit into the deep mouldings of the arch (see page 227). Later examples are often more simple. A conventional scroll can sit neatly below an entablature and the archivolt mouldings of an arch (d) and can be decorated on the outer face. If the keystone is to be recessed further into the archivolt the sides of the scrolls can be omitted and the decoration limited to the front face (e). Scale decoration has become a traditional addition to scrolled keystones.

The decorative foliage of the scrolled bracket is traditionally stylized acanthus. This can be varied to suit a particular decorative theme. Example (f) is a Roman bracket with acorns and oak leaves sprouting within the usual acanthus leaf on the outer face. Another Roman bracket, from Palmyra in Syria (g), incorporates the head of a lion.

This combination of plant and animal forms is a peculiarity of classical decoration. The addition of an animal's foot or paw to a scroll (h), to form a table leg or other support, was common in antiquity and was enthusiastically revived and expanded to include symbolic representations of the human figure (i) by Mannerist architects. The Baroque use of the bracket as a side-support for frames to openings such as windows and fireplaces, shown here (j) with carved tassels, led by a simple step to scrolls that grew out of and became a part of the frames themselves (k). A similar transformation led to the combination of scrolls and columns, usually joined together as ambiguous pilasters on either side of an opening, (l) and (m). The Baroque Ionic scrolled pilaster (m) includes a drapery festoon.

a

b

c

d

e

f

g

h i j k l m

# SCROLLED BRACKETS SIMPLIFIED

Scrolled brackets are a unique concentration of formalized architectural decor-ation. They combine scrolls similar to the volute of the Ionic capital with a complex enriched profile and the acanthus of the Corinthian order. As a decorative feature they can be heavy with architectural ornament and a display of the sculptor's art. It is not, however, always appropriate or economic to include this wealth of decoration in an architectural scheme. In common with most aspects of classical design, the specific form of the fully developed feature and the established tradition of the architectural element make it possible to reduce the quantity and scale of the detail while maintaining the identity of the element. The scrolled bracket is one of the most widespread and individual classical architectural features and a series of levels of reduction in detail has evolved.

As the modillion, the scrolled bracket is included in the upper part of the Corinthian cornice. If the Corinthian order is relatively small it is not possible to include the full range of decoration. Examples (b), (i) and (j) are from Corinthian cornices although any appropriate reduction of detail could be applied to a suitably proportioned modillion.

The scrolls themselves can have the narrow ribs that define their edges omitted and the whole body of the scroll can curl inwards. The scroll is then defined either by a groove or by the outward projection of the scroll as it coils to the centre. Examples (a), (e), (f) and (g) have scrolls defined by grooves, while (b) and (h) rely on the projection that can be seen on either side of the face.

The detail on the face of the bracket is subject to a similar process of simplification. The central bead seen on (a) and (b) can be omitted to give a continuous curved profile across the face as on (d) and (h). The face can also be flat and have simple flutes cut into it (g) or be left without any profile or decoration, (f), (i) and (j).

As the complexity of the profiles diminishes, so the leaf decoration simplifies until it disappears. The acanthus on the face of the bracket at first loses some (a) then all (b) of its detail and finally is omitted altogether. The characteristic sprouting buds that emerge from the larger scroll are either omitted or reduced to an outline (c). Fully carved isolated leaves can also be reintroduced to give added richness to an otherwise severely simplified bracket. This technique, a particular aspect of classical decoration, allows detail to be introduced economically to suggest the full decoration of the element. The lower acanthus leaf alone is fully carved on (c) and the sprouting buds in the scrolls on (f) and (h) contrast not only with the omission of detail but also with a simplification of form.

Finally the form itself can be simplified. The substitution of the smaller scroll with a rectangular detail, (f), (g) and (j), and the reduction of the bracket to no more than its profile are common. The total omission of the lower scroll (h) is unusual.

232

*a*

*b*

*c*

*d*

*e*

*f*

*g*

*h*

*i*

*j*

# Setting Out A Scrolled Bracket

The scrolled bracket can be set out in a number of different ways to produce varied shapes and one method is illustrated here. The technique for forming the scrolls is similar to that used for the Ionic capital and is an alternative to the system shown on page 87.

The height of the bracket, excluding any adjacent mouldings, is taken as eight units of measurement and the length as twenty-one. To set out the large scroll (a) take two diagonals from the outside corners and at their intersection, away from the corners and from the start of the scroll, form a square with diagonals equal to one unit. These diagonals are the circumference of the eye of the rosette. Inside this square, form another square touching the centres of the sides of the first square and, inside this square, form another in the same way. Extend the sides of the second square outwards in the order shown and, setting the compass on point 1, form an arc from the outside of the scroll, 1a, to 2a. Then set the compass at point 2 and from 2a form an arc to 3a and so on to 4a. Continue the process from point 1b (the position determined in the following paragraph) with points where the inner square cuts the diagonals of the second square until the line disappears into a circular rosette three units in diameter. With the same method but units of half the size draw the small scroll (b). The rosette, at three and a half of the smaller units, will be proportionately larger, and the line will disappear sooner.

To connect the scrolls (d) drop a line vertically from the inside edge of the rosette of the small scroll to a point A one unit below the large scroll. Divide that unit into three and make a point B two thirds of a unit above point A. Extend point 1 in the large scroll vertically upwards to a point C two units above the scroll. Join points A and C and draw an arc centred on point C from the outside of the large scroll and another centred on point B from the inside of the small scroll to meet at line AC. Draw a further arc centred on point B from the outside of the small scroll to line AC and continue this line by drawing another arc centred on point C back to the large scroll. Where this arc ends on a vertical line the inner edge of the large open scroll starts. Using the same centres as the outer edge of this scroll, turn the inside line inwards from 1b onwards until it disappears into the rosette.

Acanthus leaves and other decorations may be added to fill the spaces at the outside of the scrolls and in the gap between the scrolls. A large leaf can curl out from below the large scroll to the centre of the small scroll. This leaf will partially cover the complex curves and central fillet of the outside face of the bracket (c).

Plain cut-out brackets, (e) and (f), based on the scrolled bracket, can be formed around simple curves.

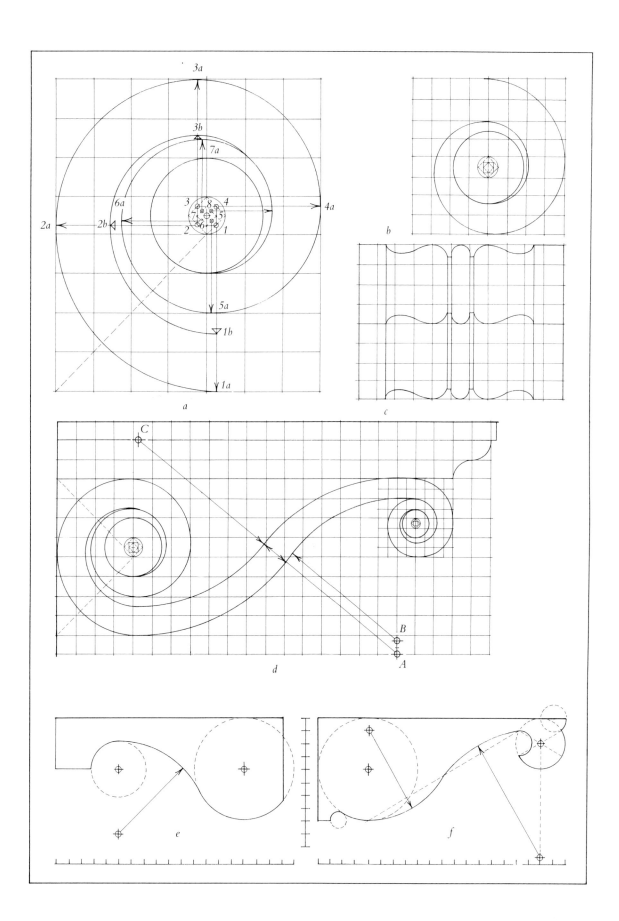

*a*

*b*

*c*

*d*

*e*

*f*

# 15. THE FIREPLACE

## ORIGINS

Although there is evidence of fireplaces from the northern Roman provinces, their incidence is rare. Most Roman buildings were heated with braziers brought into individual rooms or with hypocaust floors which drew the heat and fumes from fires through hollow floors and up flues in the walls. The fireplace as we know it is a medieval invention.

Medieval fireplaces were first built in the eleventh and twelfth centuries to replace the traditional and troublesome open hearth in the centre of the great hall. To make the fireplace, the open hearth was moved to the side of the room and a tall hood was built over it to carry the smoke to the outside. Often restricted to private rooms, these fires were luxuries, and the massive walls of aristocratic houses and castles were needed to contain the chimneys. A thirteenth-century fireplace at Abingdon Abbey in England (a) shows a typical arrangement found throughout Europe. The details are clearly derived from the architecture of the period. Two columns support brackets carrying a beam below an overhanging hood which tapers upwards to a chimney in the wall behind.

Early Renaissance fireplaces merely added classical detail to the established design. The fifteenth-century fireplace from the Doges' Palace in Venice (b) repeats the medieval pattern exactly. The columns have become distinctive classical balusters with scrolled brackets carrying a beam, decorated as a deep classical entablature, which supports an overhanging hood. The standard of decoration is very fine, reflecting the continuing high status of fireplaces.

By the sixteenth century, Italian architects had realized the creative potential of the fireplace and of the projecting chimney-breast that replaced the hood. Fireplaces now became huge architectural compositions, often dominating the room, (c) and (d). The openings could be designed according to the same principles as doors, with columns or architraves carrying entablatures or pediments. Unlike doors, the entablature was often carried on long brackets which retained the impression of the medieval projecting hood.

As the use of the fireplace became more widespread in the eighteenth century and they were introduced to almost every room, this kind of extravagance could not be justified. Designs came to be more restrained, (e) and (f), and, particularly in smaller rooms, less massive. In countries such as England, the replacement of wood with coal was a further reason for a reduction in size. The principles of fireplace design established in the previous centuries none the less remained, and the application of unusual and lavish detail continued.

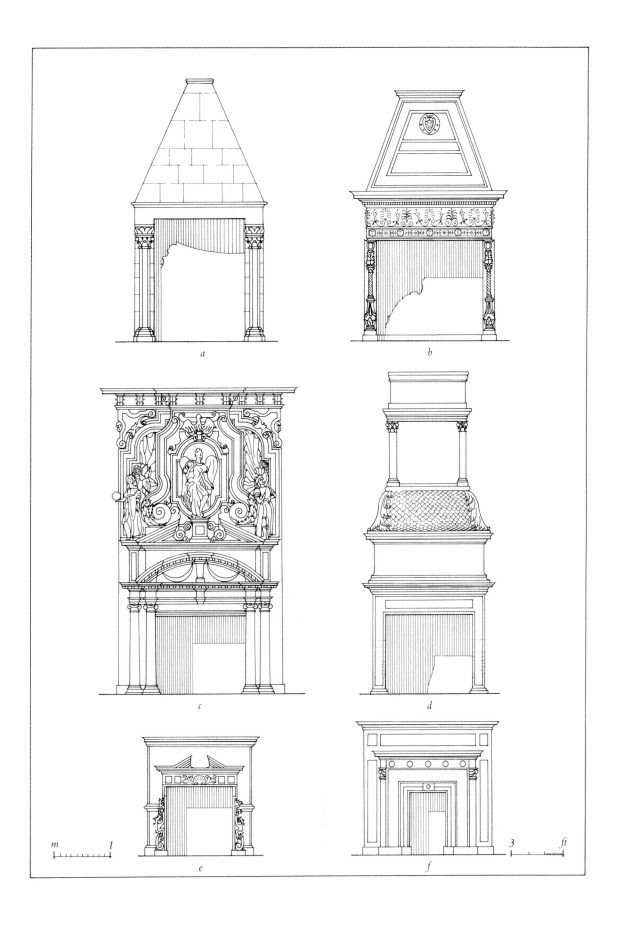

# FIREPLACES AND THE ORDERS

The design of fireplaces with the orders follows many of the same principles as the design of doors. The function is quite different, but when the only source of heat in a room was the open fire it was natural for the fireplace to become the focal point of the interior in the same way as a door is a principal feature on a façade. Fireplace designs reflect this significance and are often original and highly detailed when located in important rooms. This tradition has given the fireplace a prominence that goes beyond its function. Although the recent development of heating from a central source has made the fireplace unnecessary, the use of fireplaces has nevertheless continued but is generally limited to the principal rooms in houses to retain the aesthetic effect of a natural fire and to give a focus to a room.

One aspect of the inventive character of many fireplace designs has been the imaginative expression of the character of the orders. The Italian architect Serlio published a series of fireplace designs representing the orders in his *Five Books of Architecture* in 1547. One of the Doric fireplaces (a), while apparently a simple pair of columns and entablature, is supported on scrolls on lion's feet with the face of the scroll cut to represent the details of a Doric column. One of his Ionic fireplaces (c) has female busts on lion's feet in place of columns, to represent the legendary female origin of the Ionic order.

The orders can be represented more conventionally and the following examples are all English from the eighteenth century. A plain Doric design (b) has a simplified but regularly proportioned entablature which breaks forward over the columns and in the centre to give some variety. The entablature on the Ionic fireplace (d) also breaks forward over the columns, but the architrave has been omitted altogether, giving a larger space for decoration. A further moulding has been added below in line with the column capitals. The central panel that features on both of these designs becomes the dominant element in the Corinthian fireplace (e). The entablature also breaks forward over the columns, but the proportions have been retained by limiting the architrave and frieze to blocks over the columns. The orders can be represented without columns, but the ambiguities of cornice details can cause some confusion. The Corinthian design (g) can be identified by the modillions in the cornice, which is supported on further scrolled brackets. The frieze is filled with a rich acanthus pattern and the architrave has been reduced to a small moulding.

In the sixteenth and seventeenth centuries, fireplaces were frequently designed to the full height of the room and in two (f) or even three levels. This type of design became less frequent in later centuries but never died out altogether. It was revived as a part of the nineteenth-century interest in the early Renaissance. When the designs are of several stages the orders can be placed in their conventional sequence one above the other.

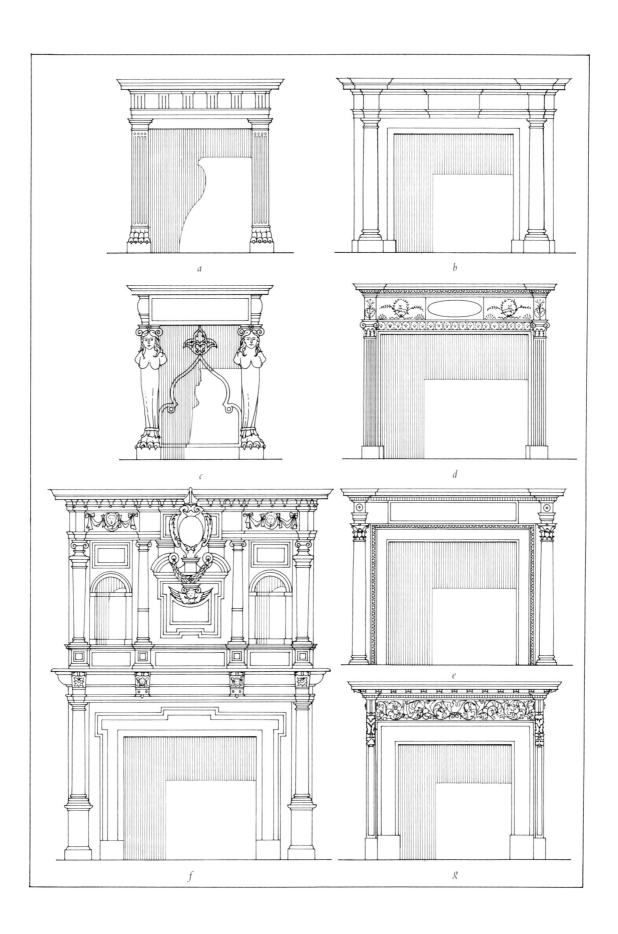

*a*

*b*

*c*

*d*

*e*

*f*

*g*

# THE FIREPLACE:
## VARIATIONS AND INVENTIONS

The fireplace can be no more than a simple architrave and play only a minor contributory role in the interior. It is, however, often the major architectural feature in a room, and is designed accordingly.

The late Baroque design (a), published in England by Batty Langley in his *Treasury of Designs* of 1740, is very simple, but is given some distinction by the double-curved cornice, the medallion relief portrait and swags. The Rococo fireplace (b) is also English, from about 1750, but is a universal type. The sides are canted outwards at an angle and in this case are decorated with elongated scrolls enriched with vine leaves and grapes. The cornice which forms the shelf is reduced to one narrow moulding which also cants at the sides and is supported on further fanciful scrolls. The decoration meets at the centre in an asymmetrical swirl. This form of fireplace, which could have more restrained decoration or a matching frame for a mirror or picture above, was very popular.

Scrolled brackets have always been a popular feature for fireplaces. Brackets can provide support for the cornice in the same way as a door-surround or be added as solely decorative devices. The large brackets on the side of the fireplace (c) are the only sculptural feature on the design. Their position set back from the opening indicates their decorative role by separating them from the self-contained central part of the fireplace. In example (d), two pairs of scrolled brackets are fitted around the ears and sides of a simple architrave. Thin brackets decorate the sides while short brackets above hold up a notional cornice and create a large frieze panel.

Scrolls also appear on a double-height English fireplace (f) designed by Colin Campbell in the early eighteenth century. They are not, however, the most significant elements in the design. The height of the two levels from the notional column base to the cornice is the same, but the total omission of the frieze and architrave and the addition of a pediment to the cornice make the upper frame dominate the composition. Although it is not immediately apparent, the scrolls above the upper pilasters probably indicate that this design is based on an Ionic order over a Doric order.

The late-eighteenth-century fireplace (e) and the nineteenth-century fireplace (g) are of contrasting proportions. The earlier design (e) has slender, square, panelled pilasters without capitals, which carry a full entablature. With the exception of the cornice mouldings, all the decorative reliefs are applied, making this a popular and inexpensive fireplace to manufacture. The later design (g), by C. R. Cockerell in 1824, is an early example of a widespread nineteenth-century pattern. Wide flat piers give the appearance of columns with the projecting sections of the cornice acting as capitals. These piers frame smaller inner columns which support a frieze panel and the same cornice with a more conventional proportional relationship.

a

b

c

d

e

f

g

# FIREPLACES AND SCULPTURE

The rich detail that is often incorporated in fireplace designs can include figurative sculpture. The importance of many fireplaces makes them particularly suitable for the display of sculpture. In common with other aspects of interior design, fireplaces often include expressive and unconventional details that are not found on the more public face of the same building.

A double-height fireplace (a) of the early seventeenth century, published by the French architect Pierre Collot, uses the opening and its surround as a base for a display of full-length figures that dominates the composition. No orders are directly identifiable although there appears to be some reference to an ascending sequence. The fire-surround is supported by two scrolls with bearded male heads immediately below a plain Tuscan or Doric cornice and the taller upper level contains female figures below a cornice that could be Corinthian. Another French fireplace design (b), published some twenty-five years later by Jean Le Pautre, has no recognizable association with an order. The surround to the opening is insignificant and two flanking brackets are virtually hidden behind the ends of oak-leaf swags. The fireplace is no more than a plinth for the two draped figures and the flaming urn.

An English fireplace (c) from the previous century has a more conventional arrangement on two levels, but the incomplete transmission of classical detail by way of Holland has given the design a characteristic individuality. Figurative sculpture is contained within Dutch Mannerist columnar figures, or herms, and has been executed with a naïve vigour. The lower order is intended to be Doric and the scrolls above the upper figures indicate an Ionic upper order. There is, however, no association between the figures and the orders and at both levels male and female sculptures alternate. The two upper panels contain small false perspectives.

The use of herms as supports has remained a popular theme for sculptural fireplaces. An early-eighteenth-century English design (d) has two bearded herms, probably representing philosophers, on each side of a relief panel with a scene from Aesop's fables. The relationship between the cornice and the architrave is conventional and places the heads precisely in the frieze, but the cornice has a Tuscan simplicity while the architrave is Ionic or Corinthian. Full figures, or caryatids, are also frequently used as supports and the eighteenth-century French fireplace (e) has a full entablature carried on two elegant, female, half-goat and half-human fauns.

In the nineteenth century the almost universal convention of rectangular openings for fireplaces was changed and fully arched openings became common. An early example (f) from 1818 includes relief sculpture of two figures of Victory, clearly derived from Roman triumphal arches. The other details are heavily simplified; the Corinthian columns have been stripped of their leaves and there is no reference to an entablature except for the suggestion of a cornice moulding.

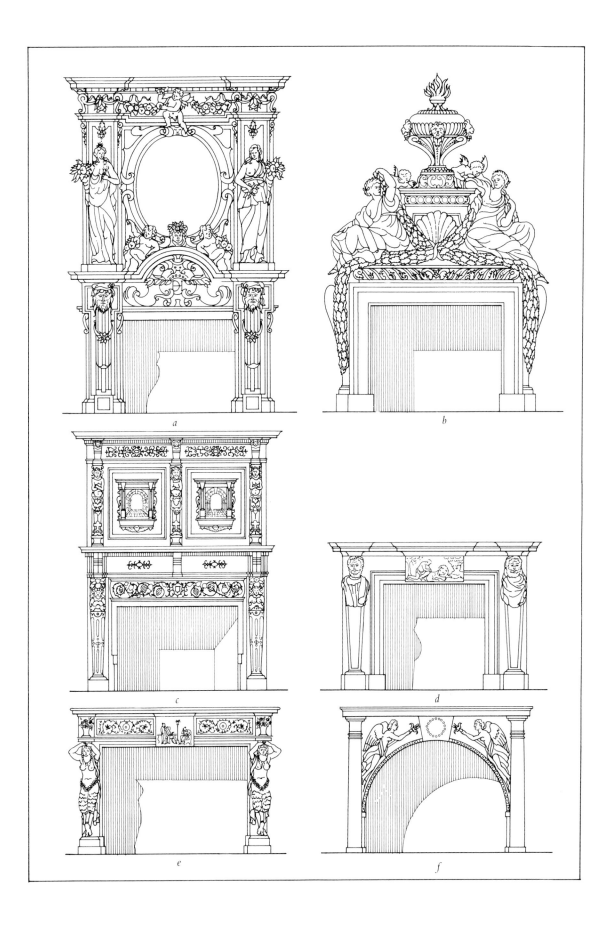

*a*

*b*

*c*

*d*

*e*

*f*

# A Doric Fireplace

To demonstrate the application of the orders to fireplaces a simple Doric design is illustrated. This shows a conventional use of the orders, although previous examples will have demonstrated that there are a bewildering number of ways of applying classical details to fireplaces.

It has been assumed that the design is for a relatively small fire-opening and the details of the order have been adapted accordingly. Mutules have been omitted from the cornice as the low level of the shelf would reduce their impact and the small size of the mouldings could make them insignificant. One alternative (b) includes triglyphs, but the other (a) omits them and has a plain or decorated rosette in the frieze above the column. The level of decoration can be increased if the fireplace is larger or a more intricate design is required. The appropriate forms are shown in the illustrations of the Doric order on pages 73 and 75.

One of the traditions of fireplace design with the orders places the details of the order around an independent frame surrounding the fire-opening. The shape of the frame is shown as a square although it could be of different proportions. The frame itself is shown as a stone surround with an ovolo outer moulding. The other parts of the fireplace could be of any suitable material, but that part immediately adjacent to the opening should be of stone or another fire-resistant material.

The height of the opening and its frame is divided into eight and a half parts to give the module. As the column base would be relatively small it is raised on a small pedestal of half a module to allow for a skirting, or baseboard, of a satisfactory height. This pedestal could be varied, but the column, shown without entasis and as a pilaster, is eight modules high. The remaining proportions follow from this division of the height, but if the width varies and triglyphs are used then the dimension will have to be calculated to fit their spacing.

To allow the projecting mouldings of the pilaster to stand free of the frame around the opening they are spaced half a module away. As the orders can appear thin at this small size it is possible to repeat this spacing on the outside to form a broad pier behind a projecting pilaster, (a) and (d). The projecting pilaster can, as shown, stand forward to provide additional support to the shelf created by the cornice. If this cornice is not to break forward then the pilaster projection should be limited to half a module and this can be seen on the upward view of the underside of the cornice (e), and the section (c).

The pilaster itself is shown as square and with a plain (b) and a panelled face, (a) and (d). The column could be half-round and have fluting and entasis. The frieze in the example without triglyphs (a) could be decorated in many different ways and the triglyphs (b) could have rosettes or other suitable decoration between them.

a

b

c

d

e

# A Corinthian Fireplace

When the orders are applied to a small fire-opening, the low height in comparison with the width required for a fire produces columns that can appear excessively slender. The proportions of Doric and Tuscan columns can be sufficiently wide to overcome this problem, but many fireplaces of the past have relied on double columns, additional piers or orders with severely modified proportions to balance the sides with detail above. In the same manner as a door, the architrave can be the principal frame and the other details of the entablature can be added above. This would produce even more slender sides for the fireplace but, when the columns are omitted, variations to the proportions of the order can be more satisfactorily accommodated. This method of applying the orders to the fireplace has been used frequently in the past and is illustrated here with the Corinthian order.

A small fireplace with a square opening has been assumed although these proportions can be varied. This type of fireplace, unlike the example on the previous page, applies the details of the order directly to the sides of the opening. The architrave, consequently, directly abuts the sides of the fire. If the fireplace is of stone or a fire-resistant material this presents no problems, but if the fireplace is of an inflammable material the architrave will need to be fire-resistant. The architrave with all its details, (b) and (e), can be created in fire-resistant material or can be simplified (a) to allow for simple slabs of stone.

This example has taken the height of the opening and divided it by five to arrive at a module for the details. This is one half of the conventional proportions of the order. A division of up to one third of the column height has often been used to increase the size of the details, particularly if the architrave alone is to be the fireplace and the rest of the entablature is to be omitted. If simple stone slabs are used for the architrave, its proportions are often increased relative to the frieze and cornice.

The architrave is shown with only two divisions, due to the assumed small size of the fireplace. These could be increased to the more usual three and decorated to provide more detail. Ears are shown with a stone slab architrave (a) but these could be added to a conventional architrave or increased in size. The frieze can be quite plain or decorated (a) and central tablets (b) are often included on fireplaces and either left plain or decorated.

The cornice includes dentils and modillions and the ovolo between them could have egg and dart mouldings added. The modillions are of a simple type but could be to any appropriate degree of detail. A method of setting them up is shown (d) at twice the size of the view of the underside of the cornice (c) which shows their spacing. Cornices are often simplified to a degree that obscures the identity of the order, but for the purposes of illustrating a Corinthian fireplace no such reduction is shown (e).

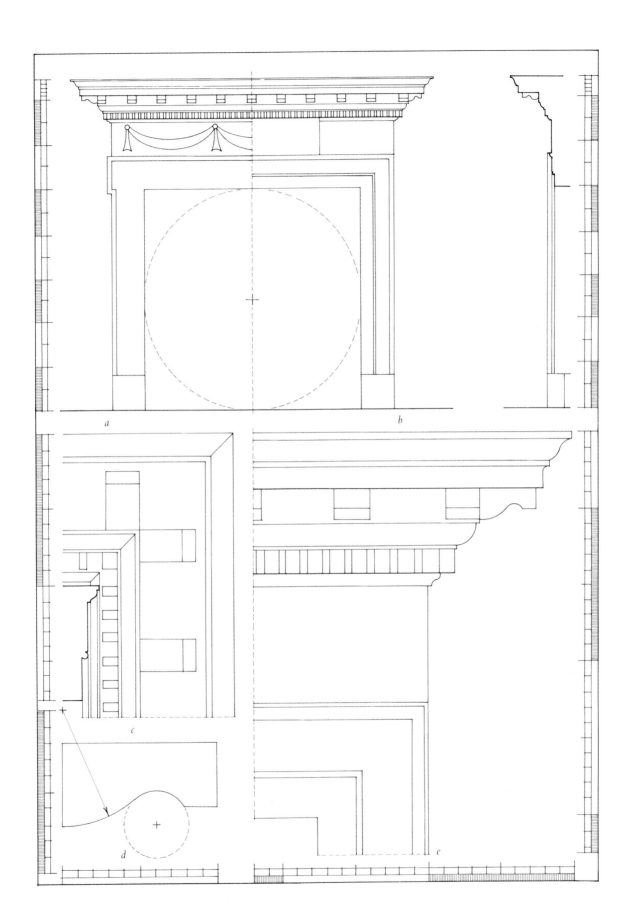

*a*

*b*

*c*

*d*

*e*

# 16. BALUSTRADES AND RAILINGS

## ANTIQUITY AND THE RENAISSANCE

In antiquity, balconies and parapets on the edge of high-level walkways or openings were either plain walls or fences. Where these ran between columns, they were constructed as independent barriers directly abutting the sides of the columns, (a) and (b). These fences were often of a lattice construction and called transennae. They could be reproduced in stone (a) or be more elaborately designed in bronze (c). There are many illustrations of railings in Roman paintings, but as they were probably made of wood or bronze they have not survived. Plain balcony walls could be decorated with relief sculpture (b).

In the Middle Ages a specific range of designs for balconies evolved which were open and gave some impression of transparency. Two distinct types developed which can both be seen in Venice, where balconies were a feature of buildings which overlooked the canals. One was a railing of small columns (e), either plain or with arches below the handrail, and the other was a wall with pierced Gothic patterns (f).

In the early Renaissance these Gothic designs were modified to incorporate classical details. Rows of miniature orders were designed to form rails (i) and Gothic tracery on pierced screens was replaced by classical motifs (j) pierced where the low points of a relief would have occurred.

At the same time a new form of railing, now known as balustrading, was invented. The form seems to have been suggested to Renaissance architects by the remains of large Roman ceremonial candlesticks (g), a number of which have survived.

The earliest Renaissance balustrading (h) has two swellings in the centre which meet at an astragal or scotia moulding. There is evidence of Roman decorative columns of this form although it is a relatively rare type of candlestick; illustration (d) is from a Roman relief. A later form (k), said to have been first used in the early sixteenth century, is clearly derived from a common type of Roman candlestick (g), a number of which are in the Pope's collection in Rome. Both these new forms of balustrade were combined with column pedestals acting as intermediate piers and, since their invention, these have become an essential element in the classical pattern.

a

b

c

d          e          f          g

h          i          j          k

# SETTING OUT BALUSTERS

---

The two types of Renaissance baluster are small columns with their characteristic bulges replacing the entasis. Their proportion, spacing and details can vary considerably and, although individual authors have suggested particular types for each order, no universally accepted link between the detail and proportion of the baluster and different orders has been established. Balusters commonly sit between piers which are, or are identical to, the pedestals of the orders. The height of the balusters is, consequently, given by the dado of the relevant order and, generally, the more detailed and slender the order the more detailed and slender the baluster. All balusters can be round as well as square, but square balusters give the appearance of greater bulk.

An example of each type of baluster of average detail and proportion is illustrated, derived from standard eighteenth-century examples.

The double baluster (a) has the given height divided into ten units of measurement and each baluster will be two units wide and spaced one unit apart. There will be a half-baluster against the dado. The top and bottom units will give the dimensions of the blocks at the capital and base, which will be square in plan. The two units above and below the centre will give the diameter of the spheres which act as the larger part of each swelling. One unit located centrally on the baluster gives the shaft, or minimum width of the baluster. The spheres at the centre are joined to the shaft with an arc centred two units out from the centre and two and a half units up or down. The intersection of the two spheres is masked by a symmetrical scotia one quarter of a unit in diameter and joined to the swelling with square fillets. The capital and base above and below the blocks approximate to a Doric capital and an Attic base. Each is one unit high and set out on one-third divisions of a unit.

This baluster can be based on broader and more slender proportions of twelve units high or more, and the detail around the central scotia in particular can be expanded with a central astragal or decoration. The principles of the spacing and setting out will, however, remain essentially the same.

The single baluster (b) has the given height divided into eight units. The horizontal setting out, shaft width, capital and top and bottom blocks will be the same as for the double baluster. The swelling is made by a sphere centred three units above the base and this is joined to the shaft with a radius centred three units down on the centre line of the adjacent baluster. The Attic base has a torus and scotia one third and two thirds of a unit high respectively. The upper torus and its fillets are one third of a unit high.

This baluster can also have broader or narrower proportions. Extra height is often given by increasing the height of the base or giving the baluster its own pedestal.

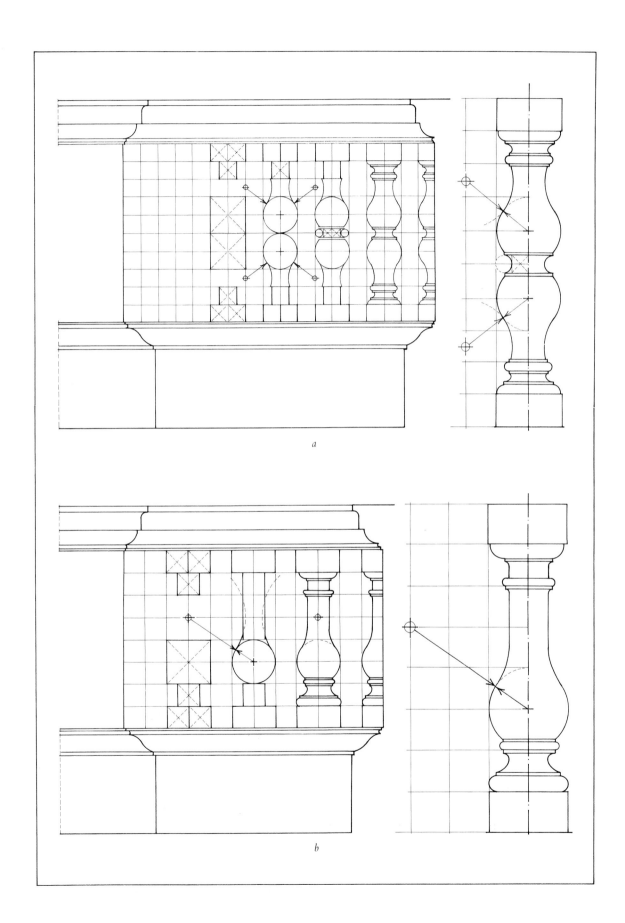

a

b

# BALUSTER VARIATIONS

Since the introduction of balusters there has been a considerable variety in design. It was not until the eighteenth century that the tradition had become sufficiently well established for authors to publish standard versions, but before long an archaeological interest in antiquity had revealed the modernity of the baluster and the revival of Renaissance and Baroque architecture stimulated more inventive designs.

Although Renaissance balusters differ in detail, the general form is consistent, (a) to (i). The double baluster, (a), (b) and (c), has only minor variations in proportion and in the degree of decoration where the two parts of the baluster meet. Although the double baluster is an earlier form, it is often combined on different parts of the same building with the single baluster. Examples (c) and (i) are both by Bramante and from the same building in the Vatican in Rome. Equally, different single balusters were used on different parts of the same building – examples (d) and (h) are both on the Villa at Caprarola near Rome by Vignola. The proportions of these balusters differ, but the major variations are the details at the capital and, in particular, the base. Balusters from the Villa Giulia in Rome (e) by Vignola have no capital, while there is more detail on both the base and capital on balusters from the Palazzo Lante (f) by Peruzzi and the Palazzo Farnese (g) by the younger Sangallo, also in Rome.

This consistency of form was interrupted in the Baroque period; the balusters on Blenheim Palace in England (j), by Vanbrugh in 1705, have the even curve of the swelling exaggerated and broken. This Baroque type became an established variant and is found on nineteenth-century (k) and twentieth-century (l) buildings. In the same period, balusters were introduced that reversed the direction of the swelling. The complex examples from Longhena's S. Maria della Salute in Venice (m) of 1630 are square in plan. This reversed form, like the broken variant, was revived in the nineteenth century (n). Other fantastic versions belong to Baroque and nineteenth-century buildings. The square rusticated balusters from the early-eighteenth-century Palazzo Pesaro in Venice (r) have an alternating taper which makes their relationship to double and single balusters ambiguous. The relationship between the baluster and the column of the relevant order, on the other hand, is made more explicit in a nineteenth-century example (q) which makes a single baluster specifically Ionic.

The Renaissance origin of balusters created a problem for neo-classical architects. The use of balusters had become so well established that they could not be abandoned in spite of, what was regarded as, an impure modern pedigree. C. R. Cockerell adapted the baluster to a vase shape with a reverse swelling on the Ashmolean Museum in Oxford (o) in 1839. An earlier solution was to substitute a specific leaf form from antiquity for a baluster (p), while the use of small Greek Revival columns (s) and small arches (t) unwittingly came closer to Gothic examples. The most authentic neo-classical baluster (u) was a version of a transenna fence from antiquity.

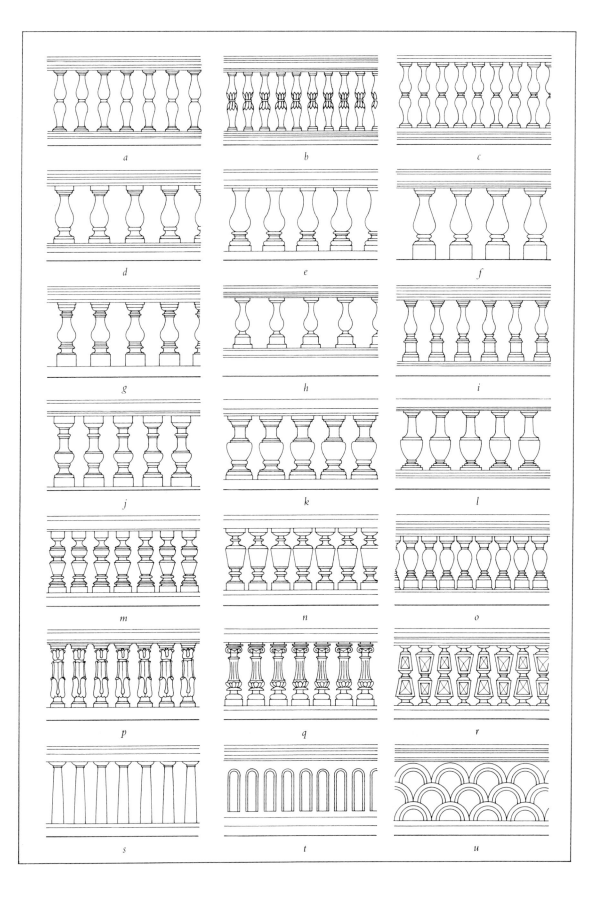

a

b

c

d

e

f

g

h

i

j

k

l

m

n

o

p

q

r

s

t

u

# PIERCED WALLS

While the baluster became the normal method of forming a parapet in Italian architecture of the fifteenth and sixteenth centuries, and in countries under Italian influence, north European architects developed the tradition of parapets formed by pierced screens.

Although French Renaissance architecture began with direct contact with Italy, it retained an individual national identity. One of the most influential native classical architects was Philibert de l'Orme. His few surviving works include a number of pierced screen parapet designs. An example from the gatehouse at Anet (a) of 1547 is made up from an interlacing series of classical scrolls which remain individually recognizable. Similar designs, but with a less obvious classical derivation (b), continued to be produced in France into the following century.

In the Protestant north, much of the spread of classical architecture was through publications from the Low Countries where Italian Mannerist books had been reinterpreted to create a fanciful architectural decorative theme known as strapwork, due to its apparent similarity to cut leather. The reliance on silhouette in pierced screen parapets made them particularly well suited to strapwork decoration and free designs on the skyline of buildings, such as on the sixteenth-century castle at Baden-Baden in Germany (c), are characteristic of northern architecture of this period. Similar parapets can also be found in Spain (d) in the seventeenth century, perhaps through a political association with the Low Countries. These designs were revived in the nineteenth century in Britain (l).

The tradition of the pierced screen continued in Britain in the sixteenth century. Rich naturalistic designs of the national Baroque style, (e) and (f), were executed on intricate internal balconies and stairs by woodcarvers whose skills have seldom been surpassed.

Later developments in Baroque architecture in the eighteenth century included variants of the baluster and other forms of parapet. In middle Europe, Baroque stairs were designed with relatively sober screen walls, cut with a form of the traditional guilloche interlacing pattern (g) or, by contrast, with a dramatic swirl of sculpted stonework, such as the screen in the Daun Palace in Vienna (h), by Lukas von Hildebrandt in 1713. In Italy, the home of the baluster, Baroque (i) and Rococo (j) pierced screens were also introduced.

The realization by neo-classical architects that screen walls and fences were the only form of protective railing in the ancient world led to renewed but more restrained interest in pierced screens and a number of designs, such as Gottfried Semper's stair for the Winterthur Town Hall in Switzerland (k) of 1863, were loosely based on examples from antiquity.

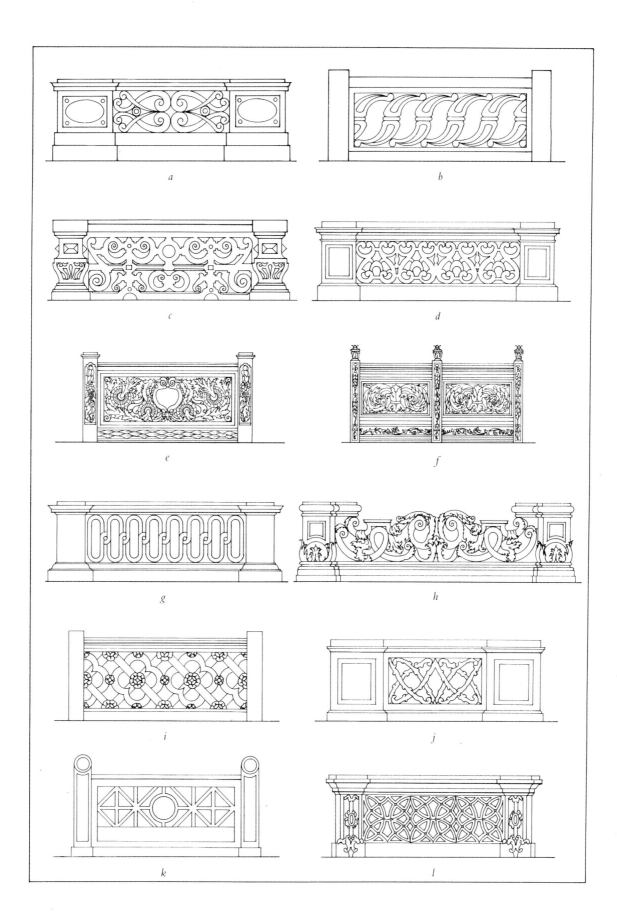

a

b

c

d

e

f

g

h

i

j

k

l

# Stair Rails

Stair rails are a form of baluster which, together with the handrail and the edge of the stair, has been adapted to suit the lightweight construction and appearance of most smaller-scale internal stairs. The principal adaptation has been a reduction in width to form a narrow rail often turned out of timber. The other details have been similarly modified.

Early timber stairs were proportioned and detailed to approximate to a sloping stone balustrade (a). The treads were concealed behind a large timber board, or string, acting as the base of the pedestal, and heavy square posts, or newels, acted as full pedestals at each end of a flight. The handrail was also large and took the form of the pedestal cornice. In the eighteenth century in Britain another type of stair (b) came into use, derived from a traditional arrangement of solid stone steps. The closed string was omitted and the ends of the treads were exposed. To ease the construction of this design in timber, decorative brackets often concealed the overlap of the treads. At the same time the rails and handrail became narrower, while the newel-posts became enlarged rails rather than piers, generally taking the form of small Doric columns. Closed-string stairs became less common, although the heavy early designs were revived in the nineteenth century.

From the sixteenth to the eighteenth century the general tendency was for stair rails to become progressively more slender. Examples (c), (d) and (e) are all from the seventeenth century and (f) is from the late sixteenth century. Their proportions are similar to stone balusters, but they are turned out of wood and follow precisely the pattern of the two types of baluster. Example (h) is also from the late seventeenth century and has a baluster form but is too slender for stone. Example (g) from the first years of the eighteenth century is similar but has a more intricate Baroque character. As rails became narrower in the later eighteenth century, (i) and (j), the two baluster forms became more difficult to represent.

In the early eighteenth century a new type of rail came into use, probably as a response to the fashion for greater slenderness. This new rail, (k) to (r), had a Doric column located over a small baluster. This allowed more slender proportions but avoided the contortion that would have made the baluster form virtually unrecognizable. At first the column itself, as in example (k) from 1709, was of conventional proportions, but as the rail became more slender the column was reduced in width. There were Baroque variations such as example (l) from 1720 where the column has a reverse taper and the column and baluster are also reversed. The columns can be fluted, (n), or twisted, as in (o) and (p); the baluster can be elaborate, (m) to (p), or simple, as in (q) and (r). Generally, as the eighteenth century progressed, the detail and baluster width was reduced until, as with (r), the rail was as thin as the timber would allow without becoming dangerously brittle.

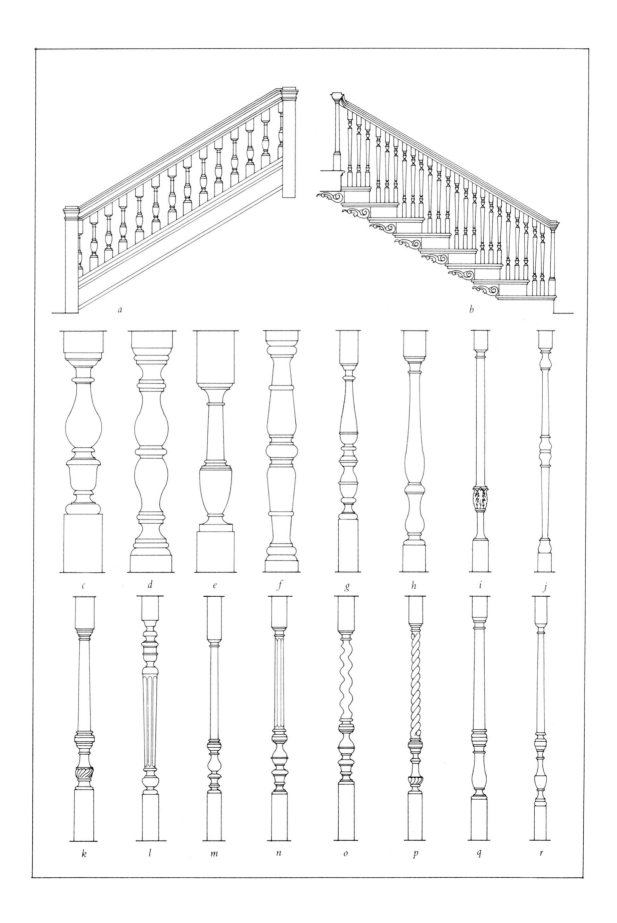

a

b

c

d

e

f

g

h

i

j

k

l

m

n

o

p

q

r

# METAL RAILS AND SCREENS

From the Renaissance to the nineteenth century, metal rails and screens have generally been of wrought or cast iron. In antiquity they were often bronze. Steel was used from the nineteenth century and in the twentieth century a number of different metals and alloys have been used. The patterns illustrated are all either wrought or cast iron, but the designs mostly derive from wrought iron. Cast iron in the late eighteenth and nineteenth century was often a mass-produced reproduction of hand-worked and higher status wrought iron. Neither material is used frequently today although steel can be hand-forged in the same way as wrought iron.

There are endless different railing designs that can be created in metal. The material can take on seemingly limitless shapes when heated and beaten, or melted down and poured into moulds. The only significant limitation to the use of metals has been the rusting of steel and the weight of most metals. Both of these problems can be overcome with the lightweight metals and rust-resistant alloys and coatings now available.

The strength and the weight of the metals traditionally used for rails has made many of the designs fine and slender, in keeping with the general tendency towards narrower rails and balusters, (b), (c), (d), (f) and (g), in the late eighteenth and early nineteenth century. The process of bending and shaping hot wrought iron by hand from thin rectangular lengths of the material has established a tradition of designs made up of curves, spirals and small flat leaf forms, (i), (j), (k) and (l). Cast iron, while following this tradition, was more brittle, but the liquid process of moulding allowed more complex patterns, (o), (p), (q), (r) and (s), in the surface of the design.

Without the joints that limit the possibilities of timber construction, slender metal railings of complex design can be made of straight pieces, (c) and (d), which require no bending. With very little forging work, simple curved designs, (a), (b), (f) and (g), can be created economically. Rich Baroque rails and posts, (i), (k), (l) and (m), often with gilding on selected areas, require considerable skill in manufacture and the flexibility of the hot metal allows continuous designs to be produced which either link a repeated rail (i) or form long individual panels (k). Late-eighteenth-century patterns are often more sparse and include a number of motifs taken from antiquity, such as anthemions, (j) and (o), and lyres (h). Elaborate and costly metal rails or posts (e), which rely more on their sculptural qualities than the nature of the material, continued to be produced in wrought iron, but similar effects could be produced more economically in large numbers from moulds in cast iron, (n), (q) and (r).

There are numerous other designs, from simple round or square cast-iron railings with spear tops to elaborate wrought panels. These examples are limited in type, period and material but illustrate the British tradition which developed at a time when the nation's industrial wealth and iron manufacture were at their peak.

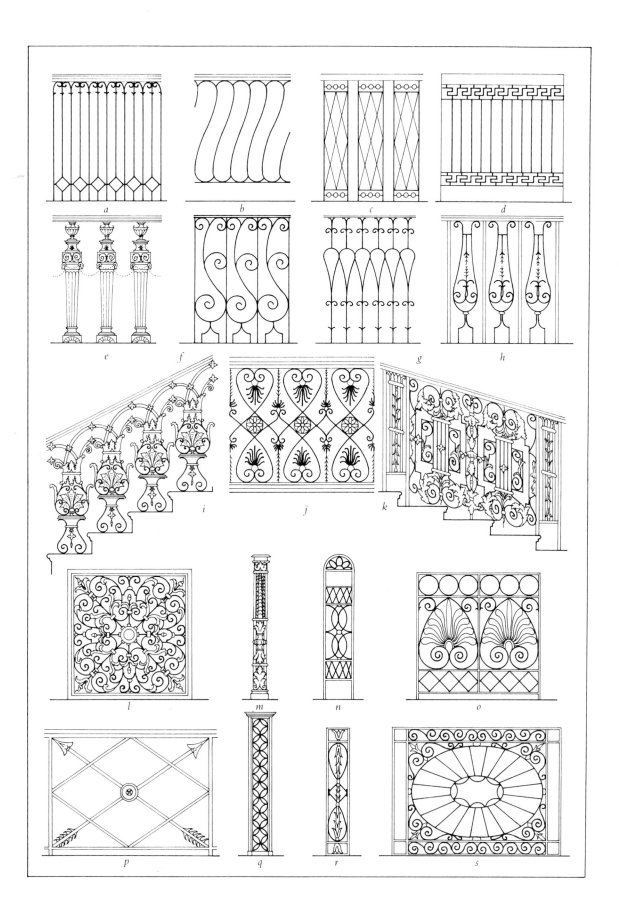

a

b

c

d

e

f

g

h

i

j

k

l

m

n

o

p

q

r

s

# TURNED RAILS

Two diameters of turned rail, which are applicable to different types of stair or balcony design, are illustrated here. Both designs could be square throughout their height rather than turned.

The proportions are taken from the height of the rail. To establish the maximum finished width of the wider rails divide the height by twelve, and for the narrower rails divide the height by twenty. Both types have a continuous central core one half of the maximum width and, particularly with the narrow examples, it is important to establish that the timber or other material used can take the necessary stresses at this diameter. In all cases the top and bottom blocks are left square and the lower block is higher. These blocks can have their projecting corners cut back to avoid later damage.

The base and capital of the double baluster (a) are each one unit high and set out on divisions of one third and one sixth of the unit. The two swellings are placed centrally between the capital and base and their intersection falls halfway across the relevant unit. The centres of the arcs that create the swellings are one unit up or down from this intersection and one unit out from the centre of the rail. The swellings return to the diameter of the core with curves centred eight units from the lower and upper extremity of the capital and base respectively.

The capital of the single baluster (d) is set out in the same way as (a). The base is two and a half units high and set out on divisions of one half and one quarter of the unit. The centre of the arc for the swelling is one unit up from the base and one and a half units out from the centre of the rail. The swelling returns to the core with a curve centred two units down from the capital and eight units out from the centre of the rail.

The capital and base of the narrow baluster rail (b) are each one unit high and set out on divisions of one third and one sixth of a unit. Due to the limited width of the rail, the swelling is limited to two small double curves one and a half units high, each based on a sphere one unit in diameter. The remaining shafts taper out to the centre from the base and capital.

The narrow column-on-baluster rail (c) has the capital set out in the same way as (b). The small baluster is four units high and has a base and capital each one unit high. The centre of the arc for the swelling is one unit up from the base and out from the centre. The swelling returns to the capital with a curve centred halfway up the capital and nine units out from the centre of the rail. The small column base is one half of a unit high and its rectangular lower moulding is left square and unturned. The column tapers up to the core diameter at its capital.

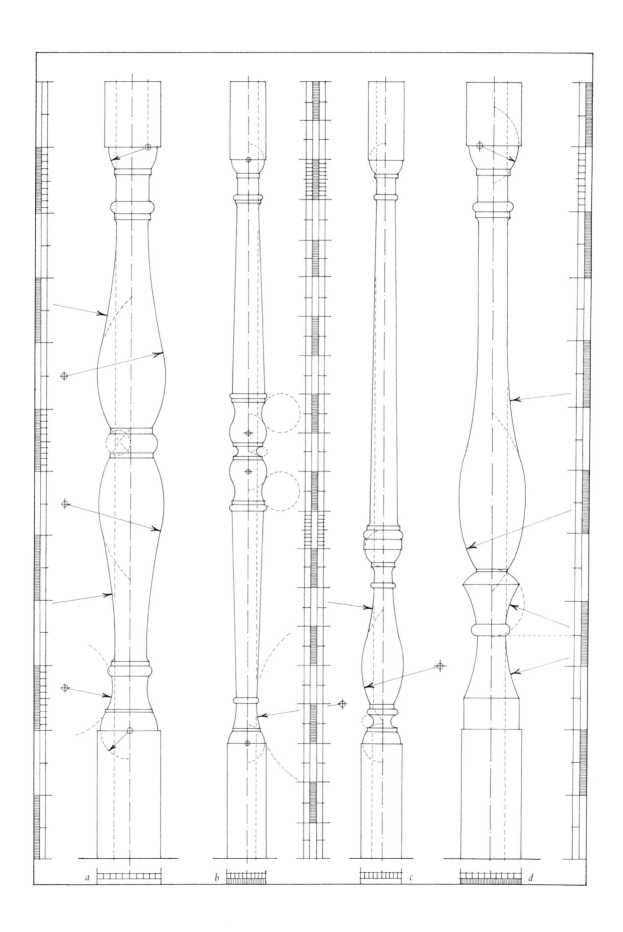

# 17. THE SKYLINE

## DESIGN FOR THE SKYLINE

In antiquity and in more recent centuries classical architects have used a number of features at roof level to accentuate buildings or parts of buildings.

The Greek temple roof had certain specific projecting features. The tiles along the ridge of the roof could have clay crests decorated with coloured leaf designs. On the pediment at the ridge and eaves, platforms were created, known as acroteria, that carried sculptural ornaments ranging from large statues of gods or mythological creatures to brightly coloured two-metre-wide discs or bronze tripods. The effect can be seen on a reconstruction of the Temple of Zeus at Olympia in Greece (a) of about 460 BC.

The design of Roman temples was influenced by the roof decorations of their ancestors, the Etruscans, which ranged from rows of horns along the pediment to groups of large clay figures along the ridge. Later Roman temples, such as the Temple of Antoninus and Faustina in the Forum in Rome (b) of AD 141, continued this tradition within the framework of the Greek temple.

Later Renaissance architects, like Jacopo Sansovino who placed obelisks and figures on the parapet of his prominent Library of St Mark in Venice (c) in 1536, were perhaps influenced by evidence of these features on ruins and coins and sculpture from antiquity.

It was, however, Baroque architects who exploited the skyline to the full. The dome, always a vertical feature, was stretched upwards by architects such as Borromini who, in the church of S. Ivo in Rome (d) of 1642, surmounted the building with a symbolic spiral ramp and open crown and placed flaming urns, balls and heraldic devices at descending levels. The English architect Vanbrugh used a series of golden balls, urns and figures to punctuate the profile of important elements, such as gates, on Blenheim Palace (e) in 1705. In London the loss of a series of Gothic spires in the Great Fire of 1666 brought about their replacement with a remarkable series of classical spires, such as St Bride's (f), designed by Wren, which made an inventive use of classical details to create powerful vertical landmarks.

The Baroque tradition was continued by architects like Garnier, who decorated each end of his Opéra in Paris (g) in 1861 with tall sculptural groups. Buildings such as these influenced the twentieth-century Baroque revival.

a

b

c

d

e

f

g

# BALLS, URNS AND PINE-CONES

The use of finials rather than sculptures as features on the roofs of buildings can be traced to antiquity through a few surviving buildings but, as such fragile ornaments rarely survive, principally through paintings and other representations. In the early Renaissance, balls and similar details were applied to the apex of pitched roofs and domes following Byzantine and Gothic practice, often as a base for a cross signifying God's rule over the world. In the late Renaissance, balls and urns became common additions to the roofs and parapets of buildings and have become, at both a large and small scale, one of the most familiar elements of classical decoration.

A large number of urns survived from antiquity and were admired and collected in the Renaissance. Examples (a) to (i) are from the Pope's collection in Rome. The quality of these vessels reflects their prestige in antiquity. Some of the finest surviving works of early Greek art are the pottery vases and urns that were mass produced not only for the domestic market but for export. Their use as containers for the ashes of the dead and consequent burial, together with the low value and durability of the raw material, are the principal reasons for their survival in large numbers. The higher status metal vessels have, however, more often been melted down as bullion. Examples (a) to (i) are all carved out of fine marble, which has ensured their survival, but the shape, detail and decoration often derives, as with pottery vases, from metal originals.

All of these shapes have been used on later classical buildings and at times have specific meaning. An urn, particularly if partially covered, can signify death. An urn with flames at the top (j) once represented charity, but in time the flames came to be no more than a standard decorative stopper. Urns the shape of (a), (c), (f) and (h) are often found on neo-classical buildings, while (j) and (k) are Baroque forms. The last example (l) is unusual and includes a block of rustication in the centre to relate to a rusticated building below. This detail is more common on balls.

The pine-cone stopper of (k) and (l) can grow to dominate the vase (p). The use of pine-cones on their own as finials (m) is a frequent classical decorative feature and derives from a famous large bronze pine-cone unearthed near the Pantheon in Rome in the Middle Ages and erroneously thought to be its finial.

The ball is the most common decorative finial, usually sitting on a base with a scotia moulding (o). This simple feature is subject to a surprising number of variations. Rusticated blocks are often added (n), the ball can be flattened to an oval, be supported on leaves (q) or issue forth flames (s) like an old-fashioned grenade. Different combinations of balls and scrolls can be made: example (t) is from the early eighteenth century and example (r) from the early twentieth century.

a       b       c       d

e       f       g       h

i       j       k       l

m       n       o       p

q       r       s       t

# FINIALS, OBELISKS AND TROPHIES

Special objects can be designed to act as features on the roofs and parapets of buildings. These finials at times derive from vases or candlesticks and sometimes are original creations. The most famous example from antiquity is on the roof of the Choragic Monument of Lysicrates in Athens (a) dating from the late fourth century BC. This elaborate composition acted as the base for the bronze tripod that the monument was designed to display. The early-sixteenth-century chapel of S. Giovanni in Oleo in Rome (b), attributed to Bramante, has a similarly complex leaf and ball design. From the same period are two candlestick finials, one from a tomb in Rome (c) by Andrea Sansovino, and another from Santiago de Compostela in Spain (h). The plain column and ball (k) and baluster and ball (l) are similar, but their simplicity has made them more popular. Many of these features have an ambiguous relationship with urns. The earliest is from Brunelleschi's dome in Florence (d) and is an original invention, while a Baroque finial with bronze representations of leaves (g) could be an urn. A combination of urn, candlestick and ball on Palladio's Palazzo Chiericati in Vicenza (e) of 1550 has been repeated and modified many times (f). Most extraordinary is an ascending series of four urns from León Cathedral in Spain (j) of 1520. While many finials have sculpted representations of flames, lamps can themselves act as features, such as example (i) by the Scottish architect Robert Adam at Syon House in 1764.

When Egypt fell under Roman control in the first century BC, obelisks (x), ancient needle-shaped religious monuments carved with commemorative inscriptions, were brought to Rome. These huge pillars were erected in the city and other smaller obelisks were imported to decorate temples as the worship of Egyptian gods became popular. The obelisk, with various other Egyptian forms, entered into the classical vocabulary. In the Renaissance the fallen remains were repaired and erected again. Since then, the obelisk has, in a surprising number of modified shapes, become a decorative feature on many classical buildings. A ball and spike like the needle, or gnomon, of a sundial is often added, (n) and (o), and flames can issue from the top, (p) and (q). They are often raised on pedestals, (n), (o), (r), (s) and (t), and occasionally on urns (q). At some time in the sixteenth century they were raised on ball or bun feet, (o), (p) and (s), and later developed curves, (m) and (s).

The ancient Greeks placed the armour of their fallen and defeated enemies on tree trunks (v). This symbol of conquest, or trophy, was adopted by the Romans as a part of their elaborate celebrations of victory and enlarged to incorporate flags, drums and other captured apparatus of war including, in sculpted form, prisoners of war. These sculptural groups have continued to be used to represent military prowess, with the addition of cannon or other weapons relevant to the warfare of the period, (u) and (w).

a      b      c      d

e      f      g      h      i      j

k      l      m      n      o

p      q      r      s      t

u      v      w      x

# 18. THE NATURAL WORLD

## THE ACANTHUS

Natural forms occur frequently in classical decoration and the acanthus plant appears more frequently than any other. The acanthus is a native Mediterranean plant and has a large leaf with a broken edge. Two species have traditionally formed the basis of decorative patterns, *Acanthus mollis* and *Acanthus spinosa*. *Acanthus mollis*, (a), (c) and (d), has a more rounded leaf than *Acanthus spinosa*, (b) and (e).

The most familiar applications of acanthus decoration are the Corinthian and Composite column capitals. The leaf form can vary considerably on these capitals and both the *mollis* (c) and *spinosa* (e) have been used. Throughout a long decorative history the acanthus leaf has been formalized, simplified and modified in many different ways. Its use continued throughout the Middle Ages and it was probably often carved by sculptors who knew neither the derivation of the form nor the plant itself. The reason for the original adoption of this particular plant form in Greek antiquity is unknown. The decorative use of most plants in the ancient world derived from their association with a god or belief in their magical powers and for this reason the acanthus is unlikely to have been introduced for solely decorative purposes. The vigour of the plant and its use in ancient funeral rites might suggest an association with rebirth or protection against evil spirits.

The leaf and the flower have formed the basis for a large number of different types of decoration and on many patterns have become so formalized that their association with the original plant is almost totally obscured.

Nevertheless, panels of leaves or individual plants can be relatively realistic. Examples (j) and (l) are Roman, while the most true to life (k) is from the eighteenth century. However, the use of the leaf and its fluted stems, or caulicoli, to create a running decoration of spiralling leaves and stalks, often turning around flowers or sprouting leaves, tends to produce a design that bears little resemblance to the plant found in nature. This pattern can sprout vertically from the base of a pilaster to decorate its face, continue indefinitely horizontally, without a point of origin or completion, or form a self-contained symmetrical panel. A large Roman tympanum (n), from the inside of an arch, has the plant meandering in a series of spirals to fill the space. These designs have proved both attractive and useful and have been repeated and modified in most periods. Examples (f), (i) and (m) are Roman, (h) is fifteenth century and (g) and (o) are from the eighteenth century.

268

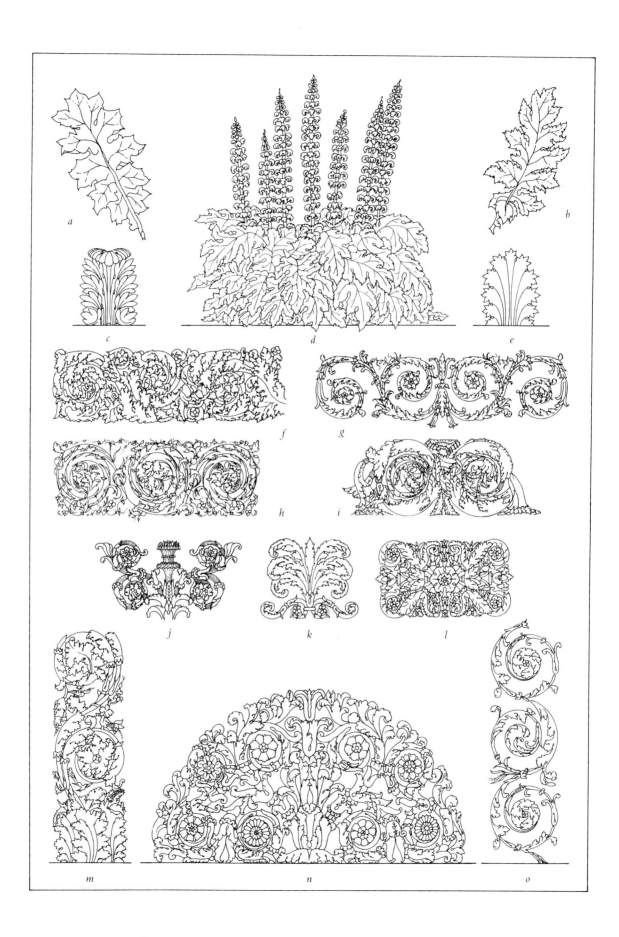

*a*

*b*

*c*

*d*

*e*

*f*

*g*

*h*

*i*

*j*

*k*

*l*

*m*

*n*

*o*

# PLANT DECORATION

There is no limit to the types of plant that can be used in classical decoration. Plant designs can be used for solely decorative purposes or can have some association with the use, ownership or location of an object or building. These symbolic connections give an added depth of meaning and interest to decoration. The relationship between specific plants and gods and the magical qualities of plants were part of the primitive mentality of antiquity. In the Middle Ages and the Renaissance this pagan animism was translated into a symbolic association of saints and plants and the conventions of heraldry. From these origins certain plant designs have become traditional classical decorations.

The laurel (d) and the olive (b) are often indistinguishable in formal design due to the similarity of the leaf shape and their small round fruit. The leaves on the olive tend to be smaller and more sparsely distributed along the branch. The laurel, or bay, is called *daphne* in Greek and is associated with the nymph Daphne who changed into a laurel when pursued by the god Apollo. The bush is associated with Apollo and the Muses and can imply artistic prowess or honour of any kind, particularly when made into a crown or wreath. As an evergreen it can symbolize eternity. The olive wreath was the highest reward at the ancient Olympic games. It is also an attribute of the goddess Minerva and, as such, symbolizes wisdom. In both pagan and Christian art, it symbolizes peace.

Both the ivy, (a) and (f), and the vine, (g), (h) and (i), are associated with Bacchus, the god of fertility and wine. As an evergreen, the ivy can also represent eternity and its clinging growth symbolizes fidelity. The persistent popularity of the vine from antiquity (g), through the Middle Ages (h) to the Renaissance (i) is in part due to the later association of the plant with Christ and the Eucharist through the parable of the vine and the blood of the Saviour. The vine also symbolizes autumn.

The oak (e) is the tree of Zeus, or Jupiter, the thunderer, ruler of the gods, and its leaves are used as a victor's wreath. The fruit of the pomegranate (c) was originally the attribute of Proserpina, who annually returned from the underworld to earth in the spring, and the multiple seeds represented fertility. In Christian symbolism this association was transferred to resurrection, but the seeds enclosed in a hard skin became symbols of chastity and the Virgin or, as many contained by one, the Church.

Some plant designs are more decorative than symbolic. Lines of fruits tied together, (k) and (l), generally indicate abundance, and different mixtures of fruits can represent different seasons. Husks, or bellflowers (j), were popular in late-eighteenth-century decoration. Mixtures of plants in vertical panels, (m) and (n), sometimes with vases or animals, originate from first-century Roman designs and were revived in the Renaissance. In sculptured relief they often decorate the faces of pilasters.

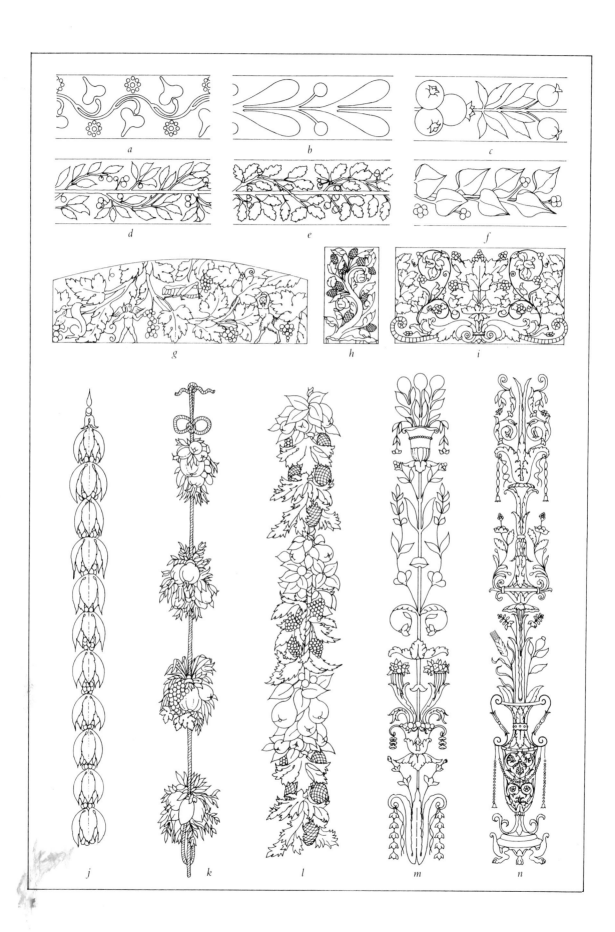

a

b

c

d

e

f

g

h

i

j

k

l

m

n

# GARLANDS AND WREATHS

The wreath and the garland have persisted as decorative forms in classical architecture since their introduction in antiquity in association with specific celebrations. While these origins have almost been forgotten, the designs retain their original appearance and much of their meaning.

The crown of leaves, or wreath, was an honorary insignia in antiquity and was made out of branches of laurel (c), oak (d), olive or some other appropriate plant and bound together with a ribbon. A laurel crown was given to the victor at the Pythian games held at Delphi in ancient Greece in honour of Apollo, while an olive crown was awarded to the victor at the Olympic Games. Victorious Roman generals and emperors received crowns of laurel or oak, and these are depicted in the hands of figures of winged Victory on triumphal arches.

Wreaths were also presented to the dead, possibly to symbolize the victory of the afterlife or to honour the earthly achievements of the deceased. Wreaths representing these functions are often found in ancient decoration. Even a cushioned, or pulvinated, frieze in an entablature could have a wreath decoration, and columns appeared to rest on wreaths when the torus moulding at the base was carved with oak or laurel tied with a ribbon, (a) and (b). The use of the wreath as a crown has long since passed, but the association with victory, prowess and death remains. Although the evergreen laurel is still used for funeral wreaths, much of the detailed symbolism of the plants is lost and the wreath is often used as simple decoration with different plants, such as the fashionable eighteenth-century husk (e).

The garland, also known as a festoon or swag, is a collection of plants, fruit, or leaves from a single plant, bound together with a ribbon and suspended, drooping at the centre, from two supports. Although the arrangement is similar to the wreath and the symbolism of the leaves can be the same, the origin is different. Garlands were used for temple decoration at festivals and sacrifices and are shown on temple friezes, together with the instruments of sacrifice, suspended between the skulls of sacrificial animals (f) or supported on large candlesticks or by cherubs. On a Roman altar (g) this religious association is given additional significance with the symbolism of leaves and animals. The combination of the oak of Jupiter and swans perhaps recalls the rape of Leda, by Jupiter in the guise of a swan, which brought about the birth of Castor and Pollux, two important Roman military gods. In the Renaissance the garland became purely decorative and lost its associations with pagan sacrifice. Masks (i), cherubs, coats of arms, lions' heads and other devices replaced the skulls and candlesticks. The garland has remained a popular decorative form and several variations in design have occurred since the Renaissance. Examples (h), (i) and (j) are from the sixteenth century and examples (k), (l) and (m) are from the eighteenth century.

a

b

c

d

e

f

g

h

i

j

k

l

m

# ANTHEMION, ROSETTE AND PATERA

I t is a characteristic of classical decoration that many of the traditional patterns adapt and abstract the characteristics of growing forms rather than attempting to reproduce nature with precision. Although some of the established designs date from a period when all representation was executed with abstracted geometric shapes, later forms, produced at a time when representation had reached a high level of sophistication, show the same freedom of composition.

Before the introduction of the acanthus, the predominant natural form in classical decoration was the anthemion. This has a conventionalized form and is said to have derived from the honeysuckle flower. A distinction is sometimes made between this design and that of the palmette, which is considered to be a simplified version of a palm leaf. The variety in palmette and anthemion design is so great that there is no useful distinction to be made, particularly as the true origin of both forms is unknown.

It is likely that these decorative themes had some significance in antiquity; the inclusion of a spiral design, from which the leaf or petal forms grow, suggests a known climbing plant. The anthemion has an odd number of leaves curling outwards or inwards to a spear-shaped central leaf. Anthemia were used singly to decorate antefixa, at the edge, and acroteria, at the corners, of Greek (a) and some Roman (c) temple roofs and the top of stele, or Greek gravestones, (b) and (d). Running patterns usually include a subsidiary narrower leaf design, (e) and (f), and the anthemion is sometimes contained in a spear-shaped frame (e). The composition of the pattern can become complex (g) and the stele crest can be elaborated to create a centralized running design (h). Although the dominance of this design declined from the Roman period, it was included in Romanesque and Renaissance decoration and enjoyed great popularity in the late eighteenth and early nineteenth centuries.

The rosette is any circular floral or plant design. The decoration of circular shapes with more or less abstracted plant forms is universal to almost all cultures and periods. Some rosettes are clearly representations of particular plants and include leaves and flowers. The Greek (j) and Roman (l) examples here may be poppies, while the Renaissance rosette (o) is hard to identify. Simple flowers with multiple leaves are common. Example (i) is Greek, (m) is Romanesque and (n) is early Renaissance; all seem to be some version of the daisy family. A Roman design (k) from a metope in the frieze of a Doric temple shows a radiant pattern of oak leaves and acorns while a late-eighteenth-century English pattern (p) is made up of long leaves or feathers.

Paterae are larger complex designs usually with a central rosette. The name derives from large ceremonial Roman dishes and the design became popular in the eighteenth and early nineteenth centuries for interiors. Examples (q), (r) and (s) are all from this date and were executed in plaster with themes developed from Roman painted, plaster and mosaic decoration.

a       b       c       d

e       f

g       h

i       j       k       l

m       n       o       p

q       r       s

# ANIMALS

Animals in many different forms appear in classical decoration. The animals that are found in the designs of antiquity generally have a significance beyond their decorative function. Ox skulls (a) and heads, and the heads or skulls of rams (c) are often added to temple friezes, altars and other objects associated with the pagan rituals of animal sacrifice (b). The heads of these animals were undoubtedly hung on the entablatures of early temples and this practice has been recorded in decoration.

Beyond this relationship between the decoration and the use of buildings, many animals were associated with individual gods or had their own attributes. The leopard, for example, is the animal sacred to Bacchus, while the elephant depicts victory or fame. In the Middle Ages and the Renaissance, bestiaries were published which listed such symbolic connections and often mixed pagan and Christian ideas. The dolphin, (j) and (n), is the creature of Neptune and, from her birth from the sea, Venus, and represents water as one of the four elements. It was also a symbol of faith for early Christians, and, through the story of Jonah, a token of the Resurrection. Similar differences of meaning occur today. The eagle (g) is the bird of Jupiter, symbolizes St Mark and represents the United States of America. The lion and the unicorn (o), here entwined in an acanthus frieze, represent Great Britain.

The lion is found in most periods and lion masks were used as gargoyles on Greek temples (e) and for many other decorative functions. The lion skin (h) is the emblem of the Greek hero Heracles and can be used as a plain decorative panel or surround for a feature such as a door or window. The sphinx was originally Egyptian but was soon adopted and modified by the Greeks (d) to represent obscure wisdom. The griffin (f) has an eagle's forequarters and the hindquarters of a lion and probably originated in India as the Greeks believed that it guarded the gold of that country. From this myth it came to symbolize watchfulness and courage and later the dual nature of Christ.

This union of the attributes and forms of creatures is one aspect of a freedom from the constraints of literal representation founded in ancient mythology and characteristic of classical decoration. The monopodium is of Roman origin and is generally found in the design of furniture. The single leg of an animal is joined with its head (m) and the junction concealed with an acanthus leaf, or different heads and feet or human forms and animal feet (i) are merged together. On the Palazzo Falconieri in Rome in 1645 Borromini alluded to the name of the family with a herm (k) on the façade that brought together an architectural column with a female bust and a falcon's head. Animals can also be partially transformed into plants. An Italian Renaissance design (n) reveals just enough of two dolphins' heads to make the plant origin of the design uncertain. Similarly, a seventeenth-century choir-stall from Paris (l) turns the already composite form of the griffin into an acanthus.

a

b

c

d

e

f

g

h

i

j

k

l

m

n

o

# THE HUMAN FORM

The human figure pervades classical decoration. The images of gods and heroes were supplemented by the convention of allegory, where meaning was conveyed by the symbolic attributes of the figures and creatures depicted.

Caryatids replaced columns on some Greek and Roman buildings. The most famous are the six female figures (b) on the south porch of the Erechtheion erected in Athens in 421 BC. These are said to represent women of Caryae, a Greek community bound to slavery as punishment for treachery in the Persian Wars. Their male counterparts are atlantes, named after the god Atlas who supported the earth. Giant male figures, called telamones, were common in Egyptian architecture, but the first known Greek atlantes (d) are from the fifth-century-BC Olympieum in Sicily. Caryatids and atlantes have taken different forms related to the prevailing style.

The cherub, also called putto, amorino and genius, is both pagan and Christian. In antiquity these winged infants were frequently shown in playful versions of adult activities, particularly wine-making (c) and Bacchic rites. In the Renaissance, pagan genii became Christian cherubs, one of the orders of angels, and were often depicted as winged heads (a).

Heads or masks appear in many different contexts. In antiquity, gods and mythological figures, (e), (f) and (i), were common, as were theatrical masks (l). This tradition continued in the Renaissance, sometimes without any specific identity, (g) and (h), but often derived directly from ancient examples, (j) and (k). Heads or masks are frequently added to the keystones of arches, (h), (j) and (k). The custom originated in antiquity, probably to keep out evil spirits, and the mask can also be related to the use or some other aspect of a building.

The herm, or terminus, was originally a boundary post or road marker, often tapering downwards, carved with a bust of Hermes in his role as a guardian deity and protector of travellers. These posts often had a phallus (m) in antiquity and were associated with Bacchic fertility ceremonies. The columnar figure was adopted as a furniture support in antiquity and could have feet (n) at the base. Herms of exaggerated proportions were shown as architectural supports in Roman paintings and copied in eighteenth-century decoration (o). In the Renaissance the herm was combined with the caryatid with varying amounts of the human form exposed, (q) and (r), and the association was made, particularly by Mannerist architects, between the human proportions of the orders and herm columns, (p) and (q). The introduction of reverse tapering on columns in the fifteenth century derives from the herm.

Human figures can be mixed (w) or physically combined, (u) and (x), with plants and animals. This decorative convention originated in antiquity and was continued in the Middle Ages. The ancient forms were revived in the Renaissance as part of grotesque decorative schemes, (s), (t) and (v).

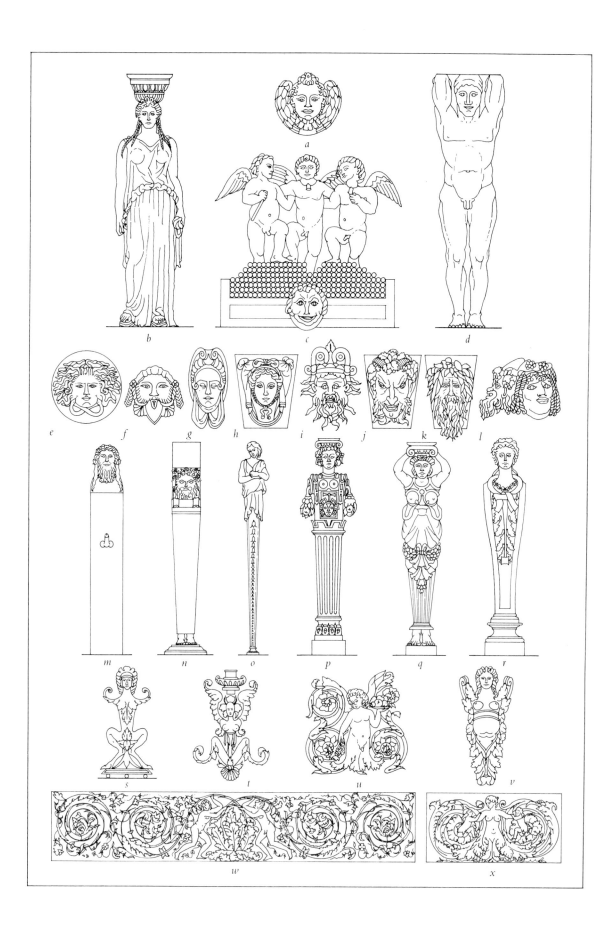

a

b          c          d

e          f          g          h          i          j          k          l

m          n          o          p          q          r

s          t          u          v

w          x

# 19. GEOMETRIC PATTERNS

## KEYS AND WAVES

There is a great variety of geometric decoration in classical design. In antiquity, shallow carving, mosaic, painting and decorative plasterwork included a bewildering variety of geometric compositions, and invention was never far behind tradition. Certain themes recur and some of these are versions of the patterns used on mouldings, shown on pages 119, 121, 125 and 127. Some other geometric forms are specifically associated with classical design.

The key pattern, also known as the Greek key, fret or meander, is a series of developments of a line moving from side to side in a succession of right-angles (a). This produces a symmetrical interlocking pattern which can be developed as alternating T-shapes (b), can then be turned down at the ends (c), halved to go in one direction, (d) and (k), and then turned round again (e). The line can be broken and other patterns inserted (f). These designs can be seen as a wandering line, or meander, or a series of interlocking shapes, or keys, which can dispense with the line and be expressed only with contrasting colours. The Greek key is found in other cultures and, from its square form and reliance on contrast, probably originated as a textile pattern.

The meaning of this design is unknown, although ideas such as interlocking hands have been suggested. A further development of the pattern, however, creates a series of swastikas (g) which, although also shared by other cultures, signified prosperity and revival in classical antiquity and was a common decorative device both in this form and in isolation. An expansion (h) or three-dimensional version (i) of the swastika design creates the impression of a maze or labyrinth, a pattern that represented Crete and the legend of the Minotaur, symbolizing the underworld and, in the Middle Ages, hell. Other fret designs from antiquity, (j) and (l), suggest a labyrinth. The simple meander can be broken or modified to turn a corner, but turning a swastika pattern can be more complicated, (m) and (n).

The wave pattern (q), also known as the Greek scroll, wave scroll, Vitruvian scroll, running dog and running scroll, is a curved version of the directional key pattern (d) and is sometimes elaborated with additional devices (r), central rosettes or foliage. This design more frequently relies on the contrast between interlocking shapes but can be shown as a meandering line (s). A corner can be turned to give a continuous direction (o) or to reverse the direction of the scroll (p).

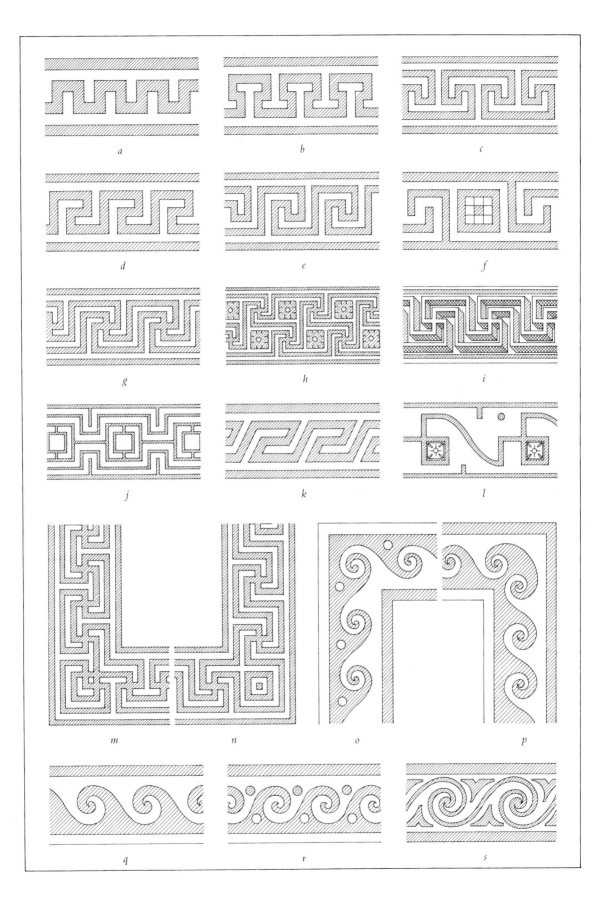

a

b

c

d

e

f

g

h

i

j

k

l

m

n

o

p

q

r

s

# GUILLOCHES, DISCS AND CONTRASTS

The guilloche, or interlacing pattern, is a decorative device that has retained its popularity since antiquity. It is the most widely used version of a series of knot designs and interlacing compositions found in classical decoration, particularly in Roman interiors. Knot patterns have been adopted by many different cultures and were taken to high levels of complexity by north European tribes and in Islamic art. It is possible that both of these artistic developments had some stimulation from Roman art. The north European tribal tradition and the classical tradition came together in the Romanesque.

The most simple form of guilloche is a running design formed of two intertwined bands which either turn tightly (a) or loosely (b) around a row of circles. These bands are often modelled to bulge outwards or inwards within a border of two flat strips and can be decorated with a rope pattern or turned over at the top and bottom to resemble a flat ribbon. The bands are sometimes brought tightly together to reduce the size of the intervening circles and a varied effect is created by flattening the discs to a lozenge shape. The resulting central space is often convex or filled with a rosette. The simple running border can be elaborated by alternating the size of the central circles or interlacing two running guilloches (c). The pattern is expanded by encompassing two rows of discs, either by winding and twisting the bands to a greater width (d), or by creating a series of loops (e), usually with a decorative detail at their intersection. A further extension to three rows of discs (f) could be repeated to occupy any width. Double and triple rows are used to enrich the torus moulding on column bases and simple arch imposts sometimes have guilloche decoration, but these are the only traditional direct application of this pattern to the orders. The design is generally applied as an enrichment to the frame around features such as coffering in vaults or as a decorative band or string course.

Circular decorative shapes can be both geometrical and natural. Overlapping discs, or coin moulding (h), can have a modelled face that resembles a gaming counter. The same overlapping pattern forms the base for a series of partially revealed rosettes (i). Many rosette designs bear only a general resemblance to living flowers and the geometric construction of the form is as evident as its natural inspiration, (g) and (j).

The durable nature of mosaics has preserved from antiquity many elaborate schemes for surface decoration. Similar patterns often appear on the few surviving painted wall decorations. These finds reveal the simple and universal fascination with geometric composition and three-dimensional illusion that has created such a variety of designs. A few of these are illustrated, (k) to (p). When this range of decorative potential is seen alongside the even greater variety of patterns that have been developed since the Renaissance it becomes hard, as with much decorative detail in classical design, to limit the patterns and features that might be called classical.

a

b

c

d

e

f

g

h   i

j

k

l

m

n

o

p

# 20. CLASSICAL DESIGN

## SYMMETRY AND AXIS

There is no formula for good design. There are, however, certain ways of organizing the layout and detail of buildings that have been developed, varied and refined within the classical tradition to become distinctive characteristics of classical architecture.

Accommodation is organized into a layout that is orderly and easily understood. The plan is usually symmetrical on either side of a line, or axis, starting at the main entrance and running straight through the building. This symmetry reflects the balance of nature and the human form. Symmetry in two directions, such as the plan of Palladio's Villa Rotonda near Venice (b) of 1550, is rare and it is more often on a single axis, such as his Villa Cornaro (a) of 1570. The required accommodation does not always lend itself to equally balanced rooms and the plan may have an irregular pattern within a symmetrical form, as does the Villa Farnesina in Rome (h), by Peruzzi in 1509. When circumstances, such as location or use, make a uniform arrangement impossible, the accommodation can be organized around linked symmetrical rooms and courts which give a clear order to the plan, as with the entrance atrium and peristyle court in the House of the Menander (c) from first-century-AD Pompeii in central Italy.

The axis is more than the geometric structure of the plan and describes the way someone would move through, view and understand a building. Greek temples focused on the image of the god with a single axis (e) while churches, such as S. Giustina in Padua (f), by Alessandro Moroni in 1532, often have a series of secondary axes. The central axis in the Villa Farnesina (h) gives the symmetry of the whole building to the irregular layout of rooms; a major axis changing direction on a secondary axis holds together the narrow town-house plan of William Wynn House in London (g) of 1772, by Robert Adam. Edwin Lutyens deliberately interrupted the central axis in many of his house plans and, as in Middlefield House in Cambridgeshire in England (i) of 1908, immediately turned it through ninety degrees to the line of the long corridor hall. Roman planning, while often based on a rigid axial layout, could be more informal. Villa plans and complex arrangements such as the baths at Hadrian's Villa near Rome (d) of AD 120, have individual groups of rooms or spaces that are relatively independent of one another but linked at various angles by a series of secondary axes.

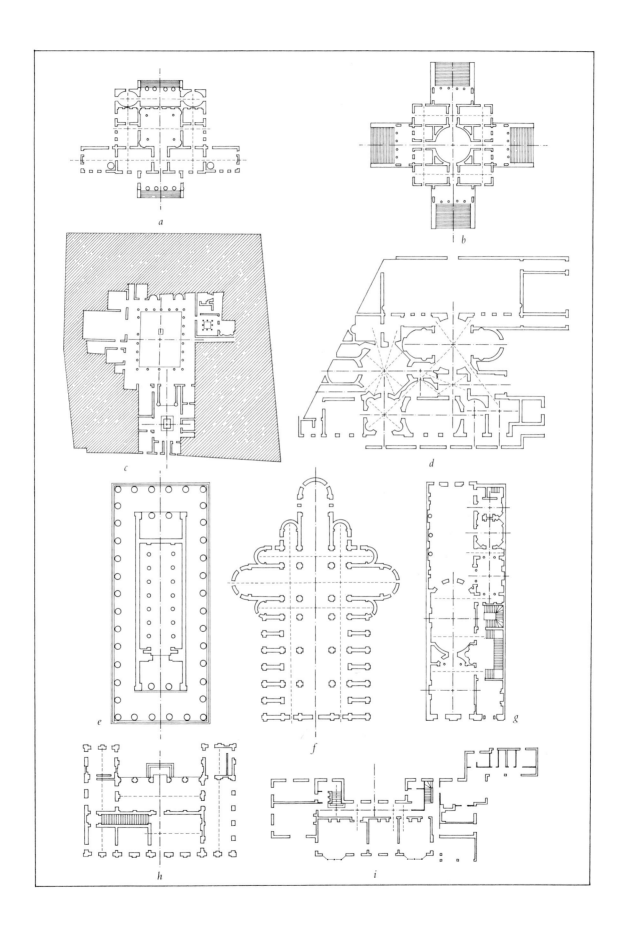

*a*

*b*

*c*

*d*

*e*

*f*

*g*

*h*

*i*

# GEOMETRY AND SPACE

The design of an enclosed area, such as a room or court, can make the space comprehensible by defining its geometry. Walls, floors and ceilings can be decorated to emphasize the geometry of the space. The construction or the function of a building usually introduces the geometric framework and, when a building has a simple form or large rooms, interior volumes can be a part of the external design.

The geometry of a dome is usually expressed in the space it covers. Two corridors in one of Nero's palaces in Rome (b) of about AD 60 meet under a simple dome. The four openings in the circular drum beneath are marked with four identical rectangular spaces where the corridors are screened with columns. These rectangular and circular spaces are brought together with diagonals and an octagon in the floor pattern. Vignola's S. Andrea in Rome (c) of 1554 is a simple rectangular space covered with an oval dome and these shapes are repeated on the exterior. Elliptical arches in the internal walls of the rectangle reproduce the shape of the oval above. The geometry of the four circles of the oval is reflected in the structure and decoration. The entrance columns are in line with the centre of each large curve and the decoration in the floor linking the columns on the side-walls also marks the line of the intersection of the large and small circles of the oval.

Changing geometry can give a different identity to a sequence of rooms, adding variety to movement through a building. The Hôtel de Montmorency in Paris (f), by Claude Ledoux in 1769, makes maximum use of a corner position by arranging the major sequence of rooms on the diagonal. A circular salon turns the axis from the line of the street towards the square room which occupies the internal corner. The intermediate oval room has no external walls and rises through two floors to be lit from the roof. Tendring Hall in Suffolk, England (d), by John Soane in 1784, has a similar series of spaces but placed along the central axis of the house. The curves on the exterior are matched on the interior, but their repetition is interrupted by a rectangular hall. Interior features reinforce the difference between the rooms.

Open courts are often designed so that the surrounding window- and door-openings and the floor levels act as a framework which defines the geometry of the enclosed volume. The court of the Palazzo Municipale in Genoa (a), by Rocco Lurago in 1564, has a rectangular plan with proportions described by the regular openings in the walls. The court lies between an entrance vestibule and a grand staircase, creating a route through the building of linked open and closed spaces. The design of the court gives added significance to the higher ground level at the head of the stair. In 1547 at Caprarola near Rome, Vignola designed the Palazzo Farnese (e) in an unusual pentagonal plan. The court is circular, but the design includes features of the geometry of the outer pentagon. Ten piers with coupled columns lie in front of the angles and centres of the walls of the pentagon.

m ⊢⊢⊢⊢⊢⊢⊢⊢⊢⊢⊢⊢ 20

a

b

c

d

e

f

50 ⊢⊢⊢⊢⊢⊢⊢⊢⊢⊢⊢⊢ ft

# VERTICAL AND HORIZONTAL HIERARCHY

On large buildings different parts, such as the entrance, need to be capable of being identified. Diverse uses, or just the monotony of height and length, can also lead the architect to seek means of differentiating elements of the design by varying the decoration. The modification of detail across a façade can give emphasis to any part of a building, either to indicate its functional importance or to improve the overall composition.

Long buildings, such as the Customs House in Dublin (f), by James Gandon in 1781, can vary considerably along their length. The details on the walls change to provide vertical divisions separating the centre and the ends. The distinct end-features, or pavilions, are made up of architectural elements from the centre and are almost buildings in their own right. These pavilions provide a satisfactory termination to the long façade but, with the intermediate walls, could be omitted to leave the centre of the building as an independent design. This sequence of separate elements builds the design up to the pediment and tall dome. Wilton House near Salisbury in England (e), by Inigo Jones in 1635, uses the pavilions as dominant vertical features which, by framing the lower building between, help to highlight the elaborate central door.

The designers of early Renaissance palaces in Italy established a tradition of separating buildings into distinct horizontal layers according to their function and varying the detail to express the relative importance or use of each floor. The defensive role of these palaces and the provision of service and storage rooms within limited urban plots put the state rooms on the upper floor. This was the noble floor, or the piano nobile. On the Palazzo Torlonia-Giraud in Rome (d), designed by Bramante in about 1500, it can be seen above the rusticated ground floor and is distinguished by its greater height and increased detail. The piano nobile was developed to become a major feature in the design of palaces, such as the Palazzo Pompei in Verona in northern Italy (a), by Sanmicheli in 1530, where the use of a fully decorated Doric order on the only visible upper floor is the single significant element on the façade. When the first floor above the ground is not a piano nobile it is often more appropriate to give a similar significance to the level of the principal rooms. In the Jenisch House in Hamburg, Germany (c), designed in 1828, Franz Forsmann carefully graded the size and detail of each floor, making it evident that the main rooms are on the lowest level.

In the United States in this century the new problem of tall buildings, often with repetitive uses on most levels, made classical architects reconsider vertical differences in decoration. Whitfield and King, in designing the Engineer's Club in New York City (b) in 1906, used a principle that was adopted for many tall classical buildings. Fine detail was concentrated on the lower floors most visible from the street while on the upper floors, seen from a distance, strong decorative features were added.

*a*  *b*  *c*

*d*

*ft* |——|——|——|——| 70    *m* |——|——| 20

*e*

*f*

# EMPHASIS AND DETAIL

The opportunity to vary the level of decoration of the orders to suit the size, significance or cost of a building gives classical design great flexibility and can be applied to individual features or details.

The design of two houses built in about 1750 in London (f) features variations in the amount of detail applied to each simple functional element. The decoration on the window-surrounds increases towards the centre. On the top floor only the centre window has a cornice, while on the floor below, all the windows have cornices with pediments on the centre three. These same three windows have small balustrades below, but only the centre window has pedestals and brackets, which increase the width of the pediment. On the ground floor identical arched openings are varied in the centre with the addition of rustication. A cornice with a pediment completes the grading of decoration towards the centre. Detail is most frequently concentrated on the centre of a building and, consequently, the entrance, but it is not always so carefully graded. The Courthouse at Saint-Lô in northern France (e), designed by Henry van Cleemputte in 1823, has little decoration except the full Corinthian central porch and door.

Central detail can be limited to the door itself. Early Italian Renaissance churches, like S. Felice in Florence (c), designed by an unknown architect in about 1450, were often the same simple structures as their Romanesque and Gothic predecessors, but the rich Gothic doors were replaced with elaborate classical door-surrounds, the fine detailing contrasting with the plain wall behind. The Savoie Palace at Mechelen in Belgium (d), by Keldermans and Beaugrant in 1520, has narrow ends without doors and the decoration is concentrated on the gable of the typical, steep-sloping roof of northern Europe. The lower two floors have no decoration except a pediment added to the upper centre window, while immediately above this window there is an ornate composition of columns, pediments, scrolls and vases.

Small buildings are often unsuitable for extensive decorative schemes, but their quality or surroundings may suggest the inclusion of some fine detail. The small house (a), built for himself in 1803 by Christian Frederick Hansen near Hamburg in Germany, is simply decorated with rustication, quoins and a cornice. There are no windows on the ground floor and the upper floor has a small plain window. The austerity of these details is contrasted with the three large windows on the principal floor, which are surrounded by Ionic pilasters, a pediment and a small balustrade. An artist's studio over a stable in New York City (b), designed by Trowbridge and Livingstone in 1901, achieves a similar effect with a large central studio window. The design is Baroque and the location of the studio on the upper floor gives the opportunity for a powerful half-round pediment supported on florid brackets over a richly detailed balcony, all of which contrast with the broad stable-door below.

*a*

*b*

*c*

*d*

*e*

*f*

# FURTHER READING

---

This book covers a large field of study and in many cases draws together information from many sources in a format that has not been attempted before. A reading list that referred to each element in the contents would be prohibitively large. The list below is, consequently, of a limited nature and only recommends further reading to amplify sections of the book which have been limited by space but are covered more extensively in other works. There are also references to current reprints or translations of influential architectural authors from the past as these are often more revealing than historical summaries.

## GENERAL HISTORY

*A History of Architecture on the Comparative Method*, Sir Banister Fletcher, Butterworth, 1933.

A well-established and extremely comprehensive reference book, more valuable for illustrations and descriptions than comment.

*A History of Western Architecture*, David Watkin, Barrie & Jenkins, 1986.

The best general history of western architecture available.

## THE ORDERS

*The Classical Orders of Architecture*, Robert Chitham, Butterworth, 1985.

A very detailed description of idealized orders, limited in scope and rather doctrinaire, but useful.

*The Orders of Architecture*, Arthur Stratton, Studio Editions, 1986.

A reprint of a 1931 edition. More broad-based than Chitham but with arbitrary choice of examples.

*Parallel of Orders of Architecture*, Charles Normand, Paris, 1819. Reprinted by Tiranti, 1928.

No longer in print but the most useful compendium of different versions of the orders. Worth purchasing if it can be found.

## PROPORTION

*Architectural Principles in the Age of Humanism*, Rudolf Wittkower, Academy Editions, 1988.

The classic work on Renaissance theories of proportion.

*The Theory of Proportion in Architecture*, P. H. Scholfield, Cambridge University Press, 1958.

A comprehensive survey of the subject.

## DETAIL AND DECORATION

*Dictionary of Ornament*, Philippa Lewis and Gillian Darley, Macmillan, 1986.

A wide-ranging and thorough survey of decorative themes and types.

*Handbook of Ornament*, Franz Meyer, Omega, 1987.

A reprint of the 1894 original. Extensive and analytical, a most useful reference book with an inevitable late-nineteenth-century bias.

## ORIGINAL WORKS

*The Ten Books on Architecture*, Vitruvius, trans. Morris Hicky Morgan, Dover, 1960.

The only treatise on architecture to have survived from antiquity. Written in the late first century BC and very influential in the Renaissance and subsequently. Architecture includes clock design and siege-engines. Much of the text obscure. A reprint of an American 1914 edition with poor illustrations, no footnotes and no commentary, but still the best translation available.

*On the Art of Building in Ten Books*, Alberti, trans. Rykwert, Leach and Tavernor, MIT Press, 1988.

The first major Renaissance treatise, published in about 1450 in Italy and structured to resemble Vitruvius. This is an excellent new translation. Not illustrated.

*The Five Books of Architecture*, Serlio, trans. van Aelst 1606, Dover, 1982.

Published between 1537 and 1551 in Italy. This was the first heavily illustrated treatise intended for practical use and the first to codify the orders. This edition is a facsimile of an anonymous 1611 English translation from a Dutch translation. The text is archaic and the translation questionable but the illustrations and format informative.

*The Four Books of Architecture*, Palladio, trans. Giacomo Leoni 1715, Dover, 1965.

Published in 1570 in Italy. Well illustrated and with a strong practical emphasis including plans of Palladio's own designs. The influence of this book is second only to Vitruvius. This is a facsimile of a 1715 English edition, the language and print are clear and the illustrations good.

# GLOSSARY

---

This is not a comprehensive architectural glossary; it is only intended to assist the reader with unfamiliar words in the text. Specialized words that are only used on the same page as their definition are not entered in this glossary but can be found in the index. Further information on many of the entries may also be found by referring to the index.

ABACUS — A flat slab on top of a column *capital*. The shape and edge *profile* vary according to the type of capital.

ACANTHUS — *Acanthus mollis* and *Acanthus spinosa*. A wild Mediterranean plant with large leaves with serrated edges. It is represented in a stylized form on the Corinthian column *capital* and other classical decorative designs.

ACROTERION — (pl. acroteria) Both the sculpture and platform for the sculpture at the apex and ends of a *pediment*.

AEDICULE — An opening or recess framed with columns, an *entablature* and a *pediment*. Originally a shrine in the form of a miniature temple front containing a cult figure.

AISLE — A space parallel to the *nave* of a *basilica*, separated from the nave by a row of columns or *piers*, often with a lower roof. Also used to describe any narrow passage in a church.

ANTEFIX — (pl. antefixa) A vertical support or decorative feature on the edge of a roof which, in its original form, supported the last tile. They are often decorated with leaf or plant designs or faces and are occasionally found on the ridges of roofs.

ANTHEMION — A formalized plant design, perhaps derived from the honeysuckle, with a series of curling leaves or petals.

APSE — A recess, generally semicircular or polygonal, often with a half-domed ceiling, off a larger space. Usually found at the end of the *nave* of a *basilica* or church and containing a cult image or altar.

ARCHITRAVE — The lower part, or beam, of the *entablature*. A door- or window-surround with the same *profile*.

| | |
|---|---|
| ARCHIVOLT | An *architrave* curved around the lower face of an arch. |
| ATRIUM | The principal room and hall of a Roman house, traditionally with a square or rectangular opening in the centre of the roof. |
| ATTIC | The space, wall or storey above an *entablature* or *pediment*. |
| BALUSTER | A short post or railing, often with one or more swellings and other details. |
| BALUSTRADING | Rows of *balusters* or low protective wall. |
| BASILICA | A hall with a large rectangular central space – the *nave* – and usually with narrow spaces along the long, and occasionally also the short, sides – the *aisles* – separated with rows of columns or *piers*. |
| BAY | One unit in a row of columns taken from the centre of one column to another. Also a division in the length of a wall often defined with columns, *piers* or *pilasters* and containing a single door, window or arch. |
| BRACKET | A projecting support. |
| CAPITAL | A carved or decorated block at the top of a column. |
| CARYATID | A female figure acting as a supporting column. |
| CLERESTORY | The upper part of the wall of the *nave* of a *basilica* which stands above the lower roof of the *aisle* and usually contains clerestory windows. |
| COFFER | A variously shaped recess in a ceiling, *vault* or dome. |
| COLONNADE | A row of columns. |
| CORBEL | A small projection in a wall, or supporting *bracket*. |
| CORNICE | The upper part of an *entablature* which corresponds to the eaves of a temple roof. Any other decorative projection that derives from the eaves. |
| CORONA | The projecting *moulding* of the *cornice* with a flat vertical face, usually below a *cyma* moulding. |
| CROSSING | The area formed by the crossing of two rectangular spaces, generally specific to the focal space of a church and often roofed with a dome or tower. |

CYMA — Literally a wave. A *profile* consisting of two joined curves alternately concave and convex and, according to their sequence, called cyma recta and cyma reversa.

DADO — Also called a die. The principal part of the *pedestal* of a column between the *cornice* and base. Also the area of wall which corresponds to this part of the pedestal when an *order* is applied to a wall.

DENTIL — Tooth-like projection in a *cornice*.

DOSSERET — An isolated piece of *entablature* above a column.

DRUM — A cylindrical wall below a dome.

EARS — Projections on the sides of the upper parts of door- and window-surrounds or *architraves*. Also known as shoulders.

ECHINUS — A projecting *moulding* on a column *capital* below the *abacus*.

ENTABLATURE — The uppermost part of a classical *order* consisting of all the horizontal elements supported by the column. It is divided into three parts: the *architrave*, the *frieze* and the *cornice*.

ENTASIS — The taper or bulging taper of a column.

FANLIGHT — A window over the top of a door.

FILLET — A small flat projecting *moulding*.

FINIAL — A vertical projecting feature at the top of a roof.

FLUTING — Vertical grooves, or flutes, usually with a concave *profile* and most commonly found running up the face of columns.

FRIEZE — The middle part of the *entablature*.

GABLE — The triangular piece of wall between the two sloping sides of a pitched roof.

GROIN — The line formed by the points of intersection of two *vaults*.

GUILLOCHE | A pattern resembling interlaced ribbons, generally linear in form.

GUTTA | (pl. guttae) Small cylindrical peg-like decorative detail below *triglyphs* and on the *soffit* of *mutules* in the Doric *order*. They became a more general decorative feature in the later Renaissance.

IMPOST | The block of stone or other material, usually projecting and often carved, from which an arch springs.

LANTERN | A small vertical cylindrical or polygonal projection with windows in a roof or dome with a roof or dome of its own.

METOPE | The space between the *triglyphs* in a Doric *frieze*, sometimes decorated.

MODILLION | Small *bracket* in the *cornice* of the Corinthian and Composite *orders* below the *corona*.

MODULE | The unit of measurement used in proportioning the *orders*. In this book the diameter of the lower part of the column is used as the module, divided into ten parts. (In other publications the module can be half a diameter and divided into thirty parts.)

MOULDING | The *profile*, or contour, of a continuous vertical or horizontal detail.

MUTULE | A flat projecting *bracket*, originally sloping with direction of the roof above, below the *corona* of the Doric *order* and decorated with *guttae* on its *soffit*.

NAVE | The large hall of a *basilica* and hence the public western part of a church.

OCULUS | A round window or circular aperture in the top of a dome.

ORDER | The five formal systems of *pedestals*, columns and horizontal *entablatures* which form the basis of all classical architecture. All the parts have a traditionally established relationship with one another and each order has its specific decorative themes. The five orders are: Tuscan, Doric, Ionic, Corinthian and Composite.

| | |
|---|---|
| OVOLO | A convex *moulding* with a *profile* resembling half an egg, sometimes carved with a pattern of alternating eggs and arrowheads or darts. |
| PAVILION | A distinct part of a building, usually on a corner or at the end of a long façade. Also a small isolated building. |
| PEDESTAL | A decorated block below a column. A similar design is used for supporting statues. |
| PEDIMENT | Originally the shallow triangular *gable* of a temple, specifically including a sloping *cornice* at the verge, or edge, of the roof. Also the same design dissociated from its original location, such as over a window or *aedicule*. |
| PENDENTIVE | A concave *spandrel* starting at a point in an angle between two walls and becoming wider to support the rim of a dome or a *drum*, so filling the residual space created when a circular dome is located in a square or polygonal plan. |
| PIANO NOBILE | From the Italian, great, or noble, floor. The principal floor of an Italian palace containing the state rooms and usually the first floor above the ground or basement floor. It has higher ceilings and enhanced exterior and interior decoration. The term has been extended to other building types. |
| PIER | An isolated rectangular section of supporting wall. |
| PILASTER | A column attached to and projecting from a wall. When the projection exceeds half the width of the column it is an engaged column. |
| PORTICO | Originally a *colonnade*, but now specifically a porch with columns. |
| PROFILE | The shape of a *moulding* or other detail shown as a section or straight cut through the detail. |
| PULVINATED | A large convex bulging, or cushion, *moulding*. Usually a *frieze*. |
| QUOIN | Block or simulated block of stone, often *rusticated*, on the corner of a building and usually in alternating long and short courses on each face. |

RESSAUT · A section of *entablature* projecting outwards from a continuous entablature over a similarly isolated column.

RIB · An arch or thin structural member supporting a vault or dome and projecting down from the *soffit*. Also used as a wholly decorative feature and to create *coffering*.

ROSETTE · A formalized decorative representation of a flower.

RUSTICATION · Rough-faced stone, stone with all or some of the joints recessed or the same detail simulated in other materials.

SCOTIA · A deep concave *moulding*.

SOFFIT · The underside of any projecting or overhead feature such as a beam. Also another word for a ceiling.

SPANDREL · The area of wall above an arch when it is set inside a rectangular opening.

SPRINGING · The level from which an arch rises.

STRING · The sloping supports for the steps of a stair. Also a horizontal line on a building, generally decorative and often projecting. A projecting course of stone or brick is a string course.

SWAG · Also known as a festoon or garland. A bundle of flowers, fruit or other objects gathered together, draped from two supports and tied with ribbons.

TORUS · A large convex *moulding*, most often found at the base of columns.

TRABEATION · The system of vertical posts or columns and horizontal lintels, beams or *entablatures* characteristic of Greek and some Roman architecture.

TRANSENNA · A latticed fence or *balustrade*, in any material, most frequently used in antiquity.

TRIGLYPH · A vertically grooved repetitive detail in a Doric *frieze*, alternating with *metopes*.

TYMPANUM · The triangular space or wall inside a *pediment*, or the semicircular space or wall inside an arch above the line of the *springing*.

VAULT — A curved roof or ceiling.

VOLUME — The space contained by a building, room or courtyard.

VOLUTE — A spiral or scrolled decoration associated with the column *capital* of the Ionic *order* and with scrolled *brackets*.

VOUSSOIR — A wedge-shaped brick or stone that, with others, radiates from the centre of an arch and forms its structure.

# INDEX

Words for which a definition can be found in the glossary are indicated by bold type.